W9-DFN-905

The Invisible Link

The Invisible Link
Japan's Sogo Shosha *and the Organization of Trade*

M. Y. Yoshino
and
Thomas B. Lifson

The MIT Press
Cambridge, Massachusetts
London, England

This book was set in Baskerville by DEKR Corporation and printed and bound by Halliday Lithograph in the United States of America.

Library of Congress Cataloging-in-Publication Data

Yoshino, M. Y. (Michael Y.)
The invisible link.

Bibliography: p.
Includes index.
1. Conglomerate corporations—Japan. 2. Trading companies—Japan. I. Lifson, Thomas B. II. Title.
HD2756.2.J3Y675 1986 338.8′042′0952 85-30033
ISBN 0-262-24025-4

This book is dedicated to Saburo Yoshino and the memory of Mary Ellen Lifson

Contents

Acknowledgments

We owe deep thanks to many people for their help in undertaking this study.

The largest and most significant group consists of the managers of various sogo shosha firms who so generously gave of their time and insight in answering our questions and who often trusted us with confidential information. Because anonymity was promised to all informants, it is not possible to thank them individually. Without their cooperation, however, our goals could never have been achieved. We thank them sincerely.

We would like to thank Dean John McArthur of Harvard Business School for his support. Professors Richard Rosenbloom and E. Ray Corey, directors of the Division of Research at Harvard Business School provided advice, vital resources, and support to the authors during key phases of the work. Mr. David Baskerville and the Weyerhaeuser Foundation must also be thanked for their essential support and encouragement during the early stages of the project. The Fairbank Center for East Asian Research, and the Program on U.S.-Japan Relations of the Center For International Affairs at Harvard University gave freely their cooperation and support. We are grateful to them. We are particularly indebted to Kay Curran for her magnificent help and support throughout the project, and to Pamela Daugherty and Sara Hazel for their secretarial support.

A group of friends and colleagues offered support, encouragement, ideas, suggestions, and help. Professors Ezra Vogel, Harrison White, Donald Warwick, Hugh Patrick, Yoshi Tsurumi, Leonard Schlesinger, Jay Lorsch, Arthur Turner, Richard Vancil, and Michael Reich must be thanked, as must be Jeffrey and Susan Weinress, Douglas Sparks, Jon Junkerman,

Hugh Newberger, Michael Ward, and Hiroshi Uchida. Our families provided essential support throughout the long course of this project. Hiroyuki Itami and Haruo Takagi ably assisted us in conducting interviews.

The Invisible Link

1

Introduction

. . . we are like the air, invisible but pervasive, providing essential things to sustain life.—Yohei Mimura, president, Mitsubishi Corporation[1]

In Georgia, a large producer of poultry learns new techniques for cutting, grading, and freezing broiler chickens. Use of these techniques will enable him to make substantial sales to a new market in Japan. The instructions come from a man wearing a small badge on the lapel of his suit jacket.

In the island kingdom of Brunei, natural gas from wells is chilled, compressed, and loaded onto specially designed tankers. Watching the loading is a man responsible for the development of the facilities. He wears another lapel badge like the one seen in Georgia.

In New York City, a new line of inexpensive shoes manufactured in Bulgaria is shown to buyers from major retailing chains. Watching carefully is the man who planned and supervised the project from design through manufacturing, importation, and marketing. He too wears the same lapel badge.

In Kenya, construction crews race to finish a new international airport which the government hopes will trigger new waves of investment in tourism and spark the economic development of a region. A similar lapel badge is visible on the suit of a man who arranged the complex logistics for the project.

In Pennsylvania, a manufacturer of electronic medical instruments works to adapt his products to export markets. Part of the changes involves using new components supplied by the same company that will act as his export agent. Once again, a man with the familiar lapel badge is his contact.

These men work for a kind of company about which most Americans know little or nothing. It is a kind of company that moves massive amounts of goods and money into and out of the United States (and almost every other country in the world) helping to determine prices, terms, standards, and innovations for a bewildering variety of products. It is among the most international types of firms, with operations spanning the globe. The name of this kind of company is *sōgō shōsha.* Its origins are in Japan. According to *Forbes* magazine, six of the ten largest non-U.S. companies in the world are sogo shosha.[2] There are only a few sogo shosha companies, all of them based in Japan. The men described here could be working for any one of them.

A sogo shosha is like no other type of company. It is not defined by the products it handles or even by the particular services it performs, for it offers a broad and changing array of goods and functions. Its business goals are equally elusive, for maximization of profits from each transaction is clearly not the major goal, at either the operating or philosophical level. There are really no other comparable firms, although important business and government leaders in the United States and elsewhere have become convinced that there should be.

This book is a study of the sogo shosha as a business institution. It focuses on the six largest firms in the sogo shosha sector, whose sales and importance are vastly greater than all the others combined. These six companies affect the lives of most participants in the world economy. From the oil used to cook french fries at a local fast food restaurant to subway cars running beneath our streets, products passing through their hands are all around us. Collectively they are the largest purchaser of U.S. exports in the world, accounting for 10 percent of our total overseas sales, 4 percent of world trade, and influencing the jobs and fortunes of tens of millions of people all over the world.[3]

These huge Japanese companies—Mitsubishi Corporation, Mitsui & Company, C. Itoh, Marubeni Corporation, Sumitomo Corporation, and Nissho-Iwai—share patterns of business strategy, operations, and organization that are very different from those of other types of business firms. Defining their business is an elusive goal, for their activities do not fit into any of the conventional categories. They could be called commodity traders, wholesalers, bankers and manufacturers, miners, venture capitalists, and many other labels. But none of these conveys a true picture of the substance of their activities.

Sogo shosha is usually translated into English as "general trading firm," "trading house," or "comprehensive trader," but these companies do far more than simply buy and sell goods for a profit. They are a unique and significant type of institution that deserves to be understood on its own terms. Rather than utilizing an inadequate translation, we will simply call them sogo shosha, with the intention of adding a new word and concept to the English language by borrowing from Japanese.*

Even in its native Japan, the sogo shosha is regarded as a somewhat mysterious entity, difficult to know about or understand but universally acknowledged as a powerful force in the economy. Overseas, where the sogo shosha companies' profile is lower and where few local citizens have an opportunity to gain a realistic picture of their status, a vast gap exists between their image and reality. In both Japan and overseas outsiders know relatively little about how and why they operate as they do.

To some extent the vacuum in knowledge and understanding of the sogo shosha is the inevitable outcome of the nature of their commercial operations, where confidentiality and secrecy are often important to business success. Information moves markets, so the natural tendency of a sogo shosha is toward circumspection about itself and its activities. But a much more important source of the knowledge gap is the complexity of the institution and the consequent difficulty in grasping its essential nature. Moreover there is a lack of readily available models, concepts, or analogs with which simply and accurately to characterize the institution.

Most of the terminology used to describe the world economy, and the processes and institutions that comprise it, were developed out of the particular historical evolution of the Western European and North American countries. For most of the last two centuries the economic actors and thinkers of these locales took the initiative in creating and defining the dynamics of process and change in the way the world produced and exchanged economic goods and services. It is therefore not sur-

* In the Japanese language no distinction is made between the singular and plural form.

Table 1.1
Japanese trading companies (in ¥ billions all years ended March)

	C.Itoh			Marubeni			Mitsubishi		
	1982	1983	1984	1982	1983	1984	1982	1983	1984
Sales	12,336	12,490	12,987	11,547	11,631	11,821	14,686	14,885	15,029
Net profit after taxes	5.01	3.08	3.41	5.28	0.35	3.74	21.13	18.23	20.32
Assets	2,852	2,820	3,105	2,968	3,092	3,387	4,412	4,523	4,868
Equity	88.05	89.00	89.00	122.63	117.70	119.20	279.79	290.17	301.96
Number of employees		7,778	7,609[a]		8,028	7,749[a]		9,793	9,318[a]
Subsidiaries abroad		17			25			28	
Branches and offices abroad		107			86			98	

	Mitsui			Nissho-Iwai			Sumitomo		
	1982	1983	1984	1982	1983	1984	1982	1983	1984
Sales	13,225	14,147	13,960	7,432	8,016	7,790	10,964	11,354	11,624
Net profit after taxes	−15.12	10.34	6,17	5.62	7.95	5.79	15.57	17.19	18.68
Assets	4,155	4,237	4,455	1,962	2,034	2,210	1,997	1,925	2,017
Equity	169.84	195.26	199.14	61.22	82.10	88.39	133.49	151.46	167.63
Number of employees		9,735	9,377[a]		6,006	5,847[a]		6,573	6,661
Subsidiaries abroad		25			20			20	
Branches and offices abroad		150			80			80	

a. Staffing levels are those as of September 1984.

prising that the concepts and words developed out of this experience might be less than satisfactory in describing an institution whose origins and development lie elsewhere. The term "trading house," for instance, although frequently applied to it, does not quite capture the essence of a sogo shosha; as a characterization of the Hudson's Bay Company or the Dutch East India Company it is perhaps much more satisfactory.

We have chosen *The Invisible Link* as the title for this study with several layers of meaning in mind. One refers to this role of the sogo shosha as organizer of other firms.[4] The sogo shosha, unique among the world's corporations, is active from the very earliest or "upstream" activities of raw material extraction or creation, through multiple stages of production, fabrication, and distribution, "downstream" to the end user, in most of the basic categories of economic commodities: food, fuel, fiber, metals, chemicals, and the end products for which they are used. Although it sometimes owns a partial or controlling interest in the corporations actually performing the activities or production or distribution, the primary role of the sogo shosha lies in the coordination or linkage of them.

Like Adam Smith's "invisible hand" of the market, and the like Alfred Chandler's "visible hand" of the vertically integrated firm, the sogo shosha provides a system of governance, channeling money, information, ideas, raw materials, products, services, and other economic goods into a coherent system of activity. The nature of this role is elusive, for it cuts across established categories of economic institutional analysis. While it is a coordinator, the sogo shosha is not a dictator or boss. It does not exercise the same degree of unilateral power over its clients as does an integrated corporation, with divisions or subsidiaries performing various activities. The clients remain, in most cases, independent firms, with the freedom to act on their own in the marketplace, rather than participate via the mechanism of a sogo shosha. The subtle and ever-changing dynamics of power between a sogo shosha and its client firms, and the utility to both of the coordinating function performed by the sogo shosha, challenge us to rethink many assumptions of the nature and boundaries of the firm and look at the basic organization of economic activity with new eyes.*

* An important branch of economics, deriving from the increasingly influential work of R. H. Coase and Oliver Williamson, is based on analyzing the

The sogo shosha, we believe, is an example of a third type of institutional form, with some characteristics of both vertically integrated firms and market. That it has been neglected by economic theorists is not surprising. In the economic history of the North Atlantic countries, trading houses, although very important in the development of the early mercantilist colonial empires, faded into virtual obscurity as significant forces during the Industrial Revolution. In Japan, however, it was different. There, the sudden forced integration of Japan in the nineteenth-century world industrial economy sparked the growth of the sogo shosha, as a response to the needs of time. Rather than dying out with the progress of industrialism in Japan, the sogo shosha grew. In the evolution of modern industrial economies, with the exception of Japan, large-scale diversified intermediaries have been a missing link. Until comparatively recently, outside of Japan, the sogo shosha has also been an invisible link.

The fact that the sogo shosha not only persisted in Japan but flourished as an engine of economic growth and change, combined with the fact that Japan, over the last century, has had the world's fastest sustained rate of increase in industrial production, GNP, and per capita income, has led many to wonder if this economic mechanism might be usefully copied elsewhere. Several countries, including Korea, Taiwan, Brazil, and the United States have enacted policies and legislation designed to promote home-grown trading companies.

But it is always dangerous to imitate complex institutions without thorough study and a willingness to learn and change quickly as unintended consequences appear. In the United States, at least, despite the initial enthusiasm and optimism which followed the passage of the Export Trading Company Act of 1982, there has been no dramatic rise of large and profitable American-style sogo shosha, and some high-profile ventures, such as Sears World Trade have, according to public reports, suffered large and embarrassing losses.[5]

The challenges of managing a sogo shosha are formidable, and increasing over time. In order to perform its role of linking external parties, the internal organization of a sogo shosha

---

implications of different choices between markets and firms in the structuring of production and commerce. Readers interested in citations of the literature are referred to the bibliographic notes at the end of the book.

must meet exacting demands. The challenge of managing complex interdependency, rapid change, and fierce external competition has been met by the evolution of a distinctive organizational system. In a sogo shosha organization it is not so much the conventional bureaucratic structures and processes, as the systematic use of informal interpersonal exchange process, that serves to govern the most important aspects of the organization's activity. These informal processes are another kind of invisible link—a real, though intangible, organization structure. The networks of interpersonal exchange activity elaborate themselves in marketlike fashion along lines that would bring joy to Adam Smith's heart. Just as the role of the sogo shosha in the broader economy challenges familiar concepts and habits of economic thought, so too does the operation of its internal organization shed light on the limits of conventional categories of bureaucratic and organizational theory.

Although the sogo shosha is a successful and fascinating institution, a major actor in the world economy, it is by no means untroubled. While overseas observers have rushed to imitate it, in Japan many are asking the question: Has the sogo shosha outlived its usefulness? In the years following the 1973 oil crisis the sogo shosha has been subjected to severe criticism increasing competition, and uncertain profits. Whether it represents an indication of things to come or a historic anomaly is for the future to determine.

2

Historical Evolution

Compared with the United States and Europe, Japan was a latecomer to industrialization.[1] Having colonized much of Southeast Asia by the midnineteenth century, Great Britain, France, and the United States expanded their spheres of influence to East Asia, until finally Japan was one of the few remaining countries to be conquered. A sudden realization of her vulnerability awakened Japan from the self-imposed isolation that had lasted two and a half centuries.

Persuaded to take action by the ineptness of the feudal leadership in 1868, a small group of young men of the warrior class overthrew the decaying feudalism, in a movement that subsequently became known as the Meiji Restoration. The overriding priority of the movement was to ensure the nation's independence, which required rapid development of the outdated military. Brief but dramatic encounters with the advanced weapons of Western nations had convinced the group that industrialization was a prerequisite to building modern military strength. Time was of the essence; building the industrial base for a modern military became the highest national priority.

This was a significant departure from the pattern of industrialization in Europe and the United States, which was characterized by gradual evolution over a much longer period. In the midnineteenth century Japan was a rather backward agrarian society. The Meiji leadership quickly realized the importance of learning from the advanced countries. Indeed, an important national goal was to catch up with the West.

Foreign trade began almost immediately or, more accurately, was forced on the struggling nation by Western countries in the intense pursuit of their mercantile policies. European and

American trading firms established offices in Japan's key ports to buy raw silk and other traditional products. For the time being, at least, foreign trade was under the complete control of these traders, simply because Japanese merchants lacked the required skills. A handful of aggressive merchants saw new opportunities developing in foreign trade, but they were able to sell only to the local offices of the foreign companies. Opportunities for blatant exploitation by foreign traders were abundant, and many humiliating experiences soon led Japanese merchants and government officials to the realization that foreign trade required substantial financial resources, special skills, and knowledge, including familiarity with foreign market conditions and a thorough understanding of business institutions abroad. The new government, with its pragmatic and nationalistic bent, also realized the importance of foreign trade as a means to pay for the purchases of new weapons, machinery, and technology and the hiring of foreign advisers. The rapid development of an indigenous institution that would be able to perform foreign trade activities became a priority.[2]

Mitsui Bussan: The Prototype

The national need to develop foreign trade independent of foreign control, together with these fresh business opportunities, soon led to the emergence of a number of firms specializing in foreign trade. Among them was the predecessor of Mitsui Bussan, or Mitsui Trading Company. Since Mitsui Bussan, popularly known in Japan simply as Bussan,* is considered to be the prototype of the sogo shosha in Japan, its evolution provides as excellent illustration. The House of Mitsui, a prosperous merchant family whose origin goes back to the late seventeenth century, was a powerful financial patron of the Restoration Movement. Its strong political connections with powerful factions of the early Meiji political leadership enabled the company quickly to become a national institution and to achieve almost quasi-official status. In fact the House of Mitsui was given the first opportunity by the new government to enter into banking, mining, and trading.

* *Bussan*, like *shoji*, is a Japanese word meaning "engaged in trade." But because Mitsui is the only major sogo shosha using the term *bussan* in its name, the company is commonly given the nickname "Bussan."

The new regime dispensed these favors to Mitsui and a handful of others, not merely as patronage to repay old political debts but also because it needed daring and progressive commercial and financial organizations, imbued with entrepreneurial spirit, to develop the nation's economy. In fact in 1876 the finance minister informed the Mitsui leadership that the privilege they had been granted by the government was predicated not on their personal worthiness but on expectation of their future service to the state.

Mitsui was sufficiently innovative that by 1887, a mere eight years after the Restoration, it had transformed its traditional money-lending business into a bank patterned after the Western model. In a society in which most of the traditional merchants were unable to cope with sudden political and economic upheavals, Mitsui was one of the few large, influential merchant houses able to respond effectively to new opportunities. Bussan was officially established as a trading arm in 1876, but at its inception the Mitsui family saw the potential risks of this venture and took precautions to protect its major holdings from the liabilities that Bussan might incur. Ironically, as we shall see later, within several years Bussan was to emerge as a central entity in what was to become Mitsui Zaibatsu. Despite its secondary status within the Mitsui family and its shaky beginning, Bussan had a grand design, again symbolic of the period. Its charter stated that Bussan was to "export overseas surplus products of the Imperial Land and to import products needed at home, and thereby to engage in intercourse with the ten thousand countries of the Universe."

The first major boost to Bussan came in the form of the exclusive right to export the output of the richest government-owned coal mine. Coal was a major export commodity of the time. The most important export market for coal then was China, where the Europeans were actively establishing modern factories, particularly textile mills. Bussan also supplied coal to foreign ships at major ports throughout Asia. The mine was subsequently sold by the government to Mitsui at a very attractive price, and it became a major source of income for decades. In fact this was a singularly important event in the development of Mitsui as a diversified financial, mining, and industrial empire. Mitsui eventually obtained the dominant share of the coal market in China. Bussan established its first overseas office in

Shanghai, soon followed by an office in Hong Kong in 1878, a mere eleven years after the Restoration.

The next major growth opportunity for Mitsui came in the promotion of the cotton textile industry. As was typical in other industrializing countries, the cotton-spinning industry became the forerunner of Japan's mass production manufacturing sector. With the use of modern technology the traditional cottage industry was transformed into a large-scale operation. The factors that led to its rapid assimilation and the growth of a modern cotton textile industry in Japan were common to countries elsewhere. A large consumer market was at hand; readily adaptable handicraft skills were present, as well as a large reserve of labor. Moreover the industry did not require a large capital outlay.

In the development of the cotton textile industry Bussan played a vital role in several areas. The initial task was to procure spinning and weaving machines abroad. England was the major source of supply. Bussan was the first to become the agent of Platt and Hargrave, the leading British producer of spindles, thus bypassing the foreign agents in Japan. Bussan also sought out other suppliers, negotiated the terms of purchases with them, and arranged for transportation and installation of the machines. At one point Bussan was responsible for as much as 80 percent of the total import of spindles. Bussan also took an active part in marketing the output of the burgeoning industry.

The Japanese cotton textile industry expanded at a very rapid rate, recording nearly tenfold growth in the number of spindles and a fourteenfold increase in the output of cotton yarn between 1882 and 1890. Such rapid growth in output soon exhausted the domestic supply of raw cotton. Bussan saw the opportunity to exploit its branch network, initially built for the coal trade, to procure raw cotton. It took the lead in importing raw cotton, first from China, as early as in 1887. The voracious appetite of the rapidly growing spinning industry required expansion to other sources, and soon Mitsui was sending representatives to India to investigate the feasibility of purchasing raw cotton directly from Indian suppliers. To promote exports, Bussan took the initiative in organizing Japanese spinners and weavers into export guilds and became the sole agent representing them. Japan's export effort was so successful that shortly after the turn of the century Japanese cotton products began to displace British products in the Chinese market. Throughout this period Mitsui was the uncontested leader in imports of cotton and exports of the finished product. By the end of the first decade of this century Mitsui was responsible for over 40 percent of the total exports of cotton goods from Japan.

To keep up with the rapid growth of foreign trade, Mitsui Bussan also expanded its ocean shipping. Before the turn of the century Bussan amended its charter to include ocean shipping and offered logistical support to client firms, ranging from ocean, coastal, and inland shipping to warehousing. Bussan also expanded its insurance businesses. Thus it began to take on the characteristics of a "full service" trading comany.

The rapid growth of both domestic businesses and foreign trade led to Bussan's opening a number of domestic and foreign branches. In the first decade of this century it established forty foreign branches, thirty in Asia and the remainder scattered in key cities in Europe and the United States, which handled 120 products. In many of these cities Bussan's offices were the first permanent Japanese presence, expanding in advance of Japanese diplomatic representation.

Within a mere four decades of its inception Bussan had become a major institution, occupying a vital role in Japan's domestic and foreign trade. In 1907, for example, its sales could be broken down into the following categories: 14 percent domestic trade, 35 percent exports, 44 percent imports, and 7 percent third country trade (trade not involving Japan). Bussan alone was responsible for 18 percent of Japan's total export and nearly 21 percent of its import.

The emergence of Bussan as a diversified trading company with a multinational network was intimately related to the development of the *zaibatsu*, a unique form of business organization created by Mitsui and several other families during the early days of Japan's industrialization. As the *zaibatsu* evolved, they became diversified groups of giant companies under the control of family-owned holding companies. Included in these groups were banks, insurance companies, trading companies, and a host of manufacturing enterprises. Mitsui and Mitsubishi developed into the largest and most powerful of the zaibatsu.

The Zaibatsu

The *zaibatsu*'s uniqueness lay in its distinctive structure, which ingeniously combined Western concepts of corporation with Japan's traditional values. The *zaibatsu* borrowed the Western concept of a joint stock company, a radical notion for the Japanese in the 1880s, and adopted mechanisms of control familiar in the West. A holding company extended over a network of subsidiaries and affiliates, through the linkages of intercorporate stockholdings, interlocking directorates, management help, personnel transfers, and bank credit. Operating decisions for the subsidiaries and affiliates were made by the holding company.

Just as basic an instrument of control as the Western form of organization were the traditional Japanese values, which emphasized hierarchical relationships, obligation, Confucian-based authoritarianism, the importance of collectivity, and discipline. In structuring its administrative system, the *zaibatsu* drew heavily on the distinctly Japanese concept of family. Traditionally the family in Japan was more than a biological kinship group. It was a network of related households, all of whose members were subject to the authority of a single head, and it was also the primary framework for structuring all types of secondary groups. Thus to the Japanese the hierarchical arrangement of subsidiaries and affiliated companies reporting to the helm of a holding company took on a special meaning.

The *zaibatsu* was indeed an ingenious invention for a society that had very limited resources but was anxious to industrialize rapidly. The institution made it possible to attain decided advantages through economies of scale in capital, technology, and management. It was another expression of *wakon yosai*, a popular slogan of the era, literally translated to "Western technology and the Japanese spirit."

In many senses the trading operations stood at the heart of the *zaibatsu*, providing information, leadership, and direction to the other subsidiaries. Trading was also highly lucrative. Bussan's relative importance in the Mitsui Zaibatsu was evident from the fact that between 1909, when the holding company was established, and 1932, the dividend paid by Bussan to the holding company amounted in aggregate to nearly 46 percent of the total paid by all of the Zaibatsu's immediate subsidiaries.

World War I gave a major boost to the Japanese economy, propelling the nation to a new stage of industrial development. Japan's international trade grew rapidly during the war, particularly with countries in Southeast Asia. Once again, Bussan was at the leading edge. Particularly notable during World War I was Bussan's ocean transportation business. In 1918, for example, transportation services provided over 28 percent of the company's total profit. Bussan's shipping businesses continued to flourish after the war; in fact its capacity was so large that as much as 60 percent of the cargoes carried were not related directly to Mitsui's trade. Bussan even diversified into shipbuilding to build some of its own ships. The shipbuilding division subsequently became an independent company. On the eve of World War II Bussan had come to boast fifty-nine branches overseas and a similar number of subbranches, and as many as 7,000 Mitsui men were employed abroad.

Mitsubishi Shoji

Even though Bussan was the dominant Japanese trading firm, it was not without rivals. Its archrival was Mitsubishi Shoji, whose evolution provides an interesting comparison.[3] Mitsubishi's origin, unlike Mitsui's, goes back only to the Restoration Movement. It was started by a bright entrepreneur, Yataro Iwasaki. He too enjoyed the strong political backing of an influential faction of the new regime. The business began in shipping, but like Mitsui, Mitsubishi, even more actively, moved into mining in 1873 under the patronage of the government. Mitsubishi needed a marketing arm for the output of its rather extensive mining ventures, and so the trading company of Mitsubishi Shoji was formed. Whereas Mitsui had a strong commercial heritage stretching two centuries back from the Meiji era, Mitsubishi's origin was rooted in nineteenth-century mining and industrial activities, which had an important influence in shaping its future.

Mitsubishi Shoji not only sold coal produced by its affiliated mines, it also represented other types of Mitsubishi-owned mines in the major Asian ports, such as Shanghai, Hong Kong, and Singapore. By the turn of the century Shoji* was success-

* Just as the Mitsui sogo shosha is popularly nicknamed "Bussan," the Mit-

fully entrenched in the domestic coal market in Japan. It supplied the National Railroad, the government-owned steel mill, the Japanese Navy, and major ocean shipping companies. The burgeoning Mitsubishi group of enterprises gradually diversified its activities beyond mining into such products as glass, paper, beer, and chemicals, and Shoji became the selling agent for the expanding group. It was not until the end of the first decade of this century that Shoji began to sell products that were not produced by its sister companies.

Despite its pioneering role in a number of industries, Mitsubishi Shoji had considerable difficulty entering the cotton textile industry, the leading industry during the early phase of Japan's industrialization. For one thing Mitsui dominated the industry and the barriers to entry were formidable for latecomers. Moreover Mitsubishi lacked experience in textiles. Like Mitsui, Mitsubishi sought to build its own *zaibatsu*, under the control of the Iwasaki family. The Mitsubishi Zaibatsu too was built around its trading arm and its financial institutions. A major difference between the two was that because of its strong roots in shipbuilding and its inability to break into the cotton textile industry, Mitsubishi stressed the development of heavy industries.

By the early twentieth century the Mitsubishi Zaibatsu had begun to develop into a formidable organization combining financial, commercial, and heavy manufacturing firms ranging from metals, chemicals, and petroleum to electric and industrial machinery and shipbuilding. World War I also gave Mitsubishi Shoji the opportunity to develop into a major sogo shosha. Between 1915 and 1918 Shoji opened eighteen branches and offices in cities including London, New York, Hong Kong, Shanghai, Calcutta, and Sydney. The range of products carried by Shoji also widened substantially by this time, including coal, metal, machinery, agricultural products, fats, fishery products, textiles, chemicals, fertilizers, and sundry goods.

As Koyata Iwasaki, a son of the founder, took over the helm in 1916, Mitsubishi Zaibatsu intensified its emphasis on heavy industries. A key element in this strategy was importation of advanced technology. In this effort Shoji performed the essen-

---

subishi sogo shosha is sometimes nicknamed "Shoji," especially when being contrasted with Mitsui Bussan.

tial tasks of identifying new technologies abroad, conducting negotiations, and facilitating technology transfer on behalf of a particular client. In those days the major sources of advanced technology were Germany and France. Shoji's offices in these countries established links with a number of leading German and French manufacturers.

In 1918 Koyata Iwasaki, then chairman of the board of Shoji, articulated the company's strategy in the following declaration:

1. Handle only that merchandise that is important to Japan's foreign trade.

2. Emphasize foreign trade; undertake domestic trade only in those cases where the volume and risks make the involvement of large trading companies essential.

3. Handle products of only leading foreign and domestic manufacturers. Whenever possible, establish close and long-term relationships with customers.

4. Extend financial assistance on a selective basis to those manufacturers with outstanding potential, and in return seek exclusive distribution agreements.

5. Confine activities to areas with potential for large volume.

6. Protect Mitsubishi's reputation.

7. Avoid entering into trading activities that may prove injurious to the interest of small firms.

During the 1920s Shoji's activities continued to grow, particularly as Mitsubishi Zaibatsu expanded. By the 1930s it even began to undertake, albeit modestly, direct foreign investment in China and elsewhere in Asia. Mitsubishi Zaibatsu's early commitment to heavy industries served it well as Japan began to intensify her efforts to build up her military strength in the 1930s. It was during World War II that Mitsubishi for the first time overtook Mitsui, its arch rival.

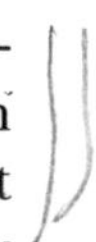

Suzuki

Examination of the evolution of the sogo shosha in prewar Japan would be incomplete without consideration of the case of Suzuki, which almost succeeded in joining the ranks of Bussan and Shoji.[4] It suffered, however, a dramatic and sudden collapse. Suzuki, unlike its two chief rivals, was based in the Kansai region around Osaka, the old commercial center of

Japan. The Kansai merchants were traditionally proud of their independence. They had kept their distance from the government, and Suzuki, unlike Mitsui and Mitsubishi, was not a beneficiary of political patronage. Suzuki, the founder, was an entrepreneur who began as a sugar importer in the early Meiji era in Kobe, a major port city in western Japan, and soon expanded his enterprise to include the manufacture of camphor and mint. Suzuki became involved in the development of Taiwan, a territory newly acquired as a result of the Sino-Japanese war (1894–95).

Suzuki also entered into industrial activities in such fields as celluloid, synthetic fibers, salt, flour milling, tobacco, beer, and steel. In 1905 it built a steel mill. In all of these activities Suzuki Shoten, its trading arm, served as the marketing agent.

On the eve of World War I Suzuki introduced its own merchant marine. By that time it had also created a number of branches abroad. Its product lines had expanded, ranging from rice, textiles, and pulp paper to copper, chemicals, machinery, and metals. World War I gave Suzuki, like Mitsubishi, an opportunity to develop into a full-fledged sogo shosha. By 1917 Suzuki's total sales had almost reached those of Mitsui Bussan, a remarkable feat.

By 1918 Suzuki had over fifty branches and offices in Japan and abroad; it was represented in virtually all the major cities in Asia and in leading trading centers in Europe and America. Its branch network stretched as far as Buenos Aires, Alexandria, and Melbourne. Suzuki used wartime profits for further diversification, and Suzuki Shoten, the group's sogo shosha, performed the familiar role of promoter and organizer of its industrial ventures. At its height Suzuki had seventy-eight companies producing a wide range of products. It had almost achieved its long-standing goal of becoming as great as the two prominent *zaibatsu*, Mitsui and Mitsubishi. But Suzuki was never to realize its dream, for it went bankrupt in the wake of the financial panic of 1927.

The development and the failure of the Suzuki group does provide an interesting comparison with the patterns of evolution followed by Mitsui and Mitsubishi. All three owed their initial success to their aggressive, sometimes daring, responses to fresh opportunities in foreign trade and industrial development. In all three cases the trading company played a vital role in developing and coordinating a network of large, diversified commercial and industrial enterprises.

But the differences are also noteworthy. For one thing, Suzuki did not have access to the highly profitable mining ventures that Mitsui and Mitsubishi enjoyed through political patronage. The mines gave the two *zaibatsu* a continuous substantial cash flow for several decades. The lack of strong political connections with the ruling oligarchy, which had come to play a role as the coordinating instrument of national development, deprived Suzuki of other privileges as well. Though its founder and subsequent management were clearly devoted to Japan's development, and did benefit greatly from Japan's own imperialistic moves, it did not enjoy the unique advantages accorded to Bussan or Shoji. Suzuki never developed its own strong financial institutions. Moreover, in comparison with the two large *zaibatsu*, it is believed that Suzuki failed to develop a strong professional management. Most critical in this regard was Suzuki's apparent inability to overcome a speculative mentality, even after it developed into a large, global, industrial and commercial organization. This propensity to seek quick profits by shrewdly playing the markets, which provided the basis of the company's initial success, was the very factor that brought about its demise. Management at Mitsubishi, in contrast, discouraged speculative activities.

Below the level of Bussan and Shoji, a number of second-tier trading companies evolved.[5] Some of them developed into sogo shosha after World War II, but during much of the prewar period they hardly qualified as such. They were smaller than the *zaibatsu* giants and had more limited product lines. Their international networks were less extensive, with branch offices only where the volume of trade in their particular products supported their establishment. Two prominent examples of this category of shosha are C. Itoh and Iwai.

C. Itoh

C. Itoh's origin can be traced to the mid-nineteenth century, when the founder began as a trader selling textile products to foreign agents in Kobe. Before World War II textiles dominated C. Itoh's business. Its size was quite modest compared with Mitsui or Mitsubishi. For example, in 1919 C. Itoh had only seven branches abroad: four in China and one each in

Manila, Calcutta, and New York. Its performance was rather erratic, subject to the fluctuations of the textile industry. Losses were particularly serious in the early 1920s; the company went through a major reorganization, but its performance remained dismal throughout most of the 1920s. It was not until the late 1930s that C. Itoh began to report steady profits and its trading activities became more diversified.

Iwai

Iwai, in the midnineteenth century, was a very modest importer of manufactured goods, such as lamps, umbrellas, and matches. A major opportunity for Iwai came when it became one of the first Japanese companies to establish direct trading relationships with English merchants, thus becoming able to bypass the foreign agents in Japan and save a considerable amount in commissions. Within ten years Iwai was importing such wide-ranging products as medicine, fertilizer, galvanized iron sheet, steel plates, and gas pipes. It increasingly emphasized trade in metals, and by the end of the nineteenth century was importing a variety of steel products from England and the United States. Early in this century Iwai became a distributor for the government-owned Nippon Steel; later it was selected to be one of the several primary distributors, thus joining the ranks of Mitsui and Mitsubishi, at least as far as the steel trade was concerned. Unlike C. Itoh, which had stayed primarily in trading, Iwai did enter into industrial ventures in a modest way, in such fields as the manufacture of steel plates, celluloid, paint, caustic soda, dyes, and chemicals. At about the same time it began a modest exporting business.

Once again, the business was small in scale compared with the two giants. For example, in 1912 Iwai's total sales were only about 1 percent of Mitsui's, and it was not until the late 1920s that Iwai enjoyed major growth. In that period the company's product lines expanded substantially, and by the late 1930s it had nine branches in China and one each in London, Bombay, Melbourne, and Sydney.

Comparison with Britain

The evolution of foreign trade in Japan presents a striking contrast to that in Great Britain, another island nation heavily dependent on foreign trade. Professor Nakagawa contrasts England and Japan in his excellent study, *Organized Entrepreneurship in Early Meiji*.[6] In England, Nakagawa notes, industrialization had progressed gradually over a period of time, and so had foreign trading activities, which went back to the days of merchant adventurers. By the eighteenth century there were in England a substantial number of foreign traders, specializing in the large-scale trading of tobacco, sugar, coffee, and slaves. Many of them owned their own fleets. Moreover the nation possessed a rather well-developed merchant marine.

In part because of the gradual growth of foreign trade, the entire English foreign trading infrastructure developed along highly specialized lines. As Nakagawa notes, in Japan both the commercial and industrial revolutions had to take place simultaneously to achieve the national goal of *fukoku kyohei*—"strong army and rich nation." Moreoever, being a latecomer, Japan faced substantial entry barriers, since key European nations and the United States had come to dominate world trade. Professor Nakagawa argues that for Japan to enter markets and industries successfully against the established competitors, large scale was essential. A combination of urgent need and lack of expertise precluded the gradual development of specialized institutions.

Large-scale foreign trade required a presence in the major markets. Moreover the urgency and lack of expertise forced the few emerging foreign trade institutions to undertake the entire range of services. The requirement for a large minimum scale and the need to provide supporting services exerted enormous pressure on these organizations to expand their product lines, since the volume in any one product was quite limited, the nation being as yet only in the early stages of industrial development.

A comparison of the development in England and Japan of the cotton textile industry—the world's first modern mass production sector—is instructive.

By the time Japan's cotton spinning industry emerged, the world cotton market was dominated by the English. English cotton spinners enjoyed enormous technical and scale advantages, supported by effective buying organizations. With the development of the cotton textile industry in Lancashire, England's imports of American cotton had expanded rapidly. Increases in volume over time had led to the development of intricate and highly sophisticated trading institutions. Along with trading, transportation and storage evolved along highly specialized lines, and the Cotton Exchange was organized. Nakagawa notes that these specialized activities functioned so well that English spinners were able to procure raw cotton when they needed it, at a very low commission.

Japan, as a latecomer to the industry, had little time to evolve specialized and sophisticated institutions. The Japanese alternative was to exploit as much as possible the few and fragile trading firms that had served to export a few commodities. Bussan's coal traders saw new opportunities in the importation of British-made spindles; its branches in China took on the new function of procuring raw cotton. The rapid growth of demand for cotton required and made it feasible for Bussan to expand its operations into the United States. Bussan bought raw cotton on its account, and through its presence in the key cotton-producing countries, it was able to scan the cotton markets on a daily basis and ensure a continuous supply of raw cotton at the lowest available price. With its ability to respond quickly to highly volatile world cotton markets, Bussan in effect performed for Japanese spinners functions comparable to those of the Cotton Exchange in England. For the spinners, Bussan and the rival sogo shosha that expanded into the cotton trade filled the gap in what would have been a very imperfect market. Providing a link to external markets in the form of exports of finished products was a logical extension of these activities.

Multiple Roles

In this evolution the sogo shosha came to perform multiple functions, including procurement of modern equipment, new technology, and raw materials; financing of these purchases; arranging for shipment; and exporting the final products. The pattern established in the cotton textile industry was to repeat itself in a number of other industries. With almost monopolistic access to advanced technologies, equipment, raw materials, and overseas markets, the sogo shosha was in an enormously powerful position. With the cash flow generated from trade, and the backing of the financial institutions of the *zaibatsu*, a logical step for the managers of the sogo shosha was to take an active part in starting new industrial ventures. Sometimes such a move was a response in the sense that new supply sources had to be created to serve the growing demand for certain products; but in others, the action was strategic, part of a larger plan to build in Japan the major pieces of a modern industrial economy. The sogo shosha, with its unique access to essential resources, contributed greatly to the ever-quickening pace of import substitution in Japan's industrialization.

Bussan and Shoji then contributed to the development of the *zaibatsu* in important ways. The sogo shosha served as a major catalyst in the *zaibatsu*'s search for new industrial opportunities and initiated new enterprises; second, once created, the sogo shosha served as a primary, if not exclusive, distribution agent. Thus the evolution of the sogo shosha began as an ingenious Japanese response to the overwhelming needs for large-scale trading organizations and led to a broader role as facilitator and even leader of the industrialization process. Its character and functions were much shaped by the distinct needs of the period. Not only did the sogo shosha become a window to the world for a nation long isolated, it came to occupy a crucial role within the domestic Japanese economy.

Inside Japan the sogo shosha promoted the division of labor in burgeoning industries saddled with a scarcity of resources. The sogo shosha gave important advantages to their fledgling industrial ventures. It enabled them to enjoy economies of scale in procuring raw materials and made it possible for them to concentrate on manufacturing, by providing them with ready access to export markets. Particularly important in this regard was the role the sogo shosha played in providing export opportunities for the myriad small Japanese firms in cottage industries, which, like their counterparts in developing countries today, faced many problems in trying to break into the world market. The sogo shosha fed them market information, helped them design products, extended credit, and, most important, developed foreign outlets for their products. The sogo shosha made it possible for scarce resources to be mobilized for foreign trade in a concentrated manner. The scarcest resources of all was experienced personnel. The sogo shosha's contribution to the nation's economic development transcended the narrow definition of foreign trade. It played a vital role as a catalyst of new industrial activities.

The Aftermath of Defeat

Defeat in World War II dealt Japan a serious blow. Her hard-won industrial base was almost totally wiped out. Industrial production in 1946 sank to less than a third of the 1930 total, and to a mere seventh of the 1941 level. For several subsequent years Japan was an occupied country. The U.S.-led occupation forces sought to introduce a wide range of economic, political, and social reforms. Among these were the dissolution of the *zaibatsu* and related economic deconcentration measures. The intricate structure of the prewar *zaibatsu*, so painstakingly built, was destroyed; family ownership and control were severed. In addition some of Japan's major companies were broken up.

The dissolution was particularly devastating to the two major sogo shosha. Mitsui Bussan was broken up into some two hundred entities and Mitsubishi Shoji into one hundred and thirty-nine. Not only were they divided into many small units, but their activities were severely restricted. The restrictions included the prohibition of the use of the names Mitsui and Mitsubishi. For several years the activities of the sogo shosha, or more accurately their very *raison d'être*, disappeared almost completely. Critical raw materials were allocated by the government. The major thrust of government aid for economic recovery was concentrated on a handful of critical industries such as steel, coal, fertilizer, and textiles. Other commercial activities were not deemed essential.

Japanese recovery, which was well under way by the late 1940s, was speeded up considerably by the Korean War. Particularly relevant to our present consideration is the rapid growth of domestic consumption and export of textile products. Once again, as it did in the early days of industrialization, the textile industry led the way. The sudden surge of demand for textile products gave a much-needed boost to a dozen or so textile shosha.

The five leading textile shosha—C. Itoh, Marubeni, Gosho, Nichimen, and Tomen—seized these opportunities. With the two erstwhile leaders decimated, they were virtually the only ones experienced in foreign trade, where they enjoyed a commanding advantage over any potential rivals. Their business expanded beyond textiles to include metals, machinery, foods, and so on. They all sought vigorously to fill the gap created by the dissolution of the two prewar leaders, as is evident in the following statistics. Between 1937 and 1943 Mitsui and Mitsubishi accounted for 28.6 percent of Japan's foreign trade, followed by Tomen (6.5 percent), Nichimen (4.9 percent), and Gosho (4 percent). In other words, the five largest firms were responsible for 44 percent of the total foreign trade. In 1951 the industry had become highly fragmented, with C. Itoh leading the way with 4.7 percent, followed by Nichimen (4.3 percent), Tomen (4 percent), Marubeni (4 percent), Kanematsu (3.1 percent), and Gosho (3 percent). The six leading companies accounted for only 16 percent of the total.[7]

The end of the Korean War created havoc in the market. A number of the shosha found themselves in a very difficult position. Many suffered severe losses in their commodity trading, with devastating results. Measures were taken by the government and the major banks to rescue the firms, but the results were not entirely successful. Several firms went bankrupt; some were absorbed by other companies. Thus in the early 1950s, just as Japan's postwar economic growth was about to begin, the first round of what was to become a shakeout and consolidation of traders had already taken place.

In the midfifties the economy as a whole quickly recovered from the temporary setback and was well on its way to beginning almost two decades of uninterrupted rapid economic growth. The government took the initiative by giving certain industries a high priority. Japan's major corporations sought out advanced foreign technologies aggressively, as they had done in the prewar era. The government objective in the 1950s and 1960s was to encourage the development of capital-intensive heavy industries. These included steel, chemicals, synthetic fibers, petrochemicals, petroleum refining, and machinery. The government did set targets and provide protection, incentives, and privileges for these industries, but much of the credit for achieving rapid industrialization goes to the private sector.

With optimistic growth potential and active encouragement by the government, the Japanese industries undertook repeated rounds of major capital investment. Real gross domestic investment, private and public, increased by an average of 13 percent a year between 1952 and 1973, and private business plant and equipment investment increased by over 14 percent. From 1957 to the mid-1960s, the share of plant and equipment investment increased from about 10 percent of GNP to 20 percent.[8] Throughout this period the private sector showed a strong sense of optimism about the growth of the economy. Business leaders were anxious to exploit this enormous growth potential by expanding their firms' operations, seeking technological improvement, and competing aggressively for greater market shares. In fact optimism was widely felt throughout Japanese industry. New demand was generated for all types of products.

This optimism became self-fulfilling. The initial growth came from the rapid expansion of domestic demand. For example, in the steel industry, domestic consumption grew from 19 million tons in 1960 to 71 million tons in 1970s, with an average annual growth rate of nearly 14 percent. The steel industry pursued an extraordinarily active round of capital investment. In the process it acquired the most modern and efficient facilities in the world. A similar feat was achieved in other industries, such as oil refining, nonferrous metal processing, and production of chemicals, petrochemicals, and synthetic fibers. By the early 1970s Japan had achieved a commanding position in virtually every basic industry.

As the nation pressed forward in building heavy industries, the sogo shosha saw great growth opportunities. In the early 1950s Mitsubishi and Mitsui began to consolidate their fragmented entities. In fact by 1954 Mitsubishi had completed its regrouping, and several years later Mitsui too once again emerged as a single entity. By 1955 Mitsubishi rose to the top, accounting for 9.2 percent of the total foreign trade of Japan.

The Era of Growth

The rapid development of capital-intensive heavy industries gave the sogo shosha splendid opportunities. Most of the raw materials, which included iron ore, coal, crude oil, pulp, and others, had to be imported. The steel industry provides an example. In 1933 Japan's total imports of iron ore were slightly over 3.3 million tons.[9] Nearly 70 percent was bought from Malaysia and China. Through the mid-1960s the sources continued to be concentrated in South Asia, namely Malaysia, the Philippines, and India. As the demand for iron ore increased rapidly, the steel industry was compelled to broaden its sources. By the early 1970s Japan's total iron ore imports reached 131 million tons. The list of sources had lengthened to include Australia, Brazil, Chile, Canada, and Peru. But the industry needed reliable sources that could supply even larger quantities of ore. With active encouragement from the steel mills, the sogo shosha sought to diversify their sources further. Also, to reduce uncertainties in supply, the sogo shosha began to participate in the financing of mining ventures by extending long-term loans and taking equity positions.

The steel industry had initially bought most of its coking coal from the United States. It became increasingly concerned, however, about its predominant reliance on a single country. Once again, the sogo shosha developed new sources in Canada and Australia. On the distribution side, the domestic demand for steel products skyrocketed. Manufacturers of machinery and ships and other major users rapidly increased their demand for steel. Growth in demand was not confined to large users, either. A virtually continuous construction boom throughout the country led to an increase in demand for a wide variety of steel products among small- to medium-size firms in all parts of the nation. The sogo shosha, as they had in the prewar period, handled the entire distribution for the industry.

Similar needs were felt in other capital-intensive heavy industries. Table 2.1 shows the enormous growth in import of raw materials between 1955 and 1973. From the point of view of the manufacturing companies, the use of the sogo shosha made very good sense. In the first place, they were preoccupied with expansion of production capacity. Given the nature of the industries, advantages of scale were obvious, and given the relative shortage of capital during this high-growth era, the manufacturers found it valuable to obtain the collaboration of the sogo shosha in the procurement of raw materials and in selling activities. It was the sogo shosha that bore the burden

Table 2.1
Import of key raw materials for selected years, 1955–1973

Year	Iron ore (1,000 Mt)	Crude oil (1,000 kl)	Coal (1,000 Mt)	Chemicals ($1,000)
1955	5,459	12,145	2,862	112,450
1960	15,030	31,121	8,292	265,202
1970	102,091	197,108	50,173	1,000,483
1973	134,723	289,699	56,855	1,865,236

Source: *Economic Statistical Annual 1978* (Tokyo: The Bank of Japan, 1979), p. 114.

of building and expanding organizations and facilities necessary to handle the ever-growing flows of products. Of even greater financial significance was the fact that the sogo shosha supplied the capital to maintain sufficient inventories of raw materials and finished products. This reduction in investment and working capital requirements made it possible for an industry to concentrate its scarce resources on expansion of capacity and purchase of the most up-to-date equipment. Thus, by working with the sogo shosha, a manufacturing company could in effect gain access to an additional source of funds.

As these industries continued to expand their capacity, exports became increasingly important. The waves of investment that caused output to exceed domestic demand also brought greater efficiency, which began to create an international comparative advantage for many Japanese producers. Japan's exports doubled between 1955 and 1960, reaching $4 billion in 1960, and they doubled again in the next five years. By 1970 the volume had grown by as much as five times.

Equally relevant to our present consideration is the fact that the composition of Japan's exports underwent signigficant changes. In the 1950s its exports consisted primarily of products of labor-intensive light industries. By the 1960s the composition had changed dramatically in favor of the products of heavy industries dominated by large, oligopolistic firms. Just as they did in the prewar era, the sogo shosha played an important role in helping their clients seek out new technologies, since once again foreign technology played a critical role in the rapid growth of the Japanese industries.

Rapid postwar economic growth and the increasingly diversified nature of the Japanese economy created new opportunities for erstwhile specialized shosha such as C. Itoh and Iwai to diversify their product lines and enter new fields. These shosha, which had formerly specialized in relatively narrow products such as textiles and metals, seized this opportunity to broaden their offerings. Particularly aggressive in this effort were Marubeni and C. Itoh, two textile-based firms, and Nissho-Iwai, strong in the metal trade.

C. Itoh and Marubeni achieved the third and fourth positions among Japanese firms, ranking immediately behind Mitsubishi and Mitsui. In the mid-1950s in both firms textiles accounted for as much as half of total sales, but by the end of the 1960s the relative share of textiles had declined to less than a quarter. Almost equally dramatic is the growth record of Nissho-Iwai and of smaller shosha such as Kanematsu-Gosho, Nichimen, and Ataka.

Still another way the sogo shosha sought growth opportunities was to develop new outlets to distribute the ever-increasing output of the large oligopolistic firms in basic manufacturing industries. To meet this problem, the sogo shosha extended financial and managerial assistance to selected small and medium-size companies. In the process each sogo shosha built quasi-controlled networks of such firms. Such relationships, commonly known as *keiretsu,* are an ingenious way of combining the market and financial power of a large firm with the flexibility, distinct skills, and lower wages of small- and medium-size firms.

Such a controlled system is particularly effective in multistage process flow industries such as steel, chemicals, petrochemicals, and synthetic fibers. It enables the main manufacturing firms to concentrate their resources and management's attention on the capital-intensive and technologically oriented phases of manufacturing, leaving the sogo shosha to undertake downstream processing and manufacturing, as well as distribution, through its network of affiliated manufacturers and distributors.

To small- and medium-size firms the danger of exploitation by the sogo shosha is not totally absent,[10] but they do benefit greatly from such associations by gaining preferential access to financing, raw materials, and, most important, to the wider domestic and international markets that are clearly beyond the reach of a single small firm.

As the Japanese economy expanded rapidly, so too the sogo shosha experienced major growth. For example, the sales of Mitsubishi Shoji increased eightfold, from ¥644 billion in 1960 to ¥5,177 billion in 1973 (table 2.2). During the same period, as shown in table 2.3, other major sogo shosha achieved equally outstanding results. According to a study undertaken by the Japan Fair Trade Commission in 1974, the six largest sogo shosha held stocks in 5,390 companies, and the total book value of the equity held amounted to ¥80 billion, or roughly $270 million. Some of these companies are no doubt other major corporations, reflecting a horizontal interlocking of stock ownership, but most represent those companies with which the sogo shosha had active business relationships. The study also

Table 2.2
Sales of the six largest sogo shosha in selected years

		(¥ billion)	
	1960	1973	1977
Mitsubishi	644	5,177	9,609
Mitsui	640	4,941	6,025
Marubeni	613	2,651	6,431
C. Itoh	545	2,831	6,333
Sumitomo	197	2,430	5,825
Nissho-Iwai	337	2,393	4,527

Table 2.3
Growth of Japan's GNP trade and the sales of the ten largest sogo shosha for selected years, 1965–1976

	1965	1970	1976
GNP	32,813	73,046	168,937
Trade			
Export	3,141	7,290	20,676
Import	3,030	6,967	19,686
Total	6,171	14,257	34,420
Sogo shosha	8,163	19,641	49,916

Source: The Industrial Bank of Japan.

shows that the six leading sogo shosha were the largest stockholders in 1,057 of these firms. The total sales of these majority-owned firms in 1973 reached $21 billion, or 30 percent of the combined sales of the six sogo shosha.

Business Groups

In the 1950s the prewar *zaibatsu* that had been destroyed in such a devastating manner began to emerge once again, though in a much altered form.[11] As Japan began to press toward economic recovery, the underlying conditions that had led to the emergence of the original *zaibatsu* were again present, in an even more compelling form. Japan's leading enterprises were concerned with modernizing and rebuilding. At the same time capital was scarce, and technical and administrative expertise was limited.

The senior executives of former *zaibatsu* firms saw the advantages of pooling their resources. Since family ownership was completely severed and holding companies were made illegal in the postwar era, it was impossible to regroup in the traditional manner. These men saw that new relationships had to be formed on the basis of much more limited cross-holding of stock and occasional interlocking directorates. They were still influenced by their awareness of the practical benefits to be derived from cooperation, and they were still bound by the sense of loyalty and solidarity nurtured in the prewar family-oriented *zaibatsu* system.

Although the postwar version of *zaibatsu* lacked tight discipline and strict central coordination in the prewar tradition, each group's banks and trading company began to assume positions of leadership and a coordination function for the group, albeit informally and considerably weaker than in the prewar era. The fact that the banks provided a significant share of capital to their member companies, at least during the high-growth era, placed them in an influential position. In this manner the Mitsubishi, Mitsui, and Sumitomo groups re-emerged. Though they no longer enjoyed the degree of power and control in the Japanese economy they had formerly exercised, the new structure made various forms of cooperation possible, such as the forming of joint ventures for entering new fields.

As Japanese business pursued its postwar strategy, another new structure emerged in the form of bank-centered groups. The forced dissolution of the *zaibatsu*, by loosening the tightly controlled economy, had encouraged the development of other large manufacturing and commercial enterprises. These enterprises, which had both prewar and postwar origins, included such well-known companies as Hitachi in electric machinery and electronics, Matsushita in electronics, and Nissan in automobiles. Since new technology was available from foreign sources and managerial resources were abundant, these companies found that, to enter new fields and expand their capacities ahead of their competitors, their most serious problem was to amass large quantities of capital. Throughout the 1950s and 1960s the stock market remained underdeveloped and could provide only a small portion of the capital needs of rapidly expanding enterprises.

Instead, their needs were met primarily by less than a dozen large commercial banks, commonly known as the city banks. These banks served as the chief financial intermediaries to channel the high level of private savings characteristic of this period into large-scale industrial endeavors. In the process the banks sought to establish close links with a selected number of large firms in various growth fields. Each bank gave preferential treatment to certain firms, which in return placed their deposits with the bank, thereby enhancing its relative competitive position. Out of this arrangement grew the bank-centered groups, of which the most dominant were Fuyo (Fuji Bank), Daichi-Kangin, and Sanwa. Each group consisted of a diversified cluster of manufacturing and service firms, among which there was a limited amount of cross-holding of stocks. Sometimes, in addition, a representative of a bank occupied a senior management position in a key client firm.

The bonds among these firms, however, remained a good deal looser and weaker than those that held together the reconstructed postwar *zaibatsu* groups. Unlike a *zaibatsu* group, a bank-centered group lacked a clear identification and a common heritage. Often the bank and the trading company competed for leadership, which hindered the development of close coordination. Nevertheless, these groups enabled non-*zaibatsu* firms to pool their resources and to share risks to an extent that would otherwise have been difficult. By casting itself in a central coordinating position, the sogo shosha provided an incentive not only to the formation but the growth of the bank-centered group.

The reconstituted *zaibatsu* and bank-centered groups competed vigorously, each attempting to participate in every major growth field. The *zaibatsu* had had a history of oligopolistic rivalry, and postwar economic reforms and rapid economic growth opened up fresh opportunities for non-*zaibatsu* firms.

Throughout the 1950s and well into the 1960s, the types of technology sought by Japanese enterprises were relatively mature ones and were available from a number of sources. To a group that already had diversified interests, there was considerable risk in failing to match a rival's entry into a major new field, because the rival group's move would pose a threat to the existing equilibrium. Then too the competitive position of a bank depended, to an important degree, on the strength of its affiliated companies. Once committed to a given field, an enterprise competed vigorously for a greater share of the market in order to increase its capacity and reap the benefits of the economy of scale. In critical industries, market share was crucial, since it was the standard criterion in the Ministry of International Trade and Industry (MITI)'s formula for approving capacity expansion.

There was also noneconomic incentives for competition among these groups. The importance the Japanese historically attach to the collectivity led to intense feelings of rivalry among the groups. Some decisions to match a competitor's moves could be traced in part to an unwillingness to be seen as anything less than a first-class group of firms.

In the face of enormous growth opportunities, the former *zaibatsu* groups and the newly emerged bank-centered groups relentlessly pursued a policy of growth and diversification. Each group was anxious to establish a foothold in every growth field. The dominant strategy of each group was to avoid being preempted by any one of its competing groups. Out of these practices has evolved the so-called "one-set policy," so aptly described by Professor Giichi Mayazaki, in which each major *zaibatsu* and banking group sought to build a set of diversified industrial and commercial operations. In each group a sogo shosha played a central role. Such group actions in turn encouraged the diversification of the group's sogo shosha.

In the two prewar *zaibatsu* groups, Mitsubishi and Mitsui, the respective sogo shosha became, in the postwar period, a focal point of coordination because of their extensive trading relationships with the former sister companies. It is estimated that in 1970 about 20 percent of Mitsubishi Shoji's business came from such member firms. Mitsui Bussan was less cohesive, with 13 percent of its total sales coming from its sister firms. The Sumitomo group created its own sogo shosha in the postwar era and undertook aggressive groupwide efforts to nurture the young company. These were so successful that within a rather short time Sumitomo Shoji had become the fifth largest sogo shosha, suggestive of the group's solidarity and relative power in the Japanese economy.

The Oil Crisis of 1973 and Its Aftermath

The decade of the 1970s proved to be an extremely challenging period for the sogo shosha. By the early 1970s the widely acclaimed Japanese economic miracle had begun to show signs of slowing down. The so-called Nixon shock, which transformed the world of fixed exchange rate into a turbulence of fluctuating currencies, was quickly followed by the oil shock of 1973. Given Japan's heavy dependence on petroleum and heavy industry, the aftermath was particularly traumatic. The Japanese economy went through a period of stagflation lasting no more than two years. Japan made a surprisingly quick recovery, but the sogo shosha, as an institution, became saddled with continuing problems. By the mid-1970s the economy shifted quite successfully from heavy capital-intensive industries to the so-called knowledge-intensive ones built around high technology. It was in this period that such industries as semiconductors, computers, and telecommunications took off. But the traditional industries such as textiles, steel, chemicals, and agricultural products had reached maturity, if not a state of decline. In fact some had lost their international competitiveness, particularly as newly industrialized nations such as Korea, Taiwan, and Singapore began to challenge Japan. Of course these were precisely the industries in which the sogo shosha's traditional strengths lay. In the aftermath of the oil crisis a sudden shortage of certain consumer products developed, and some sogo shosha sought quick gains by hoarding them, causing a tremendous public furor. In early 1974 the Fair Trade Commission undertook an extensive inquiry into the behavior of the sogo shosha, putting them on the defensive. Not long afterward Prime Minister Kakuei Tanaka embarked on his plan to restructure the Japanese Archipelago, which fueled a wave of speculation in real estate, and once again, some of the sogo shosha exploited opportunities for quick gains. These events were followed by the so-called Lockheed scandal, in which Tanaka was the central figure and Marubeni, the fourth largest sogo shosha, was implicated.

The combination of these events put the sogo shosha in disrepute, leading to the loss of public confidence. The fall of Ataka, the smallest of the sogo shosha, further eroded public confidence. Ataka, unlike its larger competitors, had remained family controlled and managed since its beginnings. Anxious to maintain and enhance its hard-won position among the ten leading sogo shosha, it took a tremendous risk in oil refining in Canada. Lack of knowledge of the industry, poor management, and inadequate assessment of risk contributed to its sudden decline. The company declared bankruptcy in 1976 and was absorbed by C. Itoh. The Ataka example heightened the public awareness of the sogo shosha's fragility.

Between 1973 and 1979 sogo shosha sales grew at a rate of 9.4 percent per annum, 2 percent below the nominal growth of GNP. The reduced rate of growth further intensified competition, resulting in the erosion of operating margins and profitability, as presented in table 1.1. For example, gross margin declined from 2.4 percent in 1973 to 1.82 percent in 1979. The sogo shosha not only had to bear the brunt of the maturing of their traditional product lines, they were also forced to expand their financing functions to rescue clients and affiliated companies in difficulty. Such difficulty was common. For example, accounts receivable outstandings hovered around three months' sales between 1974 through 1979, which was at least a month longer than the average in the 1960s. Most of the sogo shosha also had substantial funds tied up in loans, advances, and credit to their subsidiaries, affiliates, and subcontractors.

The sogo shosha's profitability continued to suffer through the latter half of the 1970s, and most of them eventually experienced losses from operations. To show a profit, they were foced to sell real estate and stock holdings.

The slowdown in growth has proved particularly difficult for smaller sogo shosha. As indicated in table 1.1, the growth rate of the top six companies has outpaced that of the smaller three. The former, given their size, historical strengths, and entrenched relationships with their sister companies and banks, enjoy substantial advantages over the smaller ones. In 1973 the top six companies accounted for 85.2 percent of the combined sales of the nine sogo shosha. Their share as a group had risen to 87.3 percent by 1979. Even more serious is the fact that the profitability of the smaller three has been significantly lower than that of the larger six. In fact many anticipate further shakeouts of the sogo shosha in the coming decade.

Confronted with fundamental changes in the environment as well as internal problems of organizational rigidity and aging managers, the sogo shosha embarked in the mid-1970s on an effort to streamline their organizations and a search for new business opportunities. Every company has undergone major organizational realignment in the past several years to reduce cost and to be more flexible and responsive to the customers' needs and to new opportunities. They have taken a variety of steps to encourage entry into new business opportunities. These opportunities are concentrated in industries such as information technology, biotechnology, and telecommunications which are unfamiliar to the sogo shosha, so they have had to reorient their strategies and structures to participate in the new markets.

The 1980s are viewed by sogo shosha management as a period of winter, a time to rationalize and restructure in preparation for the next stage of growth. As we have seen, this is not the first time they have faced such a challenge. In fact the history of the sogo shosha is one of continuing adjustment and adaptation to new opportunities.

3

Distinctive Competences

The primary function of the sogo shosha is trading—that is matching buyers and sellers of diverse products. In performing this core activity, it is entrenched in a number of key industries. Most of the sogo shosha's functions are not one-time or ad hoc transactions in which a new buyer and seller are linked for the first time but rather involve "regular" buyers and sellers on a recurring basis. Thus in various industries the sogo shosha is typically involved at different stages of the value chain, from the purchase of raw materials for a client to the marketing of the final product.

The original model of today's sogo shosha can be seen in the role Mitsui played in the development of Japan's cotton-spinning industry. It procured spinning machinery and spinning technology from abroad, and when the domestic supply of raw cotton was exhausted, it took on the functions of purchasing raw cotton abroad and ensuring the manufacturers of a steady supply of raw materials. The sogo shosha also played a vital role in stimulating demand for cotton by its actions to develop the weaving industry. It did so in a highly imaginative manner by organizing myriad small weavers who sprang up in the early days of the nation's industrialization. The sogo shosha provided the weavers with cotton and bought the textiles they produced for distribution in both the domestic and foreign markets. In these transactions the sogo shosha almost invariably extended credit to small weavers for whom access to capital was extremely difficult if not impossible.

Though the sogo shosha occasionally does engage in one-time transactions, much of its activity revolves around multi-stage involvement in vertically integrated commodity systems, particularly in basic commodities such as textiles, iron and steel, nonferrous metals, chemicals, and foodsuffs. Indeed, our study has revealed that the sogo shosha's uniqueness lies in its capacity to provide essential links between stages in a product system for a client firm. The links almost invariably involve trading but at the same time entail ancillary services.

Product Systems

By product systems[1] we mean identifiable flows of goods, services, and resources among technologically separable units that transform raw materials into finished products. The steel industry provides a clear example. Figure 3.1 shows a simplified version of the steel product system. Ore and coal must be mined, then transported to blast furnaces to produce basic steel; the basic steel is run through finishing mills to produce finished steel; and finally the finished steel is fabricated into intermediate and finished products. Resources such as money, machinery, and people are put into the system, and the output produced is exchanged for more resources.

Each basic step in this simplified version of the steel system is itself a complicated system. Consider the transportation of iron ore. Whether the ore is moved by ship or by rail, its transportation requires several steps, including loading, carriage, unloading, and storage. The activity in these systems requires the efforts of many subgroups of people and substantial resources and skills of different kinds. We can speak of the steel product system as a *system* precisely because the activities are coordinated in persistent patterns.[2]

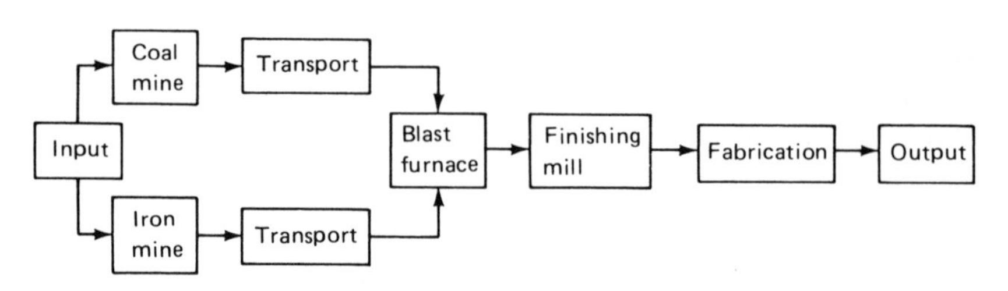

Figure 3.1
Schematic of the basic steps in the steel system

System Coordination[2]

Coordination of extremely large-scale systems, such as the world steel system, is highly complex. There are two general strategies for coordinating the basic steps down in figure 3.1. One is to locate all steps within an integrated firm. For example, U.S. Steel owns iron mines, ore transport ships, blast furnaces, mills, and fabricating plants and can coordinate the transactions among these units through an administrative hierarchy. Managers with the specific authority to do so decide how much ore should be mined, and how it should be shipped, transformed into iron, and then into steel, and finally fabricated. The other general method of coordination is markets. An independent firm carries out each technologically separate step, negotiating with the units that supply it and then with the units that are its customers; it decides independently what its production should be and what prices to charge.

In fact system coordination generally involves a compromise between the two forms, which have offsetting characteristics. On the one hand, bureaucratic administration offers the possibility of obtaining superior efficiency through rational planning and operation at the system level. On the other hand, markets offer the possibility of efficient rapid response to local conditions on the part of each unit. Both forms, however, have inherent limitations.

As administrative hierarchies grow in size and complexity, the resources that must be devoted to purely administrative functions, such as supervision, increase while the effectiveness of administration tends to decrease.[3] Instead of responding to external conditions, it responds to its internal needs. This is the well-known and often caricatured tendency of bureaucracies to become bloated, inward looking, and strangled in "red tape." In theory there is a point of diminishing returns at which further gains from administrative coordination are completely offset by the increasing costs and inefficiency of an administrative hierarchy.

Markets also face inherent limitations. In the face of the interdependence, complexity, and uncertainty of life within a dynamic system, the costs of negotiation (pricing) can skyrocket. In the face of uncertainty, each unit adds a risk premium to its prices. As goods and services move through many stages, these can snowball. When less than perfect markets exist, monopoly and monopsony costs are imposed by units with strong control of particular stages and then passed through the system. With each unit responding to *local* conditions, opportunities to act in a longer-term coordinated fashion may be lost.

This fairly simple theoretical trade-off contrasts sharply with the messy realities of real markets and real organizations. Markets vary widely in their fundamental characteristics and patterns of behavior, and so do administrative hierarchies. Most markets include administrative hierarchies as important participants, while many of the largest administrative hierarchies are broken into subunits that may compete with each other internally, rather than be fully "rational" in carrying out well-formed plans in strict accordance with orders from higher up in the hierarchy. In real life the two forms interpenetrate each other, so that it is impossible to analyze trade-offs between the two modes with any of the elegance suggested by abstract theoretical typologies. Nevertheless, we can use the trade-off between markets and administration as a tool for understanding the role of the sogo shosha in product systems.

Trade-offs between Administrative and Market Coordination

The steel product system illustrates how markets ignore benefits that are attainable by rationalization, but administrative hierarchies may lack the supple responsiveness and economy to realize these benefits fully. A blast furnace needs to be maintained with a sufficient inventory of raw materials to guarantee it will not shut down for lack of supplies. Restarting a furnace is costly and is to be avoided if possible. If the furnace operator has to go out and buy raw materials every day in the market, he risks running out of fuel or having to pay unacceptably high prices. To protect itself from these risks, a firm must bear the cost of maintaining a large enough inventory.

But if the blast furnace is part of an integrated firm, the inventory need not be as large. The firm's administrative hierarchy will plan to keep shipments from its own mines arriving regularly, so that, barring strikes and disasters, a much smaller inventory need be kept.

Administratively coordinated systems also offer the possibility of responding to changes in the environment in a more coordinated and effective way. For example, if a sudden shortage in iron ore develops and market prices soar, the price of steel will ultimately have to reflect the windfall profits received by the iron mine in a market-coordinated system. This rise in the price of steel could easily result in steel users' substituting other materials, such as plastics or aluminum, where they had previously used steel. Once this substitution is made, customers begin finding ways to use the substitute materials more efficiently. Even if the shortage of iron ore is subsequently ameliorated and prices decline for both iron and finished steel, some customers of the steel product system may be permanently lost.

In cases such as this, if a total system perspective is held by the administrative coordinator, it may make sense under certain conditions to forego some of the windfall profits at the iron stage so finished steel can be kept at a low enough price to prevent substitution by competitive product systems. Obviously this is an extraordinarily complex calculation involving detailed knowledge of the economics ~~of the economics~~ of all major applications of steel and the economics of substitute materials. The data required consist of innumerable small pieces of information scattered among many sources, and the uncertainties in predicting likely outcomes of various options are enormous. But if this information processing and coordination can be done effectively by an administrative hierarchy, it can maximize the welfare of the system more effectively than could the self-interested bargaining among all actors that characterizes market mode.

As the complexity of this task points out, however, administrative hierarchies are constantly in danger of failing to keep track of everything that is important, running the risk of a consequent suboptimal response to the contingencies that arise continually in the real world. This corresponds to the popular image of an ineffective bureaucracy, whose "left hand doesn't know what its right hand is doing." To the extent that contingencies—the infinite number of dynamic factors in the constantly changing modern world—affect what happens in a system, the flexibility of an administrative hierarchy is subject to constant testing.

Administrative hierarchies have difficulty coping with contingencies because they must transmit information up a hierarchy until it reaches someone who has authority over all of the units that could be affected. This person (or administrative unit) must assess the impact on the entire system of various alternatives, and then render a decision. The decision must then be passed down the hierarchy to the operating units involved, and then be implemented. All of this requires time. Moreover the greater the size of a system and the more people who are involved, the greater the probability that the information going up and down the hierarchy will be distorted. Finally, the greater the interdependencies among the units of a system, the more complex the process of trading off will be, and the greater the probability that information distortion will cause suboptimal decisions.

In other words, there are very real limits on the ability of administrative organizations to cope with complexity and change. Markets have the great virtue of simplifying the information-gathering and decision-making processes. Each unit operating in a market makes its own decisions. More decision units mean that distortion and complexity are attenuated. But in the process the possibility of greater efficiency through system-level management is foreclosed. This basic trade-off involved in organizing economic activity historically has been made in different general patterns in Japan and the United States during the process of industrialization.

In the United States the growth in scale, complexity, and productivity of the economy has been closely associated with the rise of the integrated industrial firm. A century ago most productive units in the economy were of small firms, selling their products to similar small firms one stage downstream. Today in place of market transactions the predominant coordinating mechanism among productive units is the administration of large-scale integrated firms. In Chandler's words, "The visible hand of management has replaced the invisible hand of markets."

Japan's economy has also been transformed into a complex industrial system, but administrative coordination of integrated firms is much less pronounced. Instead, firms are more specialized along a narrower range of functions. In a number of these industries the sogo shosha integrates the activities of separate firms into a product system, helping them realize the benefits of administratve coordination on a large scale while retaining their formal independence and some consequent flexibility associated with market-form coordination.

The Role of the Sogo Shosha

A product system coordinated by a sogo shosha is an intermediate between the poles of administrative hierarchy and market forms of coordination. It attempts to realize at least some of the benefits of both. Client firms clearly partake of market-style coordination, in that they are free to sell in open markets,* and they often use market terms as a reference point in judging the terms offered them by a sogo shosha. But clients are not completely independent either, for the sogo shosha has substantial bargaining leverage in dealing with them and often advocates forcefully the possibilities for advance in acting together as a product system.

The sogo shosha can best be understood as a coordinator of product systems. The specific role played by a sogo shosha varies with the circumstances of the product system. But in all product systems the sogo shosha's activities in multiple stages (from raw materials through finished products) and multiple functions (logistics, finance, marketing, technology scanning, and so forth) give it the broad perspective and formidable organizational and bargaining power essential to the role of coordinator. It is thus in a position to reduce uncertainty substantially for its clients, who play more limited and specialized roles. Clients at each stage can overcome the short time horizon appropriate to life within an unstable market environment and make long-range and large-scale commitments, enabling them to achieve maximum internal efficiency for their operations. At the same time they maintain their independence, which enables them to respond to the particular circumstances facing them without having to clear everything through an overarching hierarchy.

Continuing our example, the sogo shosha's involvement in the steel industry illustrates clearly the part it plays in systems management.[4] Here the sogo shosha's involvement ranges from the procurement of iron ores and coking coal to the international and domestic marketing of intermediate and finished products. Vast investments undergird the sogo shosha's role. Sogo shosha are prominent members of consortia in ex-

* Assuming they are not majority-owned, or otherwise controlled by, the sogo shosha. Most of the sales volume of a sogo shosha is accounted for by independent clients, not subject to direct control.

ploration and development of coal and iron ore. Specialized loading and unloading docks, ocean and land transport systems, storage areas, downstream facilities such as steel finishing and servicing centers, and sales offices are all part of the sogo shosha's involvement in the steel business. In 1983, for example, the Japanese industry produced nearly 100 million tons of crude steel. Next to the U.S.S.R., Japan is the largest producer of crude steel, accounting for about 15 percent of the world's total output. In the same year Japan imported over 121 million tons of iron ore and 60 million tons of coal. Japan's steel exports amounted to roughly $7 billion, accounting for nearly 15 percent of the nation's exports. Virtually all these transactions were handled by the sogo shosha.

Interestingly, although the sogo shosha are so entrenched in steel that it would be hard to imagine the industry without them, they have traditionally been relegated to a subordinate role in this business. The Japanese steel industry began under the government's direct ownership and management, and its chief mission was to supply steel for the military. Initially, only the excess ouptut was sold to the civilian sector. In the late nineteenth century the government-owned Nippon Steel, the predecessor of the present Shin Nippon Steel, designated a handful of sogo shosha as its primary agents to distribute a part of the output that was to be sold to the private sector. In view of the prevailing tradition of the relationship between the government and the private sector in Japan, the relationship between the steel mills and the shosha and other distributors was clearly hierarchical, with the latter being subservient to the former. Nippon Steel literally allocated its output among its distributors. Privately owned steel mills emerged subsequently, but Nippon Steel's dominance continued, and the new entrants followed the established leadership.

Though Nippon Steel was placed in private ownership at the end of World War II, the historical relationship to a large measure has been perpetuated. The steel mills continue to dominate the sogo shosha, even though some sogo shosha are stronger than others in this field. The mills have attempted to maintain a careful balance among the sogo shosha they deal with. During the high-growth period of the 1950s and 1960s the two major former textile shosha, C. Itoh and Marubeni, successfully established positions in the steel business, followed by the two lesser firms of Nichimen and Tomen. But following this temporary change in market participation and market share, the trading relationships soon became so well established that there was little any sogo shosha could do to increase its share in any significant way at the expense of its competitors.

The sogo shosha coordinate product systems that can be larger and more complex than the systems of almost any integrated firm.* For example, in the steel product system, a sogo shosha may be concerned with many more stages of activity than even U.S. Steel or any other integrated manufacturer. Sogo shosha organize large-scale coal and iron mines, arrange shipping, often sell or lease ships to the shipping lines, provide insurance and arrange delivery to iron and steel producers, and manage inventories all along the way. They are also involved in a wide variety of downstream fabrication and sales operations. To further coordination, they have organized groups of small- and medium-size firms into quasi-captive networks for which they provide the materials to be fabricated, market the fabricated products, and, of course, extend financing for working capital and investment. In fact it is not uncommon for steel mills and the sogo shosha to own fabricators jointly. The sogo shosha often sell steel to the very shipyards building bulk carriers to transport iron ore and coal, which will be sold or leased by the same sogo shosha.

One reason the sogo shosha have taken on the role of systems management is that Japan's economic integration with the rest of the world has involved the need for rapid structural change. As noted earlier, until the midnineteenth century Japan was virtually isolated from the outside world. Though its own economy was comparatively sophisticated for a preindustrial level of technology, few Japanese individuals or institutions were able to understand the complexities of an industrial production system and/or were experienced in dealing with non-Japanese institutions and individuals.

For industrial activity to develop in all its complexity in Japan, it was necessary that the actors undertaking technologically separable but related processes (the "units of a product system") have a stable framework in order to reduce the risks

* Obvious rivals in size and complexity are the systems of the global oil majors and the manufacturers of automobiles. Note, however, that these firms deal only in one basic product category whereas the sogo shosha span a much broader range of products and activities.

involved to a tolerable level. For example, an investment in a cotton mill required that the operator be able to tolerate the uncertainty of where raw cotton would be available at what price and quality, and where cotton yarn or textiles would be sold at what price and quality. Because international markets in both raw materials and finished goods were subject to great fluctuation, a cotton mill operator who lacked sufficient familiarity with both might be deterred from making a large enough investment in mill equipment to be fully efficient at the prevailing level of technology.

But if a sogo shosha played the role of system organizer, absorbing much of the uncertainty in procurement and marketing, the mill operator's risk could be reduced to the point at which a large investment in the most efficient equipment available became feasible. Recent scholarship on the development of the cotton textile industry in Asia indicates that the role of the sogo shosha in providing a stability for mill operators was decisive in enabling Japanese mills to outcompete contemporary Chinese mills, which paid lower wages.* By concentrating all resources on efficient production, leaving systems links to the sogo shosha, Japanese mills achieved lower costs while the sogo shosha achieved economies of scale in procurement and marketing, making the Japanese cotton textile production system globally competitive.

The experience in cotton textiles was repeated in other sectors such as steel, shipbuilding, and petrochemicals—in fact in most of the product lines the sogo shosha deals in today. The actual operators of facilities concentrated on efficient operations while the sogo shosha provided overall sysem management. This created stability for the operator: the sogo shosha acted as a buffer for risk, enabling efficient levels of investment. The operator gave up the possibility of windfall profits when markets moved favorably, but in return received the benefit of reduced exposure to unfavorable movements. Japanese operators' lack of experience heightened their perceptions

* Chao (1973) shows that Japanese mills obtained low-cost steady and consistent supplies of raw cotton via the sogo shosha. This enabled them to have long and efficient production runs. Chinese mill owners found that profit opportunities in playing volatile raw cotton markets were irresistible. Therefore their mills received irregular supplies and achieved lower technical efficiency. The Japanese mills sold their high-volume output via the sogo shosha.

of the risks involved in procurement and marketing, especially overseas, making the trade-off worthwhile.

Membership in a sogo shosha's product system often includes firms that compete with one another. For example, a sogo shosha normally supplies raw materials to several rival steel firms, and the steel manufacturers divide their business among two or more sogo shosha. Thus each side enjoys a certain bargaining leverage as a result of the ability to channel business to the firm that is most responsive to its needs. A sogo shosha product system therefore is best understood not as a rigid body whose constituent units are mechanically linked into a tightly balanced system but as a constellation of firms active at various stages of a complex production process, whose links with each other are shaped by the sogo shosha's influence. Constituent firms may buy resources from and sell output to firms outside the constellation of the particular sogo shosha that manages a system. These outside links may be with rival product systems of other sogo shosha or may consist of direct arrangements with outside firms.

In theory the transactions a sogo shosha manages are market transactions between independent firms. But the terms of many of them are different from what the outside market would dictate at the time. The sogo shosha, with its system perspective, induces members of the system to act in ways that maximize what it perceives as system welfare, in which all members want to share in the long run. For every client there is a constant tension between maximizing its own welfare and maximizing the welfare of the system. The sogo shosha acts as interpreter of system welfare and also attempts to act as enforcer of system discipline.

Value Added by the Sogo Shosha

The sogo shosha's primary value for a client is derived from the fact that a product system coordinated by a sogo shosha is intermediate between the poles of administrative hierarchy and market forms of coordination. In effect a client can realize many of the important advantages associated with both. As a "free agent," a client pays only when a sale or purchase is consummated, allowing it to minimize front-end investment of scarce resources. It also avoids having to assume the burden of high fixed costs associated with maintaining its own distribution. Thus it can frequently enjoy lower per-unit transaction costs. The sogo shosha also permits the manufacturing firm to use its ready-made facilities and infrastructure, thus making it possible to reach sources of supply or markets far beyond what the firm could reach on its own. This is particularly true with small- to medium-size enterprises. Even some of the largest manufacturers find that use of the sogo shosha makes it possible for them to concentrate their resources on production.

The client can shift more of its risk by transferring to the sogo shosha the titles to the goods handled, thereby enabling the sogo shosha to gain or lose on its own account, or it can use the sogo shosha as an agent. In the latter case the sogo shosha merely acts as a proxy for the customer in procurement and sales of merchandise and receives a fixed commission. Even under such an arrangement a sogo shosha can help reduce risk for a client through its ready access to materials sources, markets, and information on a timely basis and its ability to provide various services ranging from warehousing to transportation.

The client company can also enjoy the economies of scale offered by the sogo shosha, which as an independent entity engaged in trading in many products, often on a global scale, can spread its fixed costs over many transactions. This is particularly important because of the high fixed element in the sogo shosha's cost structure. Because it represents a number of clients, the sogo shosha can often pool its accounts. Because of its scale the sogo shosha can invest heavily in monitoring price movements in a particular commodity and so can help its clients make better decisions. Through its diversity it can spread over many transactions the risks of a particular transaction involving a given commodity. The sogo shosha can also help a client maintain a natural hedge position, since at any given time the sogo shosha as a system is likely to be engaged in selling and buying.

Through its diverse dealings the sogo shosha tends to enjoy superior access to information about a market, a customer, or a country, thus enabling its clients to assess the magnitude of risks more accurately and efficiently than would otherwise be possible. The sogo shosha is also in an excellent position, through its frequent and regular dealings, to assess the creditworthiness of a distributor. Moreover the customer is likely to be more anxious to protect his credit standing with a sogo shosha, which buys and sells diverse products and deals with a large number of parties, than with a manufacturer selling only a narrow line of goods.

The sogo shosha's diversity and its global network can, at times, help reduce political risks as well.[5] The diversity of its products and functions may place the sogo shosha in an advantageous bargaining position vis-à-vis a given country because it is usually involved in both export and import.* A host country may look upon a sogo shosha as an important link to exernal markets and may be reluctant to damage the relationship. The sogo shosha can often overcome specific constraints imposed by certain countries. This has been true, for example in Eastern Europe, where selling to the Eastern Bloc countries often requires barter, which the average manufacturer finds difficult to manage. The sogo shosha can consummate a sale to an Eastern Bloc country on behalf of its client by taking over the export of the products offered and selling them elsewhere in its system. Barter transactions have been spreading beyond the Eastern Bloc in recent years.

The sogo shosha can also reduce risks for its clients in the area of foreign exchange exposure. Because it engages in both export and import transactions, it enjoys built-in mechanisms to offset exchange losses and gains. Its expertise in managing foreign exchange transactions, coupled with the diversity in products handled and markets covered, also helps reduce the sogo shosha's total currency exposure.

The sogo shosha also provides value for a client through its enormous ability to extend credit to finance both the purchase and sale of goods.[6] For a variety of reasons explored elsewhere, debt played a singularly important role in financing Japan's postwar economic growth. Manufacturing firms sought to allocate scarce capital to the expansion of capacity and were anxious to rely on third parties, including the sogo shosha, to help finance their ever-expanding need for working capital. Many of the long-term clients of the sogo shosha are found in capital-intensive heavy industries such as steel, chemicals, petrochemicals, and synthetic fibers, in which economies of scale are so vital. The sogo shosha's financing capacity is equally important to smaller enterprises. Japan's postwar financial practices have tended to favor large enterprises in credit allocation, and smaller firms have often turned to the sogo shosha

* Sogo shosha imports to Japan exceed exports.

to finance not only their working capital needs but sometimes their long-term capital requirements as well.

The magnitude of financing extended to its clients by the sogo shosha is staggering. For example, in 1983 Mitsui's accounts and notes receivable, short- and long-term loans and advances to its clients and affiliated companies totaled $12 billion.

Further evidence of the importance the sogo shosha place on financing as a strategic instrument to create value for clients is the fact that typically as much as 60 to 70 percent of a sogo shosha's total assets is committed to financing suppliers and customers.

As is evident from the foregoing discussion, financing services provided by the sogo shosha take a variety of forms, including the extension of ordinary trade credit, advance payments, short- and long-term loans, loan guarantees, and even leasing of properties and equipment. Regardless of the form, the basic purpose is to further trade. The sogo shosha may or may not receive interest, depending on the nature of the transactions, the client, and other considerations, such as the length of commitment and the risks involved.

The following examples illustrate some of the ways in which the sogo shosha is involved in financing. Let us first examine a routine steel transaction. When the sogo shosha places an order with a steel mill for a certain amount of steel to be exported to the United States, it must pay the mill as much as 80 percent of the value of the order two months prior to shipment. The mill pays interest on the advance payment at the prime rate plus an agreed-on percentage. It generally takes 45 days for ocean transportation and another 25 for inland transportation within the United States. The usual collection period is 30 days. Therefore the sogo shosha must assume financing obligations for roughly 150 days between the time of the advance payment and the final collection.

The second example is slightly more complex. The critical role the sogo shosha has played in the Japanese textile industry has already been described. In the development of small weavers for large cotton-spinning firms or synthetic fiber manufacturers, the sogo shosha's financial ability played an all-important role because the weavers' financial resources were severely limited. For example, one sogo shosha has approximately 150 small weaving companies. These firms are primary subcontractors that control second- or even third-tier firms. In effect the sogo shosha has developed a pyramid network to mobilize myriad small enterprises.

The sogo shosha plays the pivotal role in managing this network of subcontractors, coordinating the weaving and other processing activities, either for large textile firms or in its own behalf, to produce semifinished or finished products that it distributes at its own risk. In either case, the particular sogo shosha provides not only working capital, but long-term capital as well, via equity and debt instruments.

The sogo shosha also provides long-term financing services. In fact, during the past decade or so, the sogo shosha's commitment to long-term financing has increased dramatically. Long-term financing is made necessary by the requirements of deferred payment, export sales of heavy machinery and other capital equipment, and long-term loans to overseas suppliers for the development of natural resources. Deferred-payment export contracts cover such projects as the construction on a turnkey basis of petrochemical plants, oil refineries, and other types of major plants. Some of these deferred-payment contracts are very large, up to $200 million. These loans are typically payable over a period of up to ten years. Payment of the loans is usually guaranteed by the host government or by major commercial banks in that country or elsewhere, or, in the case of raw materials ventures, payment is made when the shipment of the particular natural resource begins.

Another increasingly important financial function is project financing—that is, the development of an appropriate financial package for a major project, which may range from a large-scale mining venture to the sale of a large plant abroad. In most cases the sogo shosha's primary role is to devise an appropriate financing method, choose among various financial instruments, and help raise the needed funds. Though the particular sogo shosha involved makes a financial commitment itself, most of the funds must come from other sources. The sogo shosha's role is to make these arrangements. This often requires the participation of not only Japanese but also foreign financial institutions, and this in turn requires sophisticated knowledge of the intricacies of the foreign capital markets and financial institutions and close coordination with the client firms and with the government agencies that are almost always involved in this type of project, particularly in developing countries. In large projects or transactions the success of the entire project depends heavily on the sogo shosha's ability to put together an attractive financial package for its clients.

The sogo shosha, then, provides an extensive array of financial services. Not only does it extend trade credit and loans, guarantee loans, and make equity investments, it also helps raise funds for projects. In this respect the sogo shosha undertakes some of the functions typcically performed by commercial banks as well as those performed by merchant bankers. Of course the sogo shosha is not a banker; its financing activities, as important and as wide-ranging as they may be, are performed to support its primary activity, which is trading. Yet at the same time it is impossible to conceive of a sogo shosha without its highly effective and extensive financial prowess. The sogo shosha has traditionally enjoyed a special relationship with Japan's leading commercial banks, often referred to as city banks. As we have seen, the sogo shosha and the banks emerged as leaders in the postwar enterprise groups.

From the point of view of the bank, the sogo shosha represents an excellent way to deploy the bank's funds at a minimum of risk and cost, and without the necessity of processing a large number of small loans, as would be the case if the bank had to deal with all the individual customers itself. In addition the banks can rely on the sogo shosha's intimate knowledge of customers, which they are in a position to obtain through their trading activities. Indeed, the sogo shosha can keep themselves abreast of their customers' credit conditions almost on a day-to-day basis.

Another significant advantage for the bank is that the large volume of foreign exchange transactions the sogo shosha generates is an extremely attractive source of business. Profit aside, the amount of a bank's foreign exchange transaction has been considered by Japan's Ministry of Finance to be a critical measure of its relative strength in the international field and has been an important factor in screening applications from banks to open offices and branches abroad.

The benefits derived from the favored position of the sogo shosha in the bank's lending policies are certainly not all one-way. The sogo shosha also reap considerable advantages from these relationships. Here again the sogo shosha enjoys economies of scale. Its special ties to the banks have given it a stable source of low-cost funds; moreover it enjoys considerable freedom in the use of those funds. When obtaining loans from major banks, it is true that it must indicate broad categories of uses to which the money is to be put, but within each category it enjoys considerable flexibility. This is particularly true for working capital. Of course it must be prepared to bear the risk itself, and to this end it has developed sophisticated and careful credit evaluation procedures. The point to be noted here is that the sogo shosha does enjoy considerable discretion over the use of money. In effect the sogo shosha has become a pseudobank that obtains money at wholesale rates from the major commercial banks and retails it at a higher rate to myriad large and small clients by using the funds to support its trading activities. The sogo shosha uses financing as leverage to find new business opportunities as well as to expand its trading activities.

Last but not the least of the value the sogo shosha provides is the benefit associated with the information it can provide. Indeed, the sogo shosha is an excellent example of an institution that uses information systems as a competitive weapon. Its awesome ability to collect and process information is usually associated with the extensive telex network that links its offices throughout the world. This physical network is indeed impressive. On a typical business day the corporate headquarters in Japan of the very largest sogo shosha transmits and receives 50,000 telexes. Most of the valuable information is collected through the day-to-day work of managers engaged in a wide variety of transactions throughout the world.

Such an extensive communication network is extremely costly to replicate. Even more difficult are the intangible assets—ranging from extensive contacts and access to the right parties, to the general reputation the sogo shosha have built over decades of successful operations—that serve as a basis for effective information collection. Even more fundamental is the management system that motivates managers to search constantly for potentially useful information and makes them able to recognize the potential value of a particular piece of data and to communicate it to the right person or group. The management of the sogo shosha are in unanimous agreement that the most valuable information is obtained through day-to-day trading activities.

Thus to a client organization the benefits of using the sogo shosha go considerably beyond those associated with a specific transaction. Through its continuing relationship with the sogo shosha the client company can enjoy access to the multifaceted services the sogo shosha can provide, particularly in the areas of potential new businesses or new sources of supply or technology.

For reasons noted earlier, the sogo shosha is constantly on the lookout for new opportunities, and once it finds one, it has considerable discretion in choosing a client to whom it will give priority. A variety of factors go into the decision, but the nature of the existing ties with a particular client is surely among the most important. This uncertainty is a powerful force to tie a client to the sogo shosha on a continuing basis.

A client, a steel mill for example, may decide to discontinue the services of the sogo shosha, thereby saving the commission on certain routine transactions; presumably such savings will put the company in a better competitive position vis-à-vis its rivals. It must recognize, however, that this action creates a new risk. Discontinuing the sogo shosha's service means that the former client can no longer rely on the sogo shosha's systemwide ability to scan the world for new markets or new sources of iron ore or coking coal. Its rivals who have continuing relationships with their sogo shosha may gain certain advantages that the mill in question has denied itself. These advantages can take a variety of forms, ranging from access to attractive sources of raw materials, to entry into new markets, or those offering large contracts, to such intangible assets as the knowledge gained form these activities that can be applied advantageously to new situations. The benefits will in turn give them new capabilities that are likely to strengthen their competitive positions. What is most threatening to the former client is that the nature and extent of the advantages its competitors may gain from continuing use of the sogo shosha are impossible to measure or predict. In effect, by discontinuing the services of the sogo shosha, the client will be trading off readily measurable benefits, in the form of cost savings, for a new type of risk whose magnitude is all but impossible to measure. Few managers in large, mature, oligopolistic industries are willing to take such risks.

It is important to point out that seldom does a client use the sogo shosha for only one or two of the reasons described here. It is likely that in most cases all four factors that we have considered interact powerfully to produce value that is difficult for the client to match. The main reason the sogo shosha is willing and indeed eager to provide services beyond those associated directly with the current relationship is its desire to solidify and expand that relationship by creating new business opportunities for the client that will lead to new business for itself.

Thus far we have examined the advantages associated with scale, diversity, and preferential access to capital and information that allow the sogo shosha to provide value for its clients. These strengths cannot be realized without management and organizational capabilities. It is management that exploits the potential benefits associated with the economies of scale and diversity; it is also management that responds quickly to new opportunities and coordinates myriad activities and information on a global basis. It is then its skilled and experienced experts and managers that are the single most vital resource of the sogo shosha, together with the distinct management system it has developed to achieve a high degree of integration and coordination with a minimum of time and cost.

Coordination is a vital element in the sogo shosha's activities. Linking the buyer and seller of a particular commodity on a global basis is no easy task. Even in the performance of seemingly routine logistical services, coordination activities can be complicated. An important function of the sogo shosha is to make certain the right products are delivered to the right destination at the right time. Logistical services are particularly important in the procurement of raw materials in heavy process-oriented industries such as steel and chemicals. Raw materials are bulky, storage is expensive, and interruptions in supply can have very serious consequences.

Beyond effective and efficient management of the existing business, for the reasons we have seen, the very nature of the sogo shosha requires constant efforts to develop new businesses. But creation of new businesses cannot be routinized; it taxes the imagination, ingenuity, and entrepreneurship of the sogo shosha's staff. Over the years the sogo shosha have been able to develop, among their skilled and experienced managements, a large number of functional product, industry, and area experts. One of the most serious problems Japan faced in the early days of its industrialization was a lack of knowledgeable and qualified personnel to handle international trade, and even today a shortage persists. The sogo shosha as an institution has amassed enormous human and organizational capabilities. The capacities—the "software" of the sogo shosha—must be considered to be the ultimate source of value and the heart of the distinctive competence of the institution.

4

Competitive Dynamics and the Strategy of the Sogo Shosha

The sogo shosha's capacities, skills, and resources are formidable. Many of the factors that combine to produce its distinctive competence also constitute formidable barriers to entry. Yet despite these advantages the profits of the sogo shosha are not very high, as measured by return on sales, return on assets, or even return on equity (see table 4.1). Such low returns usually indicate a high degree of competition. This chapter examines the types of competition a sogo shosha faces and the dynamics of that competition.

Oligopolistic Rivalry

Although there are thousands of trading firms in Japan, not to mention those operating elsewhere in the world, the sogo shosha sector can be considered a peculiar type of oligopoly.[1] The six firms that form the focus of this study face competition

Table 4.1
Financial performance of Japan's leading sogo shosha

	Net profit percent of sales		Net profit total assets		Net profit percent of equity	
	1983	1982	1983	1982	1983	1982
Mitsubishi	0.01	0.11	0.03	0.37	0.43	5.60
Mitsui	0.04	0.15	0.13	0.48	2.79	9.72
C. Itoh	0.05	0.05	0.22	0.21	6.64	5.73
Marubeni	0.11	0.03	0.43	0.14	10.34	3.00
Sumitomo	0.14	0.14	0.79	0.80	10.68	12.25

Source: Nomura Research Institute.

from numerous entities in the provision of individual aspects of their services. But if we define the "product" of the sogo shosha as a comprehensive package of trade, finance, and information services, on a large scale and global basis, the number of competitive actors drops drastically. If we further qualify the definition to include the performance of a coordinating role in one of Japan's major *zaibatsu* or bank-centered groups, only six firms really qualify, a number small enough to be defined as an oligopoly.

Rivalry among the six large sogo shosha is fierce. There are three very good reasons for this. First, the sogo shosha is a marketing intermediary primarily dealing with standard products. It buys and sells soybeans, wheat, iron ore, chemicals, and textiles, all of which are mature products with virtually no proprietary technology and only limited opportunity for product differentiation. Price and delivery terms are usually the buyer's most important considerations. As a marketing intermediary the sogo shosha must be constantly aware of the threat of being bypassed by the seller and the ultimate buyer. In effect a threat of vertical integration by either a seller or a buyer is constantly present.

The second factor encouraging competition is that there are no strategic reasons for customers to enter into an exclusive relationship with a single sogo shosha. Such a relationship offers no particular advantage. On the contrary, from the point of view of client firms there are a number of incentives to maintain ties with several competing sogo shosha. A single sogo shosha, however large, does not have an equally effective presence in every market in the world for every type of product. In fact among the big six some are particularly noted for their strength in certain products and markets. Even within a given market and product category, each sogo shosha has developed its own distribution channels, outlets, and customers. Thus different sogo shosha can give the client company access to different geographic and product markets.

The use of several sogo shosha also increases the client firm's bargaining power. Moreover it helps ensure the company's access to many diverse sources of information, particularly about new markets, products, and projects, since each sogo shosha has its distinct information network. This is important because so many of the Japanese manufacturing firms look to the sogo shosha to be their eyes and ears abroad.

Still a third force stimulating the keen competition among the sogo shosha is their cost structure. As we have seen, the sogo shosha's operations entail high fixed costs. To begin with, maintaining a network of offices throughout Japan and abroad is expensive, and much of the cost associated with maintaining such a system is fixed. Buildings must be owned or leased on a long-term basis in prime locations in key business centers around the globe. Computer-based information systems must be maintained and serviced with trained personnel. Personnel-related costs are another expensive element. We have already noted that the sogo shosha's ability to mobilize literally hundreds of highly qualified and experienced personnel to a given task is a very significant competitive factor, for knowledge and skills are embodied in individuals. We shall see later that the sogo shosha has developed a unique management system to produce such effective coordination. A fundamental factor contributing to this organizational effectiveness is the permanent employment system characteristic of large Japanese firms. Virtually all of the sogo shosha's employees stay with the company for life. Such a system of employment obviously means that wage-related costs are virtually fixed. A third element of expense is financial charges. We have noted the sogo shosha's high dependence on debt, which imposes fixed obligations. A high fixed proportion in the sogo shosha's total cost structure places considerable pressure on capacity utilization.

For the sogo shosha there is yet another competing pressure to expand their volume, because the process of expansion will expose the sogo shosha to opportunities to obtain new business, expand its contacts, and perhaps to gain new expertise. Most of the new businesses come as an outgrowth of existing businesses. New business opportunities lead to other new opportunities.

In addition to these economic considerations, psychological or attitudinal considerations influence the oligopolistic rivalry among the sogo shosha to some extent. There is extreme consciousness of competitive standing among the firms—a commonly observed feature of the Japanese corporate system—and a strong desire to outdo rivals. In particular, there is keen competition to book large gross sales figures. This works particularly to the advantage of large clients able to bring high-volume transactions to a firm. Another area of particular rivalry is the race to add new types of clients, products, services, or transactions to the repertoire of the sogo shosha.

There is also a high level of competitive matching among the six major firms. Competitive matching refers to the tendency of firms to attempt to duplicate the offerings of their rivals, a commonly observed phenomenon among oligopolistic firms. The reasoning underlying the tendency toward competitive matching behavior is the same as in any oligopoly: the fear that a firm that achieves a unique product, market presence, or other capability will be able to exploit its distinctive position and compete with the others in ways for which no countering tactics are possible.

The cornerstone of the sogo shosha's strategy is the search for volume growth. To achieve this goal, the sogo shosha pursues two strategies. One is to maintain and, if possible, to expand its influence within the existing product system. The other is to create new product systems. Let us now turn to detailed examination of the first strategy.

Power Relations within the Product System

The coordinator's role in a product system gives the sogo shosha command of many powerful tools to strengthen its bargaining position with individual firms. Especially when compared with the resources of many small- and medium-size firms, the sogo shosha's power looks overwhelming. But there are also many bargaining relationships with product-system members in which the sogo shosha's bargaining position is weak or deteriorating. The sources and uses of power for a sogo shosha vary widely according to the nature of the client and situation.

Two contrasting groups of clients illustrate the range of power relationships confronting the sogo shosha. On the one hand, the small firms performing one or a few tasks, such as one stage of product fabrication or distribution, are often unable to exert much bargaining leverage on the sogo shosha. The sogo shosha's ability to divert purchases away from them or raise the price of necessary resources, its position as a creditor or shareholder, and its influence on other firms in the production chain make them feel powerless, unable to resist the terms dictated by the sogo shosha.

Particularly in many of the mature, if not declining, industrial sectors, such as textiles, the sogo shosha's role often may seem a heartless one to critics, who see it squeezing defenseless small businesses. There is a segment of public opinion in Japan that views the sogo shosha very negatively, as the ruthless oppressor of small business. There is no question but that the sogo shosha are able to exert tremendous pressures on the small businesses over whom they loom so large. Often these pressures are to reduce price, delay payment, or otherwise squeeze more net resources out of a business relationship. In a declining business the sogo shosha is allocating economic pain, not economic gain, and this is always a poorly received role in any situation.

Against the image of exploiter of small business, the sogo shosha companies prefer to highlight their ability to mobilize resources that enable small businesses to expand and modernize, even in the face of industrial decline. The textile manufacturer moving overseas, or the manufacturer buying or leasing production machinery or technology to reduce costs and prices with the help of the sogo shosha, are the types of relationships they would prefer to emphasize. Both faces of the sogo shosha undoubtedly have some basis in reality. But central to both is the asymmetry of power between the sogo shosha and many of its small clients. Size, market power, information, financial resources, and availability of alternative sources of supply strongly favor the sogo shosha. To the extent a small firm has a proprietary technology, market control, independent financial resources, or access to alternative bargaining relationships, however, it may exercise countervailing power, at least to some degree.

As a client firm gets larger, its access to resources that would give it power and influence in a relationship with a sogo shosha generally increases. But the nature of the power relationship is highly dynamic, depending on firm and industry structure, market conditions, and many other factors. The relationship between the sogo shosha and the large Japanese steel producers manifests many of the characteristics of sogo shosha relations with large powerful clients in oligopolistic industries.

Procurement of huge volumes of raw materials has, as we have noted, been one of the keystones of the sogo shosha relationship with the steel industry. Although the sogo shosha have played a major role in developing new sources of raw material, today many of the decisions on price, delivery, and other terms are made exclusively by the manufacturers, who use the sogo shosha only to handle shipping, insurance, and other logistical details. Naturally the commissions on such transactions are low, and the commission rates are raised infrequently. In Japan these commissions are often called *nemuri kosen*, or "sleeping commissions." For this part the sogo shosha are not particularly happy to play such a passive role and to receive so little compensation for it. But because the amounts involved are so large, the sogo shosha are anxious to be able to record the raw materials sales on their books. A position, even a purely supportive one, at the source of raw materials is felt to be important to the sogo shosha's overall relationship with the steel firms and its position in the steel product system.

But after the steel leaves the big steelmakers in Japan, the sogo shosha faces trouble again. The very largest purchasers of steel, particularly the automobile manufacturers, are threatening to remove another large block of sales from the sogo shosha sales roster.

Steel being a very important component of total costs, automobile manufacturers have a very high stake in obtaining the best possible prices, and are therefore anxious to bypass the sogo shosha and its commission. In dealing with automobile manufacturers the sogo shosha faces a serious problem, because it is not a part of the automobile industry system in the way that it is a part of the steel industry. Automobile manufacturers generally market their products through their own sales organizations and use the sogo shosha only in small and marginal markets. Thus the sogo shosha's influence with these manufacturers is quite limited, and the only way to protect its position in such a case is to cut its margin to an absolute minimum and to depend on the good will of the sellers, or the steel mills. To the sogo shosa, the protection of its transactions between the mills and the automobile manufacturers involves reasoning that goes substantially beyond the risk of losing a commission. For one thing the volume of business involved is substantial, and the sogo shosha measures itself in terms of sales volume. Most serious is its concern that being bypassed in such a major transaction would mean the weakening of its position in the total steel system.

Under these circumstances the client relationship becomes the key consideration. The sogo shosha's strategy in the steel industry is to make continuing efforts to maintain, if not strengthen, its position in the product system, and it does so in a variety of ways.

For one thing, the sogo shosha seeks to establish strong personal relationships with its customers. Typically those personnel of the sogo shosha assigned to work with the steel business do so for virtually their entire careers. They spend much of their time interacting with their peers in the mill. In Japan the steel community, long devoted to raising productivity, has tended to be surprisingly close-knit, despite its size. To be effective in this industry, one must be a credible and respectable member of this small group. The most important task for the sogo shosha personnel who are assigned to the steel division is to earn membership in this small and exclusive club. Such a relationship is quite helpful in protecting the sogo shosha's position in the steel product system against its competition.

Though the relationship is quite stable, there is yet enough fluidity to make it imperative for each sogo shosha to have effective communication with appropriate managers in a client company so it can engage in formal as well as informal exchange of information and views, to keep abreast of the most current thinking of the client company and to anticipate the client's future needs. It is important for a sogo shosha to have strong internal champions to promote and protect its interests within each client firm. These personal relationships can be mobilized in the event that special requests must be made, such as for preferential treatment in product allocation in case of a temporary product shortage.

The sogo shosha uses its network of investments as a source of leverage in dealing with large clients. Particularly when a sogo shosha is able to locate a key stage in the system and establish ownership or another means of influence, it may be able to achieve a degree of control. For example, when docking space is in short supply, sogo shosha-owned docking subsidiaries enhance the leverage of the parent in dealing with members of the system.

This kind of monopolistic advantage, however, is ultimately limited and temporary. For one thing, sogo shosha hold no proprietary technology, one major source of monopolistic control. Also in the long run, if the sogo shosha presses its monopolistic advantage too far, system members will be able to find alternative sources of the same goods and services by dealing in the market themselves. Dock space can always be obtained for the right price. Thus, though monopolistic control of key stages enhances the sogo shosha's bargaining power, it does not offer a full explanation of the dynamics of the power relationships between the sogo shosha and their clients.

The sogo shosha also tries to remind its clients that its value should be assessed on the basis of the systemwide benefits. An example of such a benefit is in the development of a new market. A sogo shosha can bring to a steel mill a huge order for a large construction project abroad, such as a pipeline, bridge, or industrial facility. Of course, in consummating such a transaction, the sogo shosha must work with its particular steel mill almost from the inception of the project because its technical cooperation is essential.

Another example is the sogo shosha's role in the search for new sources of iron ore and coal. As with the development of new markets, the sogo shosha undertakes such a project in close coordination with the steel mill, yet it does so on its own initiative and at its own expense. It is willing to make a substantial investment and to assume risks associated with development. For the sogo shosha there are two benefits. First, if it is successful, it will be given opportunities to handle that particular business for the mill, and second, such a project will further solidify its relationship with that mill. In effect then the fees and commissions the mills pay for seemingly routine transactions, which could well be internalized, are a form of compensation for those activities that involve considerable risk and require the commitment of management's time and financial resources. The mill benefits from the fact that the arrangement gives the sogo shosha strong built-in incentives to undertake a search for new opportunities.

The sogo shosha also makes its worldwide network available to its steel clients. This is particularly important in collecting information on new technological developments, as well as for obtaining political and market information abroad. In effect the sogo shosha offers a guaranteed and automatic access to whatever services, including information, its global network can provide.

The sogo shosha can use the multiplicity of services it can perform for a client to enhance its bargaining leverage. Creating a broad package of services for a client multiplies the information available on the client's true situation. It also gives the sogo shosha more potential avenues for exerting influence on the client. It can offer incentives (or penalties) along several dimensions, such as delivery, finance, future business, and even price. Of course it might be argued that these influence channels can be two-way streets—that the proliferation of services gives the client more leverage on the sogo shosha. With large clients, such as the steel industry, this is sometimes true. But even in a weak bargaining position, the sogo shosha will work hard to expand the range of services it offers a client. The economic structure of its costs and revenues encourage it to do this.

Because of the nature of the sogo shosha's cost structure, the incremental costs of performing an additional service for a client are small, compared with the fixed costs of getting to know the client, its business, and its suppliers and customers. Incremental revenues translate almost directly into incremental profits. This gives the sogo shosha an extremely strong incentive to maximize the range of services performed for a given client and to increase the number of clients served.

The services a sogo shosha performs for a single client are usually closely related. Inventory levels cannot readily be managed without also arranging delivery dates, while the financing of receivables cannot be handled without also assessing the credit standing of customers. The sogo shosha thus can manage a package of services with comparative ease and not much more expense than it takes to manage a single service.

Sogo shosha managers also try to price services in a way that encourages clients to use as many as possible. Managers in a sogo shosha constantly seek to expand the scope of the relationship with clients. Among the principal means they use are discovering new sources of supply or demand, arranging for innovative forms of financing, and bringing new and important information to a client's attention and helping to structure a response.

A sogo shosha thus provides major clients with a service package consisting of both prearranged services supplied on a regular basis and ad hoc services supplied as opportunities arise. The ad hoc services are used by the sogo shosha as a way of expanding its business relationship with the client. Typically clients pay only for the established services, usually on a volume-related fee scale. The new services are often provided initially without direct compensation, but both parties understand that if the ad hoc services prove valuable to the client, the client will respond by increasing the volume of business it does with the sogo shosha. Most often the ad hoc service establishes some new flow of business transactions for the client, so the sogo shosha can simply act as agent for the client on that new business flow and receive fees related to its volume. Ad hoc services thus are a principal tool for expanding the scope of a service package, generating incremental revenues and profits.

Clearly a well-entrenched position in a large-scale business such as steel is important for the sogo shosha because it gives it an essential base of business. This not only enables it partially to cover its large fixed costs, it also generates knowledge, influence, experience, and other kinds of leverage useful in enabling the sogo shosha to obtain other business in related fields. Steel is a basic product used by many other firms scattered all over the economy. As, for example, a supplier to these firms, a sogo shosha has a "foot in the door," so to speak, enabling it to be in a position to offer many other services to them and to other firms up and down the production chain.

But in the final analysis steel is a mature business, producing relatively low profits in and of itself, due to its low growth, narrow margins, and the lack of sogo shosha bargaining leverage with large clients. Not all of the sogo shosha's business lines are at this stage, however. The relationship and bargaining dynamics of a sogo shosha and its set of clients in a product system undergo a predictable series of changes over time as a product system develops, matures, and faces new competition. This pattern may be thought of as the sogo shosha service life cycle.

The Service Life Cycle: Search for New Business Opportunities

The service life cycle model[2] presumes that product systems can be created. In fact they nearly always evolve through incremental modification of existing industrial and commercial practices. However, a sogo shosha can often spot new opportunities that require the coordination of several firms to create a distinctively new set of financial, information, and product flows among them. The process of pulling together these actors, negotiating common understandings and arrangements to govern the product system, and establishing the initial flows may be considered to be the *system creation* stage of the sogo shosha's service life cycle. An example may help illustrate this process.

In Japan, as in a number of other countries, the traditional method of producing and marketing chickens had been small-scale, part-time endeavors by farm families. The sogo shosha identified the potential to replace this antiquated system with a more modern and efficient one, and imported the technology and breeding stock necessary to undertake mass production. Advancing the capital necessary for construction of huge poultry houses and processing plants, arranging for the import of grains, mixing feeds, growing and processing birds, setting up supply routes for distribution of chicken meat, eggs, and by-products, and arranging delivery are only the most basic activities of the sogo shosha in this product system. The actors include some units wholly owned by the sogo shosha, some partly owned, and some independently owned. The sogo shosha earn commissions based on the volume of goods and services and are also able to realize ownership profits at certain stages. One of the sogo shosha, Mitsubishi, has even extended its involvement in broiler chickens to include becoming the Japanese franchisee of Kentucky Fried Chicken, via a joint venture.

When a sogo shosha links previously unrelated actors in a new system, it can charge relatively high fees for its services and have those fees agreed to. This is because without the sogo shosha's entrepreneurship and participation, the system would not exist at all. From the clients' perspective the initial profits of the system are like "found money." The new system is an incremental source of profits. It required the sogo shosha to make the link among firms possible by providing the information, ideas, guarantees, and stability that reduce risks to a tolerable level. The sogo shosha may also participate in raising the capital required by members of the system to initiate operations.

From the standpoint of the sogo shosha, establishing a system is a risky investment. Time, money, and energy must be expanded well before any returns can be realized. Only when the volume of system flows managed by the sogo shosha grows large enough to cover the sogo shosha's fixed costs will a return on investment be earned. But if the system is innovative and lacks much immediate competition, or if it is able to realize significant economies over competing existing systems, it will generate a large enough total surplus that all parties to it can realize satisfactory returns.

If the system is relatively stable, however, over time the various actors involved in it will become familiar to it. Formerly unknown or threatening contingencies will be experienced and handled successfully. Routines will develop to handle the various operations necessary to maintain the system. Credit risks will decline and funds flows will become more predictable. Profits from the system will be accepted as normal by system actors and will be depended on in financial planning. Increases in profits may be hoped for or expected.

At some point some of the actors may question the justification for continuing to support the sogo shosha through the payment of high fees, as in the case of the steel industry. The impact of these pressures on the sogo shosha will vary greatly, according to the circumstances and to the size and bargaining of the firms. But over time, as the system becomes more familiar and certain to the participants, the sogo shosha's ability to command a large portion of the total system proceeds erodes. In the face of these pressures the sogo shosha must either increase the value of its services to system participants or lower the costs of those services. Failure to do either of these will eventually drive the clients to seek more profitable arrangements for managing their links with other firms and markets.

To the extent that the system is unstable, the sogo shosha can continue to justify its high fees. Its superior access to information, markets, finance, and other resources, as well as its diversity, enable it to cope with uncertainty and risk better than its clients can. But stability also means that the sogo shosha must continue to expend resources by monitoring changes, renegotiating relationships, finding new sources or new markets, and so on. Its costs rise as a result of instability. To some extent instability is similar in nature to system creation, for both require resource expenditure but create sogo shosha bargaining power. Figure 4.1 shows the effects of instability and innovation on a service life cycle model of a system and sogo shosha revenues and costs.

Against the competitive dynamics discussed thus far, the basic strategy of a sogo shosha must be to build series of relationships with major as well as minor actors across the key

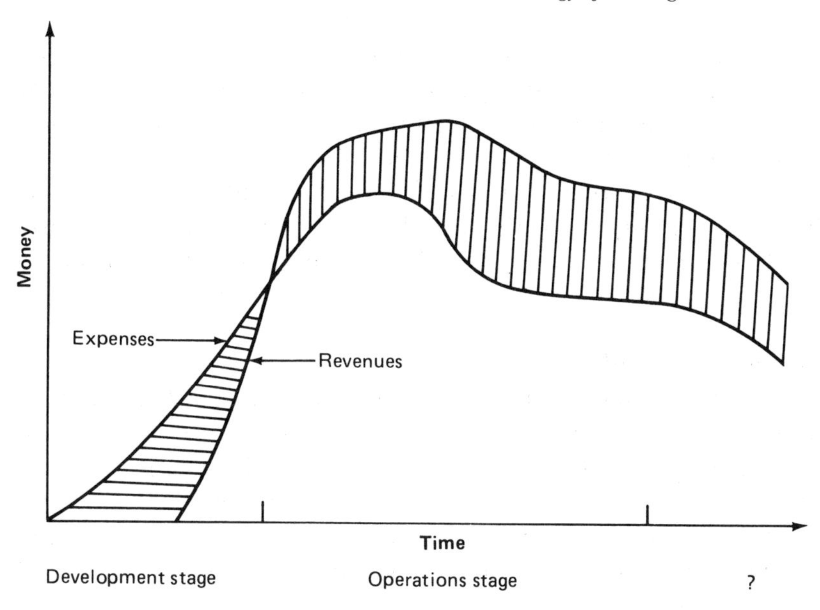

Figure 4.1
The service life cycle of a sogo shosha product system

product systems. These relationships must be managed so as to maximize the sogo shosha's capacity to adapt the entire system to the uncertainty and change.

In practice, this means the sogo shosha must always be searching for new business opportunities to add to its existing array of services to specific clients. It also means that the sogo shosha must constantly strive to identify the emerging points of greatest leverage over a particular product system and then undertake activities, such as research or investment, that give them influence or control over those points.

This thrust of activity might be described as a search for differentiated advantage. To the extent that a sogo shosha becomes the predominant or sole source of some key good or service valued by its clients, it is able to manage the product system as it seeks to. A differentiated advantage can be any resource that contributes to sogo shosha leverage over members of a product system. We have already looked at the steel system to sample the complexity of these dynamics. But in other product systems as well, the sogo shosha is pursuing several types of activity aimed at managing the system through differentiated advantage.

The sogo shosha is under constant pressure to look for ways to strengthen the existing systems and to create new ones. As we saw in chapter 2, the sogo shosha experienced major growth during Japan's high-growth period by expanding, not only in the traditional areas, but in new products and markets as well. Indeed, the high-growth period gave rise to many opportunities for development of new businesses. We shall examine a few examples.

Intermediary Role

The sogo shosha often acts as an intermediary to bring corporations together to alter traditional flows or to create new sources of production. In the early 1960s C. Itoh began actively to diversify out of textiles into other areas, namely heavy industries. At the same time the company became interested in establishing ties with major corporations in the United States and Europe.

The Japanese automobile industry offered an excellent opportunity to accomplish both of these goals. Through the 1960s the Japanese automobile industry was fragmented, and by the end of the decade it became increasingly apparent that shakeouts were imminent. Isuzu was one of the marginal producers whose future was very uncertain.[3] Its management, however, did not wish it to be acquired by another Japanese company. Seeing an opportunity to strengthen its ties with the manufacturer, C. Itoh's management concluded that the only way Isuzu could survive was to enter into some sort of working relationship with an American firm. After an abortive effort with Ford, it approached General Motors. Isuzu, though an old and respected company in Japan, lacked skills at negotiation on the international scene, and C. Itoh undertook much of this activity on Isuzu's behalf. After almost a year of highly confidential and complicated negotiations, the final agreement was reached: General Motors became a minority shareholder of Isuzu. The arrangement proved to be quite satisfactory to all the parties concerned. As a part of the agreement Isuzu gained immediate access to General Motors' worldwide sales network for certain of its automobile models, resulting in a dramatic increase in the company's exports. C. Itoh became Isuzu's sole agent for exports as well as one of its primary suppliers of steel. General Motors was not only able to establish a foothold in Japan, it also gained several new product lines, including small trucks, utility vehicles, and compact passenger cars.

Another example of creating a new system by acting as corporate intermediary is in the creation of very large integrated industrial systems with large attendant risks and rewards. Let us examine Mitsui's leadership in creating a large petrochemical complex in Iran. Mitsui took the lead in identifying the opportunity in the early 1970s. By this time the Japanese market for petrochemical products had begun to show signs of saturation and further capacity expansion was becoming increasingly difficult because of growing concern for the environment. Also a number of developing countries had become interested in creating their own petrochemical industries. Several sogo shosha quickly seized on these opportunities in such countries as Singapore, Korea, and Brazil. In the early 1970s Iran offered what appeared to be enormously attractive opportunities, particularly after the first oil crisis. The chance to gain preferential treatment on oil exploration or imports to Japan was linked to facilitating Iran's development of a petrochemical complex.

Mitsui's original plan called for construction of a complex with an annual capacity of 300,000 tons of ethylene, 1,500,000 tons of liquefied petroleum gas, and 250,000 tons of caustic soda and other derivatives. Mitsui was to provide, through various means, approximately half of the total financing required for the project and, in addition, was to extend guarantees. This was one of the largest projects that had been organized under the aegis of a sogo shosha. The subsequent political and military developments in Iran halted the partially completed project, causing dramatic and drastic alteration of the original cost estimates. Were it not for the contingencies of revolution and war, the project certainly would have been attractive for Mitsui as a means to exploit differentiated advantages. Its plan was to handle most of the export of equipment and machinery during the construction stage. Once the project was complete, Mitsui would have gained a large captive source of supply of petrochemical products, strategically located, that it could certainly have exported throughout the world. Furthermore Mitsui, as an investor, would have enjoyed handsome dividends from its equity investment in the project. Though much less tangible, the experience gained from managing a large-scale project and the relationships forged among various parties in this particular venture could have been beneficial in structuring similar projects elsewhere. Unfortunately in this case these expectations failed to materialize, and in 1981 Mitsui & Co., after a series of agonizing actions and deliberations, decided to limit its involvement.*

Diversification

Another way in which the sogo shosha have been trying to create a new system is by taking on new types of products. One example of this is machinery. In the early 1960s, as Japan was starting to emerge as a leading manufacturer in broad areas of machinery and equipment, sogo shosha firms began to recruit engineering graduates from colleges to develop new machinery businesses. The types of machinery and equipment the sogo shosha took on ranged from automobiles and consumer electronics to industrial equipment, aircraft, and tankers. Machinery has become important to the sogo shosha, particularly in exports. For example, in 1984 machinery and equipment accounted for nearly 20 percent of the total business of the Mitsubishi Shoji.

The sogo shosha's performance in what is broadly defined as machinery has been rather mixed. They have experienced limited success in automobile and consumer electronics. The sogo shosha took on the task of exporting these products in the early stage of its market development for the manufacturers. For example, consumer electronics and cars manufactured by Mitsubishi Electric and Mitsubishi Automobiles were distributed by Mitsubishi Shoji in the United States and elsewhere. For some time Mitsui marketed Toyota automobiles in some parts of the United States and Canada, but in all of these cases, as the manufacturers gained experience and built sufficient volume, they terminated or reduced their relationships with the sogo shosha. In some cases a sogo shosha was left with minority ownership of a specialized distribution operation controlled by the manufacturer.

Companies such as Sony or Honda chose from the outset to undertake their own marketing abroad. The sogo shosha were

* Mitsui and the government of Iran agreed that Mitsui would provide no more financing to complete the war-ravaged project but would help with construction and with the marketing of products.

found to be less than satisfactory in marketing products that required intensive marketing and post-sale service at the consumer level. The commodity mentality widely shared among the sogo shosha personnel did not lend itself well to successful consumer marketing. Thus today in most consumer-durable fields the sogo shosha role has been confined to small marginal markets where the manufacturer cannot set up its own distribution economically.

The sogo shosha have done notably better with ships, military hardware, and aircraft. Marketing these products successfully requires excellent contacts with a relatively small number of potential customers and high-ranking government officials. Ships, for example, represented a major growth area in the 1960s and were ideally suited for the sogo shosha's business. Major sogo shosha, particularly Mitsubishi and Mitsui, had a shipbuilding company as a member of the same *zaibatsu* group. Marketing ships requires excellent contacts and a long period of gestation. Financing almost always plays an important role, and on the production side, shipbuilding is an important extension of the steel system. Marketing ships, aircraft, and weapons systems is fundamentally different from marketing consumer durables such as automobiles. Moreover the size of each transaction is substantial. Hence the sogo shosha's network of information and communication, including political ties, becomes highly useful. Because of the large potential sales the sogo shosha are willing to make the investment of time and effort required to make the sales.

Plant Exports

The sogo shosha have achieved notable success in what is commonly referred to as plant export, in which their traditional strengths can be most effectively exploited. The sogo shosha manages an entire project of installing a large industrial plant abroad. Plant export from Japan grew in the 1970s, exceeding $10 billion in some years (see table 4.2). It is estimated that the sogo shosha collectively handled nearly 70 percent of the total plant exports. Such a project is particularly suitable for the sogo shosha for a number of reasons. A sogo shosha identifies a project opportunity in a foreign country, particularly in the developing world, and it organizes a team of Japanese as well as foreign suppliers. An important part of the project is to

Table 4.2
Plant exports, 1974–1983

	Number of projects	Total amount
1974	415	3,858
1975	489	5,241
1976	680	8,006
1977	736	8,607
1978	753	8,729
1979	743	11,785
1980	677	8,932
1981	455	12,313
1982	386	10,985
1983	316	5,992

Source: The Industrial Bank of Japan.

arrange for financing. Here again, the sogo shosha is in an excellent position to mobilize its global network and its reputation to tap the resources of not only large private financial institutions but also the public financing agencies of various countries. Once the project is approved, the sogo shosha assumes a central coordinating role in implementing it.

In these projects the sogo shosha becomes, in effect, a system organizer, albeit of temporary duration, since it typically disengages itself from active management of the facilities once they are completed. The chief attraction of such a project from the sogo shosha's point of view is that it can supply almost all the materials, machinery, and equipment. The sogo shosha sometimes does not receive special fees or commissions to organize such a project; its payoff comes in the form of business generated as a result.

Vertical Integration

Another way for the sogo shosha to create a new system, thereby gaining differentiated advantages, is to seek opportunities for vertical integration. Let us first examine upstream integration in raw materials. An outstanding example can be found in grains, a vital product the sogo shosha import to Japan.[4] Japan is the largest importer of a number of agricultural products, such as various grains and soybeans. For example, Japan imports 18 percent of the total soybeans traded in international markets, 16 percent of the maize, and 8 percent of the wheat. In the past the sogo shosha confined their role to that of importers, handling over 90 percent of food imports into Japan, but in recent years leading sogo shosha have also invested in agricultural development projects. Such projects include Mitsui's large-scale efforts to raise maize in Indonesia. Both Mitsubishi and C. Itoh undertook similar operations there, though on smaller scales. The sogo shosha have made similar attempts in such commodities as sugar, coffee, bananas, pineapples, palms, chestnuts, and oranges. These developments projects have been scattered in many countries, including Brazil, Honduras, and Spain. Another move toward vertical integration in grain trading has been the acquisition of grain elevators, silos, and other related facilities. Such an approach has been particularly important in the United States, especially in products such as grain, soybeans, and wheat. The United States is the largest grain exporter in the world, and grain trading is dominated by a half dozen major U.S.-based international grain-trading firms.

The sogo shosha face fierce competition in grain trading in the United States. In the first place, the prices for grains are determined by the Chicago Commodity Exchange. Thus the sogo shosha must not only buy from major American grain dealers at the price determined on the exchange but must sell in competition against them. A number of the sogo shosha have been trying to become integrated grain traders themselves. For example, Mitsui, as early as 1969, bought grain elevators in Montana and Oregon to serve as a base for exports to Japan. It also acquired grain elevators in Illinois to purchase soybeans and acorns. Mitsui achieved a major breakthrough in 1978 when it took over most of the grain business and facilities of Cook Industries along the Mississippi, thereby gaining direct access to the Gulf of Mexico. Cook, a major commodity trader, was forced to divest its grain business because of financial difficulties. The major American grain firms were not able to purchase these facilities because of U.S. antitrust regulations. This acquisition was considered a major achievement for Mitsui, since nearly 60 percent of the total U.S. grain export is shipped from the Gulf of Mexico, where the major American commodity trading firms own and operate elevator facilities, and as a result Mitsui was able to overcome a major entry barrier to becoming a full-fledged international grain-trading company.

Another product area in which the sogo shosha have been pursuing a strategy of vertical integration is minerals. One of the earliest efforts to achieve a limited equity position in raw material ventures was in an iron ore project in Australia. In 1965 Mitsui and C. Itoh jointly acquired 10 percent of the total equity of the project which was being developed and managed by U.S., British, and Australian interests.

Similarly Mitsui took a small share in a large copper-mining project in Bougainville. The primary motive for early investment by the sogo shosha in these projects may be characterized as defensive—that is, to assure themselves adequate sources of supply for the Japanese market in view of the rapidly increasing demand for ores.

But as markets changed, other motivations came into play. Mitsubishi entered into a joint venture with Kennecott Copper to modernize the huge Chino mine in New Mexico. With copper supplies in a surplus situation by the late 1970s, Mitsubishi marketed most of its share of the mine output in the United States and in third countries, after smelting it in Japan where the world's most efficient facilities are located. Mitsubishi's substantial investments in downstream U.S. copper and copper-product distribution facilities is benefited by this strategy, while supplies are still assured, should markets return to a situation of shortage at some time in the future. Stability of supply had become critical, and the sogo shosha viewed small equity participation as a way of enhancing their long-term competitive positions. It should be noted, however, that in these early projects the sogo shosha did not assume risks associated with the initial exploration.

Gradually, the sogo shosha began to seek greater control over product systems by participating in large-scale projects involving exploration. For example, Mitsubishi took considerable risk when it embarked on a liquefied natural gas (LNG) project in Brunei jointly with Shell. Though the project took almost ten years from the initial planning to the full production stage, it turned out to be an enormous success. Mitsubishi sells the output to major utility companies in Japan. Not only does it obtain a substantial profit from sales of the product, but the sales have subsequently become all but routinized. Mitsubishi's shipments from Brunei in 1984 accounted for roughly half of the total of Japan's imports of LNG, and a large portion of the company's profits.

Third-Country Trade

Mitsui and Mitsubishi in prewar days used their global networks to engage extensively in so-called third-country trade—trade that does not involve Japan as a buyer or supplier. In this as in other areas in the prewar era, Mitsui was in the forefront; it is estimated that its third-country trade reached as much as 30 percent of its total sales. Grain and cotton were the two most important products.

In the postwar high-growth period the sogo shosha concentrated their efforts almost exclusively on trade to and from Japan. The Japanese economy was growing very rapidly and continued to offer attractive opportunities as the nation's industrial structure underwent significant changes from labor-intensive to capital-intensive operations.

The sogo shosha's comparatively recent interest in third-country trading as a way to create a new product system was propelled by a number of forces. First and foremost was the declining growth of the Japanese market beginning in 1973. Moreover the sogo shosha's great expansion created both the need and the capacity to engage in third-country trading. They had built an extensive global presence with much-needed market contacts and networks. Major plant export projects often created the need and opportunities to obtain specific equipment and machinery from sources outside of Japan. Yet another reason for greater interest in third-country trade was the need to go to low-cost sources to defend their customer base, as Japan began to lose its competitive position as a producer of low-cost products. Yet another reason was new capacities acquired outside of Japan. The output of many of these projects exceeded the Japanese domestic demand. Mitsui's acquisition of grain elevators in the United States, for example, gave the company an opportunity to serve markets beyond Japan. Third-country trade represents an opportunity to maintain the viability of the existing product system and to build new ones, or at least to become a major player in a new system (see table 4.3).

Table 4.3
Third-country trade as percentage of total sales

	1973	1978	1983	1984
Mitsubishi	6.2	6.1	8.9	11.7
Mitsui	6.3	1.9	14.8	16.0
C. Itoh	6.3	12.0	15.1	17.7
Marubeni	5.1	13.3	15.7	16.9
Sumitomo	9.9	5.2	8.2	11.5
Nissho-Iwai	10.1	9.9	22.5	21.1

All of the activities mentioned represent logical extensions of established sogo shosha activities into new or larger arenas of competition. This is consistent with the competitive dynamics model described earlier in this chapter.

Clearly one of the key issues facing the sogo shosha is whether these responses will be adequate to preserve its institutional role into the next decade and century. Although systems instability helps a sogo shosha vis-à-vis its clients, instability also challenges its own management capacities.

5

The Organizational Challenge

The strategy of a sogo shosha requires it to manage exceedingly complex systems governing the flow of goods and services from raw materials to ultimate consumers. Not only must it perform this role more efficiently than its customers could on their own, it must also continually seek new ways to add further value, by innovating new business schemes for existing customers, by adding new clients, or by enabling existing customers to cope more effectively with change and uncertainty, among other means. The preceding chapters have analyzed the economic, business, and strategic factors underlying the sogo shosha's assumption of these roles. This chapter will begin our consideration of the organizational means that are employed by the sogo shosha to carry out its tasks.

Development and Operations

In essence the sogo shosha is a linkage mechanism, competing with markets as a means to link buyers and sellers into multistage systems. However, unlike markets, the sogo shosha must continually seek not only to carry out existing linkages smoothly and efficiently, it must also be able to seek out new linkages for its customers. Without this latter activity its ability to maintain its fees, and therefore its existence, would soon diminish.

The creation of new linkages by sogo shosha is possible because the range of its activities continually exposes its managers to a wide variety of opportunities to imagine new combinations of institutions and resources. This gives them the impetus to create or modify systems. We can label this creation of new activity as *development,* for the ability of the sogo shosha to grow, or even maintain its present strength in existing systems, depends on it. On the other hand, the relatively routine performance of facilitation of existing linkages in existing systems will be labeled *operations*. The routine processing of documents and purchases of stable commodities are examples of operations.

The two are analytically distinct but are inextricably bound together in practice. It is the very act of becoming familiar with resources, people, and opportunities via operations that creates the possibilities for development. Somehow a sogo shosha organization must balance both functions, performing each effectively. Building and managing an organization that can do this is a central challenge to the sogo shosha.

The necessity of performing operations and development places unusual demands on the managerial organization of a sogo shosha, whether considered in isolation or in comparison with other types of multinational enterprises. The sogo shosha must be flexible enough to respond to the almost random development of opportunities that appear in markets, technologies, policies, and other widely diverse spheres of activity. Yet its responses must be highly systematic and coordinated, often within a short time frame. It is impossible to routinize the search for many of these opportunities, especially the truly unusual and significant ones.

Initiative must usually be taken at comparatively low levels of the organization by managers widely scattered throughout the world. The most common type of opportunity, a chance to make a deal on especially favorable terms, requires that a group of traders coordinate a complex and varying mix of services within the firm: financing, shipping, insurance, storage, delivery, and other customer services. These traders will usually be separated by geographic distance, and sometimes they will also be separated by product "distance"—that is, they may be trading rather different commodities both of which happen to be involved in a large transaction.

Most sogo shosha trading is done not for the firm's account but rather for the accounts of clients. Therefore close liaison with the client organization must take place, if the sogo shosha is to know its needs and keep it informed of what trading is taking place on its behalf. Virtually every trade involves two halves: buying and selling. When the sogo shosha is working within a product system in which its client ties are extensive, a single transaction often involves buying from one client and simultaneously selling to another client, further complicating the coordination that must take place.

Information Processing[1]

The coordination performed by the sogo shosha requires above all that information be available to the people who need it. The sogo shosha organization must be able to obtain, check, channel, and act on information. It may be thought of as an information-processing mechanism. The following points are the most significant aspects of the information-processing task of a sogo shosha:

1. Large amounts of information are generated in diverse product and geographic environments.

2. Some of this information must be selected and transmitted to selected other persons in other environments.

3. Information or decisions originating in one area can be very important to other areas.

4. Diversity is high.

5. The scale is large.

6. The number of decision points is large.

Returning to a steel system example, information on nickel shipments and mine development in New Caledonia might be of great importance, not just to nickel department personnel but also to a wide group of other traders within a sogo shosha. This is because New Caledonia is a major global source of nickel, which is a basic ingredient of many forms of steel. The markets for steel products, iron ore, coal, shipping, and machinery, among others, are all potentially influenced by developments in the steel industry, and activity in New Caledonia can, under certain circumsances, be an advance signal of changes to come.

Learning by means of the firm's telex system that certain parties have been making inquiries about long-term contracts for nickel, a sogo shosha manager in Japan who deals in machinery might hypothesize that someone is undertaking a feasibility study for a new steel mill. Checking for similar activity in ore, coal, and shipping markets, it might be possible to confirm the hypothesis, to deduce the magnitude of the project, and possibly to identify the principals. Alerted to the possibility of selling the steelmaking equipment of his firm's clients who make such capital goods, the manager could create a task force to involve the sogo shosha as deeply as possible in this proposed new project. Ultimately the sogo shosha might hope to act as agent for procuring raw materials for and selling the output of the new mill. In the long run the value of a small piece of information from remote parts of the world could be immense.

However, because so much information is generated every day, it is clearly impossible to report everything to everyone. Selecting the relevant information for the appropriate person is an essential first step. The dangers of information overload are as great or greater than the dangers of not reporting sufficient information. A representative who is buried under too much information is incapacitated for many functions, whereas one who lacks critical information is handicapped only in dealing with the items of business related to that particular information.

Coordinating Service Packages and Making Trade-Offs

Coordinating the sogo shosha service package to the potential steel mill builder in the preceding example would raise severe organizational problems. Certainly a number of competitors could offer to perform the same kinds of services as the sogo shosha departments of this example might undertake. The competitors might be other sogo shosha or specialized firms. Therefore a good deal of bargaining with the new steel mill's managers would have to take place. It might be necessary to cut the price of the steelmaking machinery in order to ensure that a total package, including long-term resource procurement, could be sold.

Underaking such bargaining means that the sogo shosha must have some mechanism for making trade-offs between the interests of its own subunits and those of its clients. In this example the price cut would hurt both the plant export section of the sogo shosha and its machinery-making clients, if the price cut is passed on to them.* Meanwhile, the interests of the

* Depending on the nature of the relationship with this set of clients, the sogo shosha might fully or partially absorb these price cuts.

resource procurement sections and their client mines would be helped. Not only must these trade-offs be made quickly, but effective operating relationships must be maintained within the sogo shosha and with its clients. Bitterness and recriminations could easily result. There is no particular reason why simply working for the same company leads automatically to harmonious relations, much though managers might wish it to be so.

Carrying the example even further, not only must the different product lines of the sogo shosha be coordinated but also the different geographical units. For instance, it is possible that the output of a new steel mill in Brazil might adversely affect steel mills in Japan that had been exporting to the Brazilian market. These steel mills might well be customers of the sogo shosha. In this instance some coordinating and trading off might have to take place between sogo shosha representatives in Japan, some of whom are losing steel exports while others are gaining machinery exports, and those in Brazil who are losing steel imports but possibly gaining a new major Brazilian client. Figure 5.1 presents a highly simplified schematic rendering of some of the coordination that must occur with the major actors in this example. If trade-offs cannot take place across geographic as well as product lines, then the firm cannot effectively deliver complex service packages.

Similar conflicts occur in ongoing product systems management. In an existing broiler chicken system, for example, a continuing issue is the price of chicken feed. World grain markets, after all, are subject to fluctuation in prices. To what extent should these fluctuations be passed along to broiler houses, who would in turn pass along their increased costs to processors, and so on? Because chicken is rising in popularity in Japan, all parties to the system have an interest in avoiding disruptive price fluctuations. On the other hand, substitutes for chicken, such as beef, fish, pork, and bean curd, are also fluctuating in price. The grain-importing section of the sogo shosha may want to pass along all prices increases, and no decreases, whereas the section distributing chicken meat may want exactly the opposite policy. Both sections would recognize the importance of maintaining good relations with the broiler houses that buy the feedstuff and sell the live chickens. If these clients are squeezed too hard by rising feedstuff prices and low broiler prices, the whole system could be disrupted. The sogo shosha must be able to make a constant stream of judgments

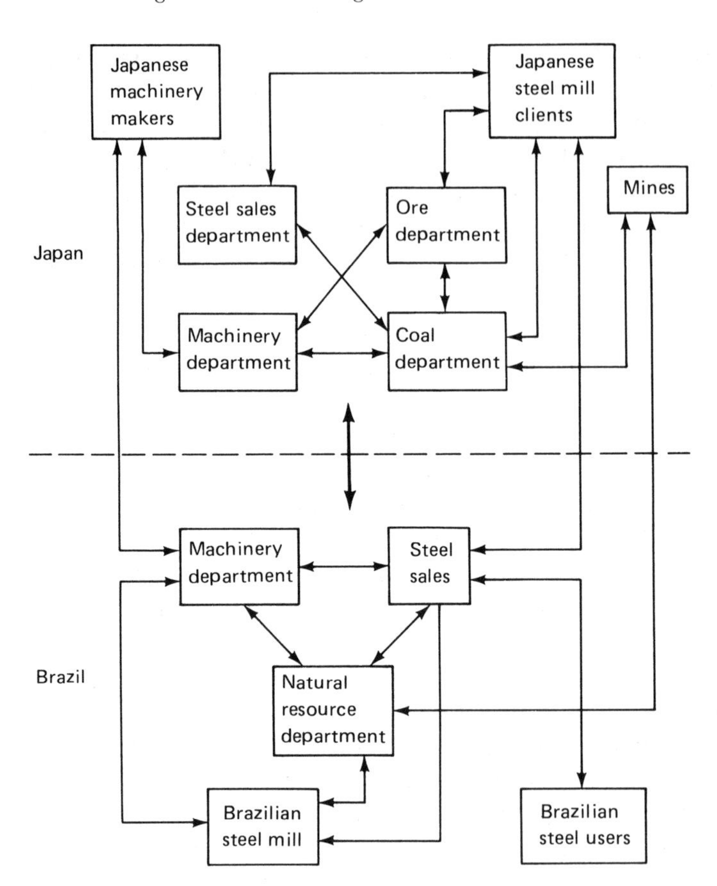

Figure 5.1
Schematic of major lines of coordination in a steel system deal

on what policies to pursue. Its own interests and those of its clients are continually affected.

From the preceding discussion we can identify three basic categories of tasks that must be accomplished by the sogo shosha:

1. Gathering and channeling information.
2. Evaluating the profit potential created by the information.
3. Acting to realize the profits.

Each of these is itself a complex set of activities requiring coordinated decisions and actions among a group of people separated by geography and product line concentration.

Two aspects of the sogo shosha make these tasks particularly difficult to undertake. One is the changing nature of its business. Unlike a manufacturer, there is no machinery to define and regularize activities. Whether a sogo shosha manager will buy or sell, whether he will work with manager A or manager B is entirely contingent on developments external to the firm. Furthermore the necessity of development activities means that the substance of activity must change over time, sometimes quite quickly. It is therefore difficult for a sogo shosha organization to be very definitive in establishing enduring procedures to enable managers to accomplish these three basic tasks.

The second aspect that creates difficulties is the great diversity over *two* dimensions of a sogo shosha's operations. Geographic differences create obstacles to effective working together. A manager who works within Saudi Arabia must necessarily think and care about different things than a manager working in Japan, even though both work for the same firm. Similar barriers exist between managers working in grains and those to heavy machinery. Even the most sophisticated American multinational firms dealing in relatively well-defined businesses such as manufacturing and banking find that managing diverse areas and products is a continuing challenge.

Routine and Strategic Coordination

The operations of a sogo shosha can require highly sophisticated and complex integration of disparate organizational units, but it is useful to remember that not every action on the part of a sogo shosha manager demands the utmost in organizational capacity. Repetitive transactions (those we earlier labeled operations) or development activities involving only minor changes, or extensions of existing business activities and ideas, can sometimes be accomplished using established decision rules and frameworks and involving comparatively few and comparatively low-level managers. This type of activity may be thought of as "routine coordination."

However, development activities pertaining to many new business opportunities, such as undertaking new functions, expanding the roster of clients, or making a substantial financial commitment, are not so simple from an organizational standpoint. There are complex risks to be weighed, many possible perspectives to be heard, and hard trade-offs to be made. When an action requires assigning a significant orgnizational resource to a use in which the risks and trade-offs involved must be appraised by multiple organizational units, we label such integration a "strategic coordination." An aggressive policy of seeking new business opportunities requires greater strategic integration. A less aggressive policy is comparatively easier to manage, consisting more of routine integration. Every sogo shosha organization must be able to handle substantial amounts of strategic integration if it is to avoid gradual liquidation of its business lines.

Because organizational resources are not infinite, strategic integration inevitably means giving resources to some parts of the organization and not to others. In other words, it is both a political and a business issue. The sogo shosha's role in international trade and the Japanese economy has been, and continues to be, highly dynamic. Within the career spans of today's top-level sogo shosha managers, sectors such as textiles and steel have gone from the position of being high-growth sectors to that of mature, stagnant, or even declining business lines. The adjustment to this reality is part of the process of strategic integration. It goes beyond the issue of resource allocation into highly complex and inevitably subjective qualitative weighing of priorities, activities, information, and personnel.

For the sogo shosha, then, there is a crucial balance of business activity and attendant organization requirements. Operations generates profits and makes only routine coordination demands on the organization. But development activity, with its more complex strategic coordination needs, is a necessary ingredient to preserve the future of the institution. Strategic coordination is not only more complicated and subjective, it also has the potential to be internally divisive.

Formal and Emergent Organization

Most Americans, if asked to describe the elements of an organization that make it work, will point to rules, procedures, ranks, and other clearly defined elements of what we will term *structure.*[2] By structure is meant any aspect of the organization that is written down and codified and that can therefore be changed by persons with appropriate formal authority. The structure of an organization can also be called the *formal organization.*

But there are other aspects to organizations that are equally (if not more) important in determining the actual behavior of members and therefore overall organizational performance. Although often thought of as "process" (as opposed to structure), such things as the shared assumptions, the vocabularies of words that take on special and rich meaning to those inside the organization and the widely understood "way of doing things here" which everyone must pick up on and use to be effective are enduring artifacts of the organization as much as its formal structure. These elements are rarely precisely analyzed, and members of the organization are often not even conscious that they exist, except when a newcomer's ignorance of them causes them impatience or amusement. These aspects of an organization can be called the *emergent organization,*[3] for they are not a product of conscious design but rather emerge as a necessity for accomplishing things.

Every organization has a formal and an emergent aspect to it. But the balance between the importance of the two varies considerably from one organization to the next. To continue with our method of dichotomizing concepts for clarity's sake, we can consider two polar types of organization:[4]

1. An organization where formal structure plays the major role in determining the trade-offs, making decisions, and coordinating activities. Though individual discretion is naturally present and essential to this type of organization, the important point is that such individual discretion is closely defined, so that it is clear who has the authority to decide on issues, goals, and work procedures.

Not only is decision-making power clearly divided up among company management, but company communications are also regulated. "Channels" exist, and in theory communication outside of channels is unnecessary. The underlying concept is that the tasks the organization must perform can be known and somehow broken down into measurable subtasks. When bureaucracy or bureaucratic procedure are spoken of in the pejorative sense, a stereotype of this model is often what is being referred to.

Of course no organization exactly matches this model, but military organizations are sometimes cited as the closest familiar approximation. Organization theorists have coined the term "classical model" to refer to this type of system.[5] Reliance on such formal structural methods is also sometimes referred to as "administration by hierarchy."

2. An organization where *people* are given the greatest possible individual discretion to define and achieve their tasks and where consequently rules and procedures are at a minimum. Naturally some rules are inevitable, such as rules concerning salary, but the theory behind this type of organization is that the individuals performing the tasks should know best what is appropriate and can be relied on to take all necessary steps. Situational judgment is required, and the flexibility to achieve it requires less structure.

An important element of such an organization is the kind of people who make it up. The people may be thought of as the key element of the organizational "design," and the effort and resources that might go into writing job descriptions in an organization on the classical model would be devoted to recruitment and development of staff in an organization of this second type, which we shall label the "participative model."

An important factor influencing the way people fulfill their roles in participative organizations is the pattern of their experience over the course of their careers. Since they have greater discretion to control their activities, their previous experience becomes an important guide for them in determining what to do. Thus the structure of career paths is an important element of the organization design.

Another basic element of an emergent organization that systematically influences members' discharge of their functions is the organizational climate or culture: the sum of general experience, values, expectations, vocabularies, and other factors that is shared among members and transmitted to new members. Although intangible, corporate or organizational culture can be a real and very effective force in molding and controlling managerial behavior. We shall return to this topic shortly.

Professional service organizations such as law firms are often participative organizations,[6] especially in matters directly relating to the performance of client services (the *line* functions, as opposed to the purely *staff* functions such as billing, salary, and administrative). Organizations generally adopt a participative style when the line operations require considerable case-by-case discretion and when the organizational or external environments encourage the maintenance of high standards of performance by the organization's members; such organizations are common in the professions. The sogo shosha in many respects looks like a type of professional service organization. But, although its members require considerable case-by-case discretion in performing development activity, there is no outside professional standards organization, such as the bar association, to enforce professional standards and provide a vision of professionalism. If any set of values or procedures exerts a guiding influence on sogo shosha managers, it is likely to be derived not so much from a professional body of standards but rather from organizational culture or the broader ethnic culture of Japan.

Culture and Organization

Anyone who has ever had the opportunity to observe similar types of organizations operating in different cultures knows that culture does affect organization in many ways, large and small.[7] Even military organizations, which tend to be tightly structured around the classical model, differ considerably from country to country, and culture seems to have something to do with this.

In recent years the literature of Japanese management and culture has multiplied. The quality of this material varies widely, from the simplistic and inaccurate to the sophisticated and penetrating. Because our focus is on the institution of the sogo shosha, which happens to have evolved in and still is based on a Japanese cultural environment, it is useful to consider the general role of culture in its organization. But it would divert us from our central purpose to attempt an inclusive review of all the relevant aspecs of Japanese culture that have an impact on the sogo shosha. Insted, in this chapter we will confine ourselves to an overview of the general role of culture in organizations and to consideration of two very broad aspects of the Japanese cultural environment that have particular relevance to the sogo shosha organization: the role of law as an integating mechanism and some important characteristics of the Japanese language.

As yet there is no useful framework for explaining what effects culture has on organizations. More organizational theorists have preferred to focus their attention and energy on studying organizations within one culture. Much of the work that does exist comparing organizations in one culture with similar organizations in other cultures has focused on government bureaucracies rather than on business organizations. As multinational corporations grow, and especially as non-American firms come increasingly to global prominence, the importance of the role of culture in business organization is sure to be reflected in further studies that will refine and expand the range of tools available for analyzing culture and organization.

At the moment, however, some formidable issues await the serious student of the subject. The first is the lack of a widely shared understanding of exactly what culture is. One search through the literature of anthropology uncovered no less than 164 definitions of culture.[8] Fortunately this book does not aim to make any fundamental statements about the general relationship beween organization and culture. We only want to understand the role of culture in the sogo shosha. Therefore we can afford to be less than fully precise in our definitions. As a working concept we will use one of the earliest and most inclusive notions of culture, drawn from the pioneering anthropologist E. B. Taylor, who called culture "that complex whole which includes knowledge, belief, art, morals, law, custom, and any other capabilities and habits acquired by man[sic] as a member of society."

Three things about Taylor's definition are particularly noteworthy. First, he considers culture as a *whole*. That is, all parts of it are interrelated. Change one part and the other parts are affected. This is analogous to reciprocal interdependence within organizations. Second, culture is acquired by being a *member* of society. Culture cannot be acquired exclusively by studying it; some crucial aspects, at least, can only be learned through the shared experience of membership. Third, culture includes things that are formally written down, such as laws, and also things that are not, such as customs. To use our earlier terms, culture has both a formal and an emergent aspect.

The fact that some of the concepts useful for describing organization are also useful for describing culture is not surprising. In some senses culture is part of a large organization, a society. Culture provides the rules, the symbols, the meanings, and other aspects of the framework necessary to make a society work. Perhaps this overlapping of culture and organization as concepts has much to do with the difficulty of studying their relationship to each other. It can be very difficult to discover the relationship between two things that are sometimes indistinguishable.

One way around this problem is to take the same approach to it that Taylor took toward culture. That is, don't try to specify completely the relationships among the constituent elements of the phenomenon being studied; instead, treat it as a *whole*. The interrelationships are far too numerous and situationally dependent to enable us to specify fully all aspects of their complexity. If we see them as related, and if we can say something about their relationship in a specific context, then we will have done all that we can.

When applied to organizations, this "holistic" perspective is sometimes called the "institutional" approach. The focus is on a particular organization, and the method is to trace the dynamics of the relationships among values, environmental demands, formal structures, culture, and anything else that is important to understanding what is going on. The image is not of a static entity in which it might someday be possible finally to understand and specify all the relationships observed. Rather, it is understood that institutions are dynamic systems, constantly adapting themselves to change. Because the constituent parts are interdependent, such adaptive change necessarily causes relationships among the parts to change. Thus the most we can hope for is some sense of what the patterns are and what the general directions of change might be. Far from being a social science, this is at best an art and at worst an exercise in frustration.

The institutional approach well suits our goal of understanding the sogo shosha. It also provides us with a set of expectations about what we will find. Rather than specific relationships that can be quantified or even directly specified, we will be seeing patterns of qualitative relationships which will require the reader to participate actively in sensing the complexity and subtlety of the way the pieces of the puzzle fit together.

One of the best examples of the institutional approach can be found in the work of French sociologist Michel Crozier. He posits that there are two sides to every organization: the "utilitarian rationality" of the formal organization and "the means of social control, which are determined by the primary behavior and values characteristic of the cultural system of which the organization is a part."[9] These two categories correspond to what we have called the formal and the emergent system. Crozier tells us that when the two sides of an organization are in conflict, the result is "the bureaucratic phenomenon"—red tape, ineffectiveness, frustration, and the like. It is this conflict between the two sides of organizations that Crozier explores with richness and brilliance.

Our approach is somewhat different. We are seeking not the conflicts but to understand how the two sides of the sogo shosha harmonize sufficiently well to enable it to compete with markets and with the internal capabilities of its clients' organizations as a form of product systems integration. This is not to imply that the sogo shosha is a perfectly harmonious system, it too has its share of dysfunction. But unlike the state-linked organizations Crozier studied, the sogo shosha could be replaced if it did its job with less efficiency than existing alternative organizational means.

Further Crozier seems to limit the influence of culture to the emergent system. It is true that culture has its most direct, pervasive, and important effects on this aspect of an organization. But culture also influences selection of elements of the formal system. Some cultures emphasize hierarchy more than others, and formal organizational structures in such cultures tend to have more levels of hierarchy, for example. Culture tends to influence strongly many aspects of what might be called the personnel systems of formal structures. Pay differentials, recruitment practices, promotion rates, and other such matters vary widely across cultures. These personnel systems also have a strong influence on the emergent system. So culture enters organizations through a variety of means, and influences organizations in many ways.

Organizational Culture

Culture's effect on organization is not limited to the influence of national culture on formal and emergent systems. As we noted, organizations tend to develop their own narrower cultures shared by their own members. Just as people do in societies, people in organizations face common situations and problems. Specialized meanings, values, and customs develop in order to facilitate coordinated action. If we think of organizations as systems of human interaction, then such interaction systems must depend on a "shared basis of normative order."[10] Sharing a basis of normative order (knowing what things mean) is considered to be a key element of a cultural system. In an organization, signals generated by the formal structures must be interpreted and acted on by members of that organization. Only by sharing in a system of meaning can they do this with consistency. In other words, the organizational culture becomes a filter through which members perceive each other and the organization as a whole.

Organizational cultures obviously derive in part from the national or ethnic culture(s) of their members but augment this base with distinctive forms. This organizational culture serves to distinguish members from nonmembers, who may well share the same ethnic culture. Organizational culture is thus both necessary to getting things done in an organization and also a mechanism of maintaining organizational identity.

Limits and Extent of Culture and an Explanatory Factor

There is an understandable though unfortunate tendency among some students of Japan and Japanese ways to cite Japanese culture as a residual explanation for almost any observed social phenomenon, including managerial phenomena. The strength and homogeneity of Japanese culture makes this approach seem persuasive, and the sheer mystery and complexity of alternative explanations sometimes makes this the easiest course. It is hoped that the present study will avoid falling into this trap. Culture will be a major artifact of analysis, but it is the interaction of culture with other factors that is intended to be the focus. Culture is, in other words, a causal factor, not an ultimate cause.

This kind of warning about the possible abuses of culture as an explanatory factor should not lead to the absolute avoidance of the use of culture in explanations of behavior, however. Culture must be seen in its relationship with emergent and formal systems, and the interplay among these factors should be elucidated. These intentions will underlie our examination of sogo shosha organization in the next chapters.

But before we go into such details, we first wish to examine the roles of formal and informal systems and the role of culture at a much higher level of organization—that of Japanese society. Two principal motives are behind this brief excursion. The minor one is to provide background information on the nature of law and custom in Japan that is helpful in understanding the legal-social environment of the sogo shosha. The major one is to show that the pattern of reliance on culturally influenced emergent patterns of integration and conflict resolution is by no means unique to the sogo shosha. Rather, the use of such emergent integrative mechanisms is characteristic of Japanese society. The sogo shosha's system has deep roots in the culture and society of Japan, though it has adapted this cultural heritage carefully to serve the needs generated by its own business situation.

Integrating Societies

Just as the differentiated business units of a firm have to be integrated or coordinated with each other, so the various parts of any society have to be integrated with each other. Societies achieve integration in ways that are in accord with their own history and development.

They can rely on formal procedures, or they can use emergent, largely culturally determined integrative mechanisms. All societies, like all organizations, use both; it is the relative emphasis that varies. Japan and the United States rather sharply contrast with each other in this regard. The United States has a history of ethnic diversity, and so it has developed a system that uses rules and laws extensively as a way of governing relationships and settling disputes, that is an integrating mechanism.* However, the fact that law is so well adapted to diversity has perhaps had something to do with the great reliance Americans put on it as an integrative medium. Japan, on the other hand, with its ethnic homogeneity, its status as an island country, its two and a half centuries of isolation until the mid-1800s, and with its own particular culture proclivities, has developed many alternative social and cultural integrative mechanisms, so that rules and laws have not had to be so extensively developed.

Among the key elements that integrating mechanisms must provide are agreed-on channels and vocabularies for communication and agreed-on methods and standards for dispute resolution. One great virtue of written law is that once everyone agrees on the rule of law, an enduring body of rules and interpretations can always be referred back to, and one can know how things ought to be done or resolved. For a country such as the United States, whose many ethnic traditions might yield very different intuitive senses as to what is proper in any situation, it is most vital to have a common grounding in law, so that disputes can be settled in a way that everyone perceives as fair.

However, in Japan, a highly developed cultural sense of what ought to be done in many situations has emerged through the many centuries of cultural growth and homogenization that have taken place in that isolated archipelago. As a result the necessity of developing a legal system to enforce conformity and resolve disputes has not been as strongly present. Over 1,300 years of near isolation has made culture virtually as certain a reference point in many disputes for Japanese as law is for Americans.[11]

Law and Culture as Integrating Mechanisms in Society

The contrast between Japanese and American sensibilities about law is instructive in many ways, for it illustrates how two cultures go about accomplishing the same ends, each relatively successfully and each in accord with its own social and cultural

* It is not meant to imply that diversity is the only reason for the development of and reliance on law in the United States. Clearly, the English legal tradition has been extremely important, among other factors.

heritage. There are many analogies with corporate managerial systems that are both appropriate and useful.

In the United States, law is used to regulate many essentially private relationships. Contracts are a favored format for establishing relationships, and the courts stand ready to enforce contracts that may be only implicit or verbal in some cases. The American system is based on the theory that adversary relationships are inevitable and should be presumed to exist, so that the "truth" may be discovered in the dialectic between opposing sides as each is forced to make its position explicit in the adversary process.

In Japan, traditional law held the group, whether a family or a collectivity of neighbors, to be the relevant unit of responsibility.[12] The individual's behavior was to be regulated by informal social processes within the group. Law in Japan did not generally regulate the behavior of individuals, only groups; this offers a stong contrast to Western ideas of the responsibility of the individual before the law. It also alerts us that emergent processes within a group have historically played a major role in integrating the individual into social systems that transcend face-to-face interactions.

Even after the legal reforms of the Meiji era a century ago and the reforms sparked by the American occupation of Japan, very great differences remain, and there are still many functions that law in Japan still has not taken over from emergent cultural and social mechanisms. These include functions that are routinely handled by law in the United States. As any American businessperson who has had experience administering contracts in Japan can testify, Japanese attitudes toward contracts differ sharply from American ones. The contract is regarded as a basis of discussion perhaps, but Japanese businesses tend to feel that any long-term relationship must develop subtleties and complexities that cannot possibly be expressed in a confining document written at the outset. A communication of any sort can only be understood in the context of its sender. A contract between two firms, divorced from the dynamic continuing interaction of individuals representing those firms, lacks meaning and is difficult to live with comfortably for most Japanese. Therefore contracts cannot possibly be regarded as the final word in any relationship.

The Japanese legal system, as well as the American one, reflects its own culture; as a result contracts do not have quite the same legal standing in Japanese courts as they do in the United States. As Tokyo University Professor of Law Takeyoshi Kawashima has stated, "The contractual relationship in Japanese law is by nature quite precarious and cannot be sustained by legal sanctions."[13]

The culture and law both put a premium on compromise as the basis for dispute settlements. There is a tendency to regard unilateral imposition of will as inherently unjust, regardless of the working of a contract. Good will, and the culturally presumed norm of harmonious relationships rather than the clash of opposing parties in an adversary relationship, is looked upon as the engine of dispute resolution.

The prevailing forms of dispute resolution in Japan lie outside the legal system in the realm of information and formal mediation.

The Japanese Language

When describing Japanese organizations, it is necessary to discuss briefly some of the special characteristics of the Japanese language and of Japanese-style interpersonal communication, for communication is vital to integration, and the Japanese language is rather unusual in certain respects.[14]

The long period of isolation from the outside world, which has had such important effects on Japanese society, has also affected the language. It is highly idiosyncratic, full of phrases and usages that have meaning only in a particular context. The grammar is deceptively simple: for example, there are only two tenses, past and nonpast.* The net result is that there are few rules by which meaning can be precisely pinned down.

The basic number of sounds employed in Japanese is very small compared to most languages, and homonyms abound. Because of the large number of homonyms, understanding a particular word's meaning requires a knowledge of the general context. Another consequence of the small number of sounds in Japanese is that Japanese people are very poorly equipped to deal with the task of pronouncing or hearing other languages, as they have not been trained to distinguish many different sounds.

* A specifically future tense does not exist but must be inferred from the context.

All this adds up to the fact that Japanese are considered to be quite seriously handicapped in distal communications (i.e., with outsiders). On the other hand, however, Japanese is, for most foreigners, one of the most difficult languages to learn, and there are very few Westerners who speak it with any real fluency.

Further Japan is what one anthropologist has called an "endogamous society," implying that the inhabitants share so many aspects of consciousness and experience that explanations via the medium of language become unnecessary in many situations. Rather than saying something outright, one might merely have to supply a nuance.

This ability to communicate meaning indirectly or nonverbally has been reinforced and developed by two previously mentioned characteristics: groupism and the primacy of vertical relations. Because groups are so important, potential clashes of will—especially clashes between subordinate and superior—have to be avoided. If relations between two people in a group are allowed to become sour, it can easily affect the harmonious functioning of the entire group. Given the importance of the group commitment, really fundamental clashes can have serious and lasting consequences for many people.

Thus, Japanese has evolved into a language that is often described as "elliptical," in which meanings are first hinted at, allowing time for a reaction to be sensed. If the reaction is favorable, then the statement can be strengthened, and a bond of agreement built between the two sides to a conversation. Direct expression of one's opinion, voiced in one's own name, is often considered to be forward or impolite at best. Thus a Japanese language discussion has been likened to a game of catch: one person throws out a tentative thought, and the other, if he agrees (or catches it) throws it back, perhaps with some strengthening or modification.

In this process nonverbal cues are often at least as important as the actual words themselves. There are many Japanese folk expressions which reveal the importance of nonverbal communications. *Haragei* (literally "art of the belly") refers explicitly to the nonverbalizable element of meaning, which must be present if true understanding is to be achieved. There is a definite and quite widespread flavor of distrust of words alone, and a feeling of necessity to go beyond mere words in communication. Another expression, "the eyes tell more than the mouth," illustrates this point.

It is considered the hallmark of a leader to withhold judgment until others have spoken. Even then the leader must avoid wordiness. The Japanese distrust people who are too smooth and wordy.

Naturally in Japan as elsewhere there is often an imperative need to present a disagreement in the course of a discussion. Various methods for doing this without directly disagreeing personally with a previously expressed opinion, especially the opinion of a superior, have evolved. The simplest method is to mention, but not support, a third opinion, preferably the opinion of an "authority" of some sort—but at least the opinion of someone not present—that disagrees with the previous view. This allows one to avoid expressing personal dissent and yet to plant the seeds of disagreement in the discussion.

Of course everyone involved in the discussion recognizes the ritualistic nature of this charade. Yet everyone also agrees on the importance of maintaining the fiction. Non-Japanese may be tempted simply to dismiss all this as archaic formality, but the fact is that these linguistic patterns have evolved out of necessity, as part of a complex and interconnected ecology of human relations.[15]

It is widely accepted in Japan that one qualification for being a leader or an important person in an organization is to know how to remain silent, while effectively drawing out the views of subordinates.[16] At the same time the leaders must also sense the direction of a discussion and promote consensus. Given the characteristics described here, one can readily see that a superior who prematurely expresses his own views in a direct fashion may foreclose the possibility of productive discussion taking place in the group. Similarly an effective subordinate must know how to read his boss's nonverbal cues and understand what directions the discussion ought to take.

Organizations develop their own characteristic shared understandings, which become incorporated in both verbal and nonverbal communications. These shared understandings enormously facilitate communication, for they can obviate the need for much of the "ritual" conversation that is aimed at establishing the all-important context in which the wor
should be interpreted. The importance of these shared und
standings is one reason why most Japanese companies hire o

fresh graduates and shun the hiring of people from other companies.[17]

The very qualities of shared understandings and acceptance of a common framework that promote effective communication within an organization tend to hinder communication with those outside.

The prerequisites for effective and efficient communication can only be produced by having face-to-face communication over an extended period of time and by sharing an initial starting point of a somehwat common background. As ethnically homogeneous as Japan is, the idiomatic nature of the language, the importance of sharing understanding, and the heightened role of group membership have all led to the emergence of semidialects in Japanese. A graduate of an elite university and a day laborer, for instance, would each tend to communicate, within his own group, in a pattern that would be difficult for the other to follow. Japanese society is divided into subgroups, based in large part on educational background, which obviously influences communications patterns. The leaders of Japan's most important businesses and governmental organizations are, including the sogo shosha, predominantly drawn from a handful of elite universities. Graduation from one of these schools is a virtual prerequisite to a high-level post in government or industry. Communications ease is an important factor in the cohesiveness of this educational elite.

From the preceding discussion of the importance of nonverbal cues, it should be clear why face-to-face discussion is preferable to telephone or letter as a means of communication. In fact one notable aspect of most Japanese offices is the relative lack of telephones, each of which is commonly shared by several people and of typewriters. Though telephone conversations and written correspondence are used, much more reliance is placed on face-to-face discussion.

Of course once people have established a basis of effective communication and know each other fairly well, a great deal of meaning may be transmitted in just a few words on a telephone, or even via a telex. Despite the cumbersomeness that the Japanese language imposes on newly established communications patterns, it is a very effective medium between those who have previously established a solid basis of understanding.

6

Administrative Structures

This chapter will examine the formal organizational structures of the sogo shosha. We have already noted that formal organization is only part of the story of how any firm administers itself. The informal or emergent organization of the sogo shosha is also important and will be the subject of chapters 10 through 13. Prior to that chapter 8 will examine the personnel or human resource policies and practices that shape their informal system. Hence the purpose of this and the following chapter is both to examine what administrative structures and practices exist in the sogo shosha and to assess their usefulness or adequacy in the light of the task requirements and the administrative burden of a sogo shosha. In this way we can better understand the background and importance of the informal organization analyzed in the next chapter.

Similarities and Differences among Soho Shosha Organizations

The organizations of each of the six largest sogo shosha are by no means identical. All are highly diversified global organizations, though each firm has its own particular set of choices around the organizational issues that confront it. Yet there is enough similarity among them that useful generalizations can be made about formal and informal organizations. Three separate factors underlie this basic similarity.

First, the sogo shosha share a common set of historical and cultural roots in Japan. Certain organizational features, such as the recruitment, upon graduation from college, of male managerial staff employed up until retirement, are quite usual among large Japanese companies and are therefore seen in all of the sogo shosha. Despite its multinational spread the sogo shosha, as we have stressed, is still primarily a Japanese institution, and this imposes certain kinds of uniformities on its organization.

A second factor is the common functional demands faced by each of the sogo shosha organizations. Given the intensity of competition for market share among the individual firms, they must quickly match the services supplied by their rivals. Thus the sogo shosha find themselves undertaking the same kinds of tasks and needing the same kinds of coordination among their parts.

Manufacturers who face nearly identical functional demands often end up investing in similar production technologies. But for a sogo shosha, aside from the sophisticated computerized global telex networks of each of the firms, the basic production technology is *organizational* in nature: the ability to obtain information and coordinate activity. Thus, though it may be possible for two steelmakers each possessing basic oxygen furnace technology to match each other competitively while maintaining somewhat dissimilar human organizations, for a sogo shosha common functional demands much more directly imply organizational uniformity.

A third factor underlying organizational uniformities is the amount and intensity of interaction among the sogo shosha firms. They are fierce competitors, jealously guarding both details of their organizations and trade secrets from each other. But large numbers of managers at all levels of the firms are in contact with managers of rival firms daily, in the course of participation in the same markets, as a result of joint venture undertakings such as overseas resource development projects, and as a result of living overseas in often tightly knit Japanese business communities. Moreover the largest clients use the services of two or more sogo shosha and are thus able to compare their organizations, often sharing their observations with sogo shosha personnel. Despite intense concern for the protection of corporate secrecy, it is difficult for one firm's organizational innovation to go unnoticed by its rivals for very long. When these innovations are successful, there is naturally pressure to match it.

Although our main emphasis here is on tracing the common features of formal organizations, we shall not hesitate to point out the differences that do exist when they are significant, and we will refer to a range of practices that exists among the firms. Sometimes it will be possible to identify specific firms when commenting on the differences. But more often, due to the confidentiality that surrounds any outsider's access to sensitive organizational data in this industry, we shall confine ourselves to broader generalizations. Since our purpose is to identify the underlying logic of the organizational systems, in our view this lack of firm-specific detail does not present major problems.

The Structure of Incorporation

In any discussion of formal organization of large firms, a very important distinction between the legal structure of incorporation and the administrative structure of management must be understood. Particularly in the case of multinational corporations, the two are not always identical.

Any corporation operating in several countries faces a number of options in determining the legal status of its overseas arms. The most basic alternatives are either to incorporate the operation in the host country or to make it a branch of the parent, incorporated in the home country. The choice of which form to use is a complex one, depending primarily on external circumstances such as host country regulations and attitudes, tax implications, and access to local financial markets. As far as the firm's administrative system is concerned, however, the choice need not make a great difference. As long as 100 percent ownership of the local corporation is maintained, information, authority, funds, and other components of the corporate lifeblood can flow across the boundaries of incorporation. The legal structure of incorporation need not, and for multinational firms in particular, often does not, have a determinate influence on the process by which administration occurs.

Each of the big six sogo shosha actually consists of a network of legally incorporated entities. There is the parent corporation legally domiciled in Japan and hundreds, even thousands, of separately incorporated units, legally incorporated in Japan and overseas. The vast majority of these "other" corporations are beyond our immediate concern here, for they are engaged in specialized activities ancillary to the business of a sogo shosha. We shall refer to these others as subsidiaries and affiliates.*

But a significant number of corporations are actually locally incorporated arms of the global trading network, functioning as part of an integrated worldwide administrative entity. They must be closely coordinated on a daily basis with the operations of other units of the firm, located in various nations.

The fact that a sogo shosha operation overseas is locally incorporated does have some important effects. Taxation issues are greatly influenced by corporate domocile. Legal status is also affected, with important consequences (see chapter 7). And corporations do keep their own books, have their own directors, and can be given an identity. Although there is some movement in the direction of devolving more power to local trading subsidiaries (see chapter 7), still in balance it is the international administrative processes that give life to the sogo shosha's strategy, and it is on these that we will focus our primary attention as we describe the sogo shosha organizations. Our review of major structures will begin at the top, with the board of directors.

The Board of Directors

At the top of the sogo shosha's hierarchy is a board of directors which, as in the United States, is responsible to the shareholders for the management of the firm. However, these boards are quite large, with forty to nearly fifty members. This is about twice the number of people on most boards of large American firms. Clearly a group of this size requires fairly structured procedures in order to be able to cover its agenda, and it cannot meet very frequently.

Another difference is the Japanese boards' composition: as in most large Japanese firms, virtually all members are senior executives of the firms, charged with regular operating responsibilities in addition to their duties as directors. Thus the sogo shosha's board of directors is really as much an organ of management as of the shareholders. Membership on the board of directors becomes a way of recognizing outstanding managers and of broadening their perspective of the firm to include

* Subsidiaries and affiliates will be treated separately in sections of this and the following chapter.

corporate strategy and operations. Indeed, membership in the board of directors is usually the very definition of top management.

There is further a hierarchy within the board. About half of the members are just "directors" (*torishimariyakuin*) which is the lowest rank. Above them come "managing directors" (*jōmu torishimariyakuin*) and "senior managing directors" (*semmu torishimariyakuin*). At the very top of the hierarchy are the executive vice presidents, the president, and the chairman of the board. To each successive level accrue increases in salary and responsibility, and the mandatory retirement age is usually raised with each step upward as well. In effect the hierarchy reflects the seniority of a firm's directors in addition to the other factors mentioned.

There are only a few outside members on any of the boards at any time. These outside directors are most often the presidents of the main banks supplying funds to the sogo shosha or else the presidents of closely affiliated members of the same *zaibatsu* or bank groups as the sogo shosha itself. Their presence on the board symbolizes the closeness of the interfirm relationship and permits top level coordination of significant issues in the relationships. But unlike American boards of directors, there is no pretense that the outside board members somehow represent the interests of shareholders in opposition to the interests of mangagement. Managers and shareholders are presumed to have harmonious interests, in that both want to see the firm prosper and grow in the long run.

The managerial character of the boards enables them to be used more operationally than most American boards. Since the members are familiar with the daily conduct of business, they can use the board to pass on a much wider variety of issues than would be possible in an American board. However, because the large size of the boards would make them unwieldy as operating committees, executive committees comprising the more senior group of directors in Japan are generally designated to handle a wide range of issues.

Practices vary from firm to firm, but executive committees are generally called on to render final judgment on an astounding number of decisions, ranging from credit lines to promotions. One possible explanation for this role is that the executive committee is the one place where managers familiar with and representing the real diversity of geographical and product interests of the firm can gather to deliberate and decide issues affecting the entire firm. But even an executive committee that meets three or four days a month is limited in the number of issues it can actively and intelligently decide, given a membership of about twenty managers.

As a result in most cases the executive committee really serves to ratify and accept responsibility for the recommendations made to it by the director(s) with operating responsibility for the issue at hand. Judgment, however, is called for from the executive(s) closest to the matter under consideration. Often this executive has a personal stake in the outcomes of the decision—for instance, a request to increase the budget of a unit under his supervision. Other members of the executive committee must factor this into their evaluation of his opinion. Naturally it is possible for other executives to speak up on issues, especially if they strongly disagree, so that other details may be brought to light. But as we have indicated, time pressures would rule out the possibility of debate as the normal process. For most issues the executive committee member closest to the problem would have the most decisive say. Although it will often accommodate members who wish to stake their credibility on an issue, the executive committee in effect usually ratifies the decision of the members closest to an issue and educates other top managers about how the decision being made will affect all important areas of the firm.

Basic Organizational Contours: Product and Geography

As we mentioned earlier, the organization of a sogo shosha consists of many specialized units and subunits. Within each sogo shosha choices are made on how to constitute these into coherent groupings. Two possible forms of organizational division stand out: units can be grouped according to finer segments of product lines or according to finer divisions of the world into geographic segments. Clearly the product organization mode fosters greater coordination among managers working on the same or similar products, whereas the geographic organization mode occasions greater coordination among managers working in the same or related geographic areas.

A sogo shosha needs to coordinate both modes of organization. For instance, steel traders in Seattle and Kinshasa are affected by the same group of suppliers and the same markets and cannot blithely sell the same lot of steel to their respective customers. But the steel traders in Seattle must also coordinate their visits to customers, such as Boeing Aircraft, with the work of machinery, aluminum, and other traders who call on Boeing. Likewise, their counterparts in Kinshasa and elsewhere, dealing in copper, machinery, or other commodities, must coordinate their common clients and also their interactions with the governments, banks, shippers, and all the other elements of the local commercial environment that they share.

The common approach of all six major sogo shosha therefore has been to implement both geographic and product groupings. The result two hierarchies are not isolated from each other; rather, each manager reports to two bosses, one in each hierarchy. Technically this type of administrative structure is known as a matrix.[1] It is considered one of the most difficult types of arrangements to live with. But a matrix system brings the distinct advantages of flexibility and responsiveness to businesses that are willing to pay a price for these virtues. The balance of power between product and geographic hierarchies and the maintenance of effective leadership can pose critical problems for any matrix organization.

Each sogo shosha has dealt with the problem of balancing product and geogaphic interests in its own distinctive way. In some, such as Mitsubishi, the product groups are reputed to be predominant in influence, whereas in others, such as Mitsui, the geographic hierarchy is regarded as exercising more influence. Overall, product-based organizations tend to predominate. But generalizations such as this must be regarded with extreme caution. Key individuals are capable of mobilizing corporate resources, almost regardless of their current location in one or the other of the hierarchies. Over the course of their careers managers can expect to rotate from one hierarchy to another. And the situation of each company continually changes as management responds to the exigencies of business. At one moment it may be necessary to delegate unusual authority to a product unit, as might be the case in a global commodity shortage or a technological change, and at another moment, such as following a political upheaval, a geographic unit may need to predominate in key decisions.

The real balance of power between geographic and product hierarchies is based as much on external contingencies, current concerns, personalities, career path patterns, and a firm's traditions as on the details of its formal management system. There is thus a continuing ambiguity of authority and power inherent in the matrix form of organization. When sensitively and properly managed, this becomes a source of strength because it forces managers to make their decisions in the light of multiple factors reflecting the real complexities of the firm's situation. But it requires a high order of interpersonal skill, a willingness to look beyond the immediate issues to see the longer-term perspective, and a tolerance for ambiguity to avoid a degeneration into a state of continual bickering and organizational paralysis. The nature of the organizational dilemmas inherent in a sogo shosha's matrix organization will become clearer as the details of organizational structure and process are examined.

The Product Organization

A sogo shosha with a product-based structure is divided into six to nine basic groups. Each group trades in one major commodity such as ferrous metals, energy, foodstuffs, machinery, textiles, and chemicals. In addition to these commodity divisions, there is often a construction division, which handles large construction projects, and a general merchandise division, which handles commodities that do not fit into the product systems handled by the other groups.

Each of the product groups is headed by a top level executive, usually a managing director or senior managing director; the exact rank of the executive often reflects the relative sales level, profitability, or growth prospects of the product area. Each product group is comprised of divisions that are subdivided into departments and further subdivided into sections. These are the basic levels and units of the organization, with examples of each level of subdivision:

Product group, or *bumon* (e.g., foodstuffs group).

Product division, or *hombu* (e.g., commodities division).

Department, or *bu* (e.g., oil and fat department).

Section, or *ka* (e.g., soybean section).

In addition to the sections there are often teams that are only temporary. These teams are not organized as formally as sections. Some firms are increasing their use of teams to the point of reducing their use of sections, as a way of decreasing rigidity and fostering cooperation. In some other firms the difference between a team and a section may only be semantic. But it is nevertheless significant. As we shall see, the section itself is a major institution of socialization.

It is quite common for the head of a subunit to have an assistant to help with the management duties, but the assistant is never the person to whom subunits one level lower in the organization formally report. Officially sections report to the department chief over them, not the assistant, even though in practice, the assistant department chief may sometimes be the person with whom they most often are in contact. It is rare to have a span of control wider than five or six; no more than six sections would report to a department, and no more than six departments would report to a division.

There is more variety among sogo shosha in the organization of staff functions than in product organizations. Some firms consolidate staff areas into one or two groups that have the same status as product groups; others leave staff units at the division or department level, but reporting directly to the executive committee or the president. Staff units include obvious functions such as corporate planning, personnel, accounting, legal affairs, finance, credit, electronic data processing, and auditing that are to be found in any corporation of any size. But they also may include separate staff units concerned with the mapping and coordination of long-term plans in specific problem areas or opportunities of special significance to the entire corporation. These may be centered around particular geographic units such as the Soviet Union, China, the Middle East, or Brazil, around products and technologies, or even the development of a major new client. They are kept distinct from the line operating units which conduct day-to-day business in these areas, so as to allow a longer and broader perspective and more top management information and input. In some cases staff units may be centered around issues of functions that cut across product areas, such as insurance, shipping, or collection of overdue payments.

Domestic Branches

The Japan offices of a sogo shosha are of course more a part of the product axis of the matrix than the geographic. This is because there are none of the peculiar problems of operating in the international business environment where national governments, foreign exchange, language, customs, and other issues must be dealt with. Also in Japan diversity is not so great, so to some extent domestic branches operate just as they would as if they were physically located in the Tokyo headquarters.

Among the domestic branches the Osaka, and to a lesser extent, Nagoya offices maintain a special status. Osaka is not only the second largest city, but historically it has functioned as the premier commercial center of Japan. In fact two of the sogo shosha—C. Itoh and Marubeni—were originally based in Osaka and have only in the last decade or so moved their headquarters to Tokyo, which has decisively become the business center. Nagoya, the third largest city, and a major center for the machinery and textile industries, maintains a lesser, though strong, claim to special treatment as the home of important clients. In each of these offices can be found senior executives and divisional or departmental units supervising groups of sections in each of the basic product areas.

Other domestic locations have mostly specialized offices, with relatively few subunits and relatively low levels of responsibility. The number of domestic locations of a sogo shosha may be sixty or more, but the total number of personnel employed in them is comparatively small, about 10 percent of the total staff, and has been falling in recent years. Because of the ease and speed of transportation and communications within Japan, it has been feasible to concentrate personnel and power in the headquarters, which has been growing in absolute and relative size.

Among the overseas offices the regional headquarters cities are at the top of the heriarchy. Below them come full-service offices, capable of doing all kinds of business. Then come one or more levels of subbranches, depending on the firm. Many offices are limited by either the host country or the firm itself so that they may not actually sign contracts and book business, even though as a liaison or representative office, they may have conducted part or all of the preliminaries to doing business. Sometimes these subbranches are formally attached to a larger full-service branch.

A subbranch is more economical to operate for two principal reasons, one external and one internal to the firm. Without signing contracts and booking business, the office usually needs fewer licenses, must file less paperwork, and otherwise need not commit as many resources to a specific location. Being of lower status, the office can be staffed by lower ranking personnel who are much cheaper to employ.

A manager rotated into an overseas office from Japan has two supervisors: the head of the local office where he is working and the head of his product group's operation in the regional headquarters city to which his branch reports. For a Pittsburgh machinery representative, for example, this second boss would be the head of the machinery department in New York, the U.S. regional headquarters. Maintaining a balance between these two lines of authority may be a continual problem for the sogo shosha as it may be for any other matrix organization. But in the sogo shosha's case the complexity of the problem is increased because the regional product group head, say the machinery department chief in New York, is also part of a matrix and so has two bosses: the head of the regional office where he works and the head of his product group in Tokyo.

Each sogo shosha has about 100 overseas offices, and these employ several hundred to slightly more than a thousand Japanese managers, or about 10 to 15 percent of the total managerial personnel. A small percentage, about 3 percent of the managerial personnel, may also work overseas in nontrading subsidiaries. We shall describe these subsidiaries and their roles shortly.

The composition of the local overseas work force is heavily skewed toward nonmanagerial jobs, though in various offices there are some non-Japanese who have risen to positions of managerial responsibility. In some countries, particularly the United States, this has led to some serious problems for the sogo shosha (see chapter 14). But with these few exceptions, most local staff are employed as secretaries, clerks, sales representatives, drivers, porters, and janitors. There is no large blue- or white-collar labor force. Nevertheless, the overseas offices do have a significantly higher ratio of support staff to managerial staff than do the domestic Japanese offices. The ratio is highest in low-wage countries such as India, where custom and necessity require the employment of clerks to perform jobs that might be unnecessary or automated elsewhere. Drivers, porters, and others who perform personal services are relatively numerous. But even in high-wage countries such as West Germany and the United States, managers enjoy much larger support staffs than they do in Japan. Support staff in these countries tend to be more semimanagerial, serving in sales, accounting, and so on. One explanation why the overseas managerial staff is more highly leveraged or stretched thinner than in Japan is the high cost of maintaining expatriate managers. But also important is the need to employ people familiar with the local environment to enable managers to perform their functions with maximum effectiveness. We will examine personnel and human resource aspects of staffing later in the chapter.

The Overseas Geographical Organization

Overseas branches, unlike domestic ones, are organized along the geographic axis of the organization. Typically branches are aggregated into about six major geographic regions, namely North America, South America, Europe and Africa, the Middle East, Australasia, and East Asia. The importance of these overseas regions and of the geographical axis as a whole varies somewhat from firm to firm and from region to region. In general, Mitsui is known for having the greatest autonomy in its overseas geographic units.

In these regions the headquarters office is usually in the major commercial city, such as London, New York, São Paulo, Hong Kong, or Sydney. The headquarters office is divided into departments that reflect the basic groups of the product hierarchy. Each of these regional headquarters product departments supervises the overall product strategy in the region, keeping watch over the activities of traders operating out of the branch offices.

Large offices in major overseas cities other than the regional headquarters may also be divided into product departments reflecting the full range of activity of the firm. But when Paris, Los Angeles, Singapore, and other regional subcenters are excluded, relatively few of the branch offices can support a full complement of personnel in all product areas. In Pittsburgh, for example, metals and machinery are likely to be represented, not textiles and foodstuffs.

The Structure of Work Responsibilities

Work at the sogo shosha is structured in very different patterns from those most Americans are accustomed to. Below the level of *kachō** ("section chief"), individual job descriptions or "job slots" do not exist. A section (*ka*) usually has from four to eight members. These members do not have any specific responsibilities as far as the formal organizational design is concerned. In fact the duties of the section itself are only vaguely specified. For example, one firm's organizational manual description of the duties of the soybean section reads as follows:

1. Handle the import and domestic trade in soybeans.
2. Handle the domestic distribution of soybean flour.

By American standards these are terribly unspecific instructions. It is entirely up to the *kachō* to determine how best to utilize his staff to accomplish these general tasks. Whereas there is a strong tendency in American managerial practice to refine the responsibility of subunits and individuals as far as is practically possible, the design of the sogo shosha is extremely loose if not vague. Even "loosely decentralized" conglomerate firms in the United States tend to use much greater specificity in defining the mission of their constituent units. Participative organizations try at least to specify the ends to be served in as much detail as is possible, but in the case of the sogo shosha the formal organization ends at the section level. Individual job slots do not appear at the bottom ofthe organization chart.

The way in which individual responsibility is allocated and individual effort controlled will be examined at length later. It is important for the moment to keep in mind the striking flexibility inherent in such an unspecified organizational design. As the earlier example of a complex steel transaction

* The original Japanese title *kachō* will be employed when referring to the position of section chief, even though English, not Japanese forms will be used when referring to most other terms. We do this to give emphasis to the difference between the executive responsibilities of this position and the type of executive responsibilities common in American organizations.

pointed out, flexibility is absolutely vital for a sogo shosha to be able to seize ad hoc opportunities in its transactions as it develops and operates systems.

The Network of Subsidiaries and Affiliates

Besides trading activities a sogo shosha is also involved, via a network of separately incorporated entities, in a number of other business lines. In general, these business lines are related to trade but are more specialized and less complex than the sogo shosha's functions. Most of these companies were founded or purchased as the outgrowth of the trading business. But many have been taken over by the sogo shosha after they defaulted on credit lines owed to it. By assuming management responsibilities in such cases, the sogo shosha hopes to achieve a turnaround and regain the funds it advanced, and perhaps go on to operate the business profitably as well as avoid disruption to a well-established product system.

A sogo shosha has a few hundred subsidiaries and affiliates with about half in Japan, and half overseas.[2] In number of employees they dwarf the sogo shosha, for their operations are more labor intensive. One hundred thousand people or more may work for a single sogo shosha firm's subsidiaries and affiliates. The total equity investment in these subsidiaries is in the hundreds of millions of dollars, so the average equity stake is about $1 million per firm. In addition to its equity, however, the sogo shosha has also "invested" a substantially larger sum in these firms in the form of credit advances. This money is also at risk in the subsidiaries and affiliates, since there is no real recourse in the event of default. When equity and credit invested in this network are added together, they equal a sum that is usually larger than the sogo shosha's own equity.

We may define subsidiaries as companies wholly owned by the sogo shosha and affiliates as partially owned but considered to be under the same effective management control. Often the sogo shosha may own less than a majority of equity but still effectively control an affiliate through its loans and through channeling purchases and sales.

There are several reasons for using subsidiaries and affiliates as vehicles to perform certain functions, rather than leaving them to be performed by the trading network. A separate corporation can be used to limit the parent's financial risk in situations where the business risk is substantial. The sogo shosha's exposure to risk is limited to its equity and credit advances. A separate company may have access to a different segment of the Japanese labor market than the sogo shosha, which must hire first-rate staff and pay high wages and benefits. A subsidiary or affiliate can also develop specialized skills to a degree that is difficult for the parent, with its need for broadly experienced personnel who can serve as integrators of its organization and product systems. Affiliates also allow joint-venture partners to participate in the risks and rewards of various business lines, thereby solidifying important business relationships with these partners. Finally, separate companies may have access to additional sources of financing that cannot be tapped fully by the parent. For example, overseas affiliates with local equity investors may have access to government-sponsored, low-interest loans, and in Japan an affiliate may be able to borrow from a bank that has already reached its legal loan limits on borrowing by the sogo shosha.

There are basically five types of subsidiaries and affiliates:

1. Resource development affiliates in such fields as mining, paper and pulp, and agricultural products.

2. Sales organizations that handle specialized products such as certain types of textiles or machinery.

3. Support service organizations such as warehousing and forwarding agents.

4. Manufacturing firms whose raw materials and output may be handled by the sogo shosha.

5. Financing organizations that are set up to deal in specialized services and financial markets.

Subsidiaries and affiliates are usually established at key points in the product systems that the sogo shosha manages. With its broad perspective the sogo shosha is often able to see where profitable opportunities lie in product systems. If the bargaining relationships with the other actors in the product system permit, it can establish a subsidiary to reap the rich potential profits of the key functions. Sometimes the bargaining relationship is such that major clients are able to insist on being joint-venture partners in an affiliate, so as to share in the profits inherent in carrying out major functions.

Yet there are also instances when a necessary function in a product system does not seem likely to yield very great profits. In such instances the sogo shosha may be compelled to advance the capital necessary to establish a subsidiary in the interest of getting the entire system functioning. The bargaining leverage of the sogo shosha would then be used to try to compel other system members to join it in financing an affiliate organization.

In still other cases the sogo shosha may establish a subsidiary or affiliate in a key function primarily for the value of the insider-based detailed information which it could provide. By running its own manufacturing operations in certain industries, for example, it is able to gain in-depth knowledge of the economics of each aspect of production. The manufacturing operation itself may not yield significant profits, but the parent can put the knowledge it gains from this operation to use in enhancing its ability to bargain successfully with other members of the system. Subsidiaries and affiliates often enhance its bargaining leverage in this way.

Although the businesses of these subsidiaries and affiliates are closely tied to that of the trading network, they do not require the same degree of integration that the trading network does. Subsidiaries and affiliates are usually more closely integrated into trading operations than clients are, but they are less integrated than the subunits of the trading network itself. Subsidiaries and affiliates are also different from the trading operations in several fundamental respects. Their businesses are usually much better defined, due to such things as their higher fixed investment in capital facilities, their stable technologies, their ties to brand identification, and their relatively limited and stable functions. We shall return to the division of labor between the trading network and the subsidiaries and affiliates later in this study.

7

Administrative Processes

Planning and Control Systems

Formal organizations use planning and control systems to gather information and then use that information as a basis for forming policies, plans, and goals that help coordinate activity and for measuring and enforcing compliance with these goals throughout the organization. The planning system is a way in which the activities of managers can be adapted to change, for planning involves assessing what the future holds for the organization and what the organization's response should be. To the extent to which the environment is diverse, the planning system will require input from diverse subunits of the organization. Changes in the subunit's environment also help determine how often the planning process must take place. The planning system involves flows of information in two directions: "upward" from subunits to the planners and "downward" from the planners back to subunits that must carry out activity.*

Control systems are the means by which organizations formally provide incentives and disincentives for members to behave in ways consistent with the goals specified in the planning process and by which organizations measure compliance. A control system also involves flows in two directions. The data measuring compliance flows "upward" and rewards and penalties flow "downward." Once again, the frequency with which

* Planning most often occurs at high levels in organizations, but the formal rank of planners is not necessarily higher than that of the subunits submitting data to them. "Upward" and "downward" are therefore not fully adequate terms to describe the direction of flows, although they are not too misleading in most cases.

this occurs is normally linked to the rate of change in the environment but should also be related to the time span of feedback. It makes no sense to measure and reward performance of a task that hasn't yet had any measurable effect.

Planning and control systems are fundamental tools of formal organization. They provide important signals to all levels of an organization, signals that can be used to guide behavior in more effective directions. The degree to which planning and control systems are developed and elaborated within an organization is one important indicator of the weight of formal organization relative to emergent organizations. An even more important indicator, however, is the degree to which planning and control systems are actually *used* by members of the organization as a guide for their own activity.

In this regard Mitsubishi is generally the most prone to emphasizing formal procedures and planning, whereas Mitsui is known for allowing key individuals and units wider discretion in mapping their future and implementing operations. In fact a popular saying goes: "Mitsui for people, Mitsubishi for organization" (*Hito no Mitsui, sōshiki no Mitsubushi*). The other firms fall somewhere in between these two, with the exact position changing from time to time. Often when a firm experiences problems, such as bad debts or declining sales, it will strengthen planning and control mechanisms as a way of reasserting central control.

But a powerful factor mitigates against such centralization in even the most planning-oriented sogo shosha: the managers closest to daily operations know best what ought to be done. The greatly diversified operations of the sogo shosha makes this even more imperative, especially when rapidly changing events require on-the-spot responses. As we shall see, planning and control, though not insignificant, play a supportive—not dominating—role in the administrative process of the sogo shosha.

Top-Down and Bottom-Up Planning.

The usual planning method of the sogo shosha is for the executive committee or the board of directors to issue a ten- or twenty-year strategic plan. High-level planning staffs assist in gathering and analyzing data for this plan, but the final responsibility for making trade-offs and hard choices lies at the top of the firm. Each year this plan is revised and extended, so that it becomes a rolling plan. It is primarily a macroplan; it forecasts world economic trends and indicates which opportunities the sogo shosha should pursue. Top management, with its global and multiproduct system perspective, is supposed to be able better to identify large-scale trends and opportunities and to guide lower levels in the pursuit of these.

The business of a sogo shosha is highly dependent on economic activity throughout the world, and on trade levels. These are factors that the sogo shosha has relatively little power to influence. Thus its economic analysis is a means of formally recognizing that business plans must be in accord with trends in the world economy. When trade grows, so will business opportunities. When trade in petroleum rises while trade in textiles declines, the sogo shosha must respond by managing its efforts and resources accordingly.

The long-range plan sets goals for such basic items as sales growth, profits, capital expenditures, growth in shareholders' equity, shifts in product line emphasis or geographical composition of sales, the opening of new offices, additions to personnel, research and development, and changes in the network of subsidiaries and affiliates.

Top-down planning thus is important to the process of allocating resources among the different parts of the firm. We will examine this aspect of it shortly. For now, we may simply state that the long-range plan partly serves to spur on the operating units to ambitious goals. As one top planner commented: "We can readily determine what our expenses will be for the coming year for salaries, investments, and financial charges. Then we need to set goals which aren't too conservative and safe."[1]

The long-range plan does not usually deal with the section level of the firm. Departments or branches are the lowest level it details in some firms, and in others, the division or subregion. Thus as a formal control mechanism it does not reach very far into the organization. Yet it should not be supposed that lower levels of management are not influenced by the plan. Branch and group managers know of and share their superiors' commitment to the goals announced by the plan, though often it may not be clear in the long-range plan how an individual manager buying rubber in Malaysia, for example, ought to comply in his daily conduct of business. The long-range plan mainly provides a frame of reference for other signals and incentives of other mechanisms, among them the short-range planning and control systems.

In general, the long-range plan goes through an iterative process as units down the line are asked to respond to preliminary versions of the long-range plan. It often serves to set an agenda or prioritize various types of goals. There is little or no unilateral imposition of plans from staff units divorced from the operating realities.

Short-range plans are usually produced from the bottom up, with sections estimating their business prospects over the next quarter or half year. These are operating documents, with slogan-level policies (e.g., "tighten inventory" or "add market share"), budgets, profit and loss projections, and human resource allocations.

The difference between the bottom-up, short-range plan and the top-down, long-range plan is reflected in each plan's intent. Since the long-range plan communicates to the firm the strategic priorities of top management, naturally it is top-down in character. The short-range plan, which is meant to inform management of specific business conditions facing the firm as perceived by managers actually dealing with customers, starts with data from such lower level operations.

In some firms the short-range plan doesn't reach down to sections and subbranches; in other firms it does. Whichever approach is taken, it is the department chief (*buchō*) who is most responsible to senior level for the smooth implementation at the section level.

Strategic Planning

The heavy reliance on formal analytical tools popularized by some American consulting firms has never enjoyed quite the same vogue in Japan as it has in the United States. Certainly in the sogo shosha, and perhaps in many other Japanese companies as well, this reflects a preference for consensus processes rather than isolated pronouncement from oracular planners as a mode of decision making. It also reflects a related conviction that only line personnel, actively involved in day-to-day operations, can have a sufficient grasp of business dynamics.

But there are two types of strategic planning processes that can be considered close to the practices of many large American firms. One is the exercise of very broad macroeconomic forecasting, especially as it relates to overall growth rates of world trade and to the relative growth of basic business sectors in which the sogo shosha has, or contemplates having, an important involvement. Both specialized staff groups and line operations may be involved in this, though, ultimately, it must be recognized that such forecasting is hazardous. In effect, what counts most is not the formal technical exercise itself but the longer-term process of discussion, bargaining, and consensus-formation for which it serves as a partial basis.

The single most important decision that depends on this forecasting is the recruitment of personnel. The number of new graduates to be hired largely depends on overall anticipated business growth in the long term. The educational backgrounds to be sought is influenced by the perception of the rise of certain business areas. Currently, for example, a larger proportion of graduates with some technical background in computer sciences, electronics, biosciences, and related fields is being sought, due to the perception that these will be future growth areas for the sogo shosha. But the decision to do so is not the outcome of a specific planning process so much as a longer-term process of perception and consensus building.

The other major area in which a strategic planning process can be said to take place is the commitment of a firm to large-scale projects and investments. Here again it is not so much a single strategic planning system but a longer-range, less definable process that is important. Each firm, though, differs in the relative role of influential individual decision makers, formalized studies and procedures, and informal consensus processes. As we have mentioned, the commitment of large-scale resources is inherently a political process, so it must be assumed that informal discussions, bargaining, and evaluations will be important.

Nevertheless, there may be a very considerable effort made in some firms to review and check important proposals formally. In Mitsubishi, the firm known to be most formalized in its decision-making approach, a department head described the process leading to a major investment as follows:[2]

> About ten years ago we launched a study team to recommend long-term strategy for this business. We knew that product supplies were limited, while demand was growing slowly but steadily between 2 and

3 percent a year. We had somehow to be certain that we could obtain a dependable supply for Japan in times of shortage.

We also wanted to be able to deal in third-country trade in the product. The long-term loans we'd traditionally extended to commodity producers usually limited us to exporting only to Japan. We felt that our best opportunities lay in expanding our business beyond Japan, whose consumption was growing slowly.

There were three reports of this study team over a ten-year period. During this period membership on the study team changed, but because we were all rotating within the same division, there was a continuity of thinking and commitment, regardless of the specific membership. Gradually we narrowed our focus and our list of potential countries and partners, and a consensus emerged that we should approach a particular natural resources company. We had been dealing with them regularly since before World War II and were currently in a consortium together which is engaged in deep-sea mining of manganese nodules on the ocean floor.

After repeated approaches from us through an overseas operation of ours, the other company proposed a venture to us. We went to the Investment Administration Office to get their suggestion about whom to send to this partner to study this specific proposal. We ended up sending two teams in February 1980, one technical, and one financial and legal, with eight people altogether representing six departments and three engineers from a major client of ours involved with this commodity. There were lots of things brought back by these teams that had to be studied carefully to determine whether the partner's proposal would really be beneficial to us. For such purpose I had to ask general managers of various departments to provide specialists from their staff to form a study team at a working level.

After the selection of the team I went to the personnel department to let them know that a new team had been created. We also formed a similar "core" team here in this department to monitor it closely, and a smaller team was organized within our overseas trading subsidiary in the partner's country. Naturally it was necessary to do a lot of consensus building before starting the project in a formal way. When it came time to start formally, Mr. X, the division head, and I went before the Project Comprehensive Policy Committee to explain our ideas and answer questions. There were a lot of questions on which they asked for further study. The above-mentioned "core" team, fully assisted by the interdepartmental team, tackled these questions, spending a lot of time and effort. On the basis of this team's work, Mr. X wrote a letter to the partner setting out the terms under which we would consider participating in the venture. Then we started the negotiation, and by May we had exchanged memoranda on the project. Following the execution of the memoranda, we proceeded to the complicated negotiation of drafting up a formal contract, and in December 1980 we signed the contract.

Accounting and Control

As might be expected, keeping track of all the business flows of a sogo shosha requires a high level of investment in accounting systems. A corporate staff unit ensures basic uniformity across the firm, but typically there are many accounting issues and functions that are handled at the product group or departmental level. Trade, financial, and accounting practices can vary across the wide range of products handled by a sogo shosha.

These systems enable each section to produce a monthly set of accounts, including a profit-and-loss statement. These are monitored closely by the departments, and department-level results are monitored by the higher levels. Such data are important to management, but typically, they are not regarded as seriously as are profit center data in U.S. companies. As is true in many Japanese firms, there is greater interest in and willingness to wait for long-term results. There is also a basic recognition that a dynamic and largely uncontrollable trading environment may influence short-term results, so it makes little sense to hold people directly accountable in the short run. Simple profit performance is only part of the story. As one Mitsubishi planning manager commented: "While we look like a profit center organization on paper, in fact we're closer to an informal qualitative evaluation system in practice."[3]

But profit performance cannot be disregarded in the long run. Top management must decide which units of the firm should grow, and the best data to use in determining this is profitability in the long run. This means that units of the firm see themselves at least partially in competition with each other to maximize their own profit contribution. While top management seeks to avoid any hint of disharmony or destructive competition, it is often necessary for different units to share the proceeds of a single transaction or set of transactions.

For example, a machinery department may make a large sale of an industrial plant, perhaps a petrochemical complex. One key to its success would have to be its ability to get good prices for the metals that would be used in building the machinery. This might require a special effort on the part of ferrous and nonferrous metals divisions. Similarly, if the petrochemical plant were in an oil-producing country, one significant payoff for the firm could be the enhanced ability of its energy division to buy oil from the country on favorable terms.

When through the effort of one unit, another unit gains an advantage that produces an income stream for it, the first unit often asks that it share in the income stream. In other words, ferrous and nonferrous might share in the machinery department's commission on the petrochemical plant sale, and the machinery department might get some commission or other share in the energy department's purchases of oil, at least for a while.

These kinds of special arrangements must naturally be negotiated. We shall examine this process more fully in the next chapter. For now, let us note that such negotiations must occur when the firm develops new business involving more than one unit or product system. This makes them a regular phenomenon but not a part of the daily operating routines.

The conventional wisdom of American management thought would hold that frequency, immediacy, and direct relation to reward are all highly desirable attributes of a control system.[4] The sogo shosha's control system makes data available on a monthly basis. But since so much of its trading business takes place within global commodity markets which can change daily or hourly, and since very large losses can be incurred in a very short time, the formal control system cannot be judged to be terribly frequent. Immediacy refers to the time span between performance and review. With formal review every six months, and informal monthly reviews, the system also cannot be seen as highly immediate, either. As for direct relation reward, there is none. The fact that a firm the size of a sogo shosha has managed to develop and continue functioning without the aid of such a control system tells us that some other mechanisms must be serving the basic function of monitoring, guiding, and motivating behavior, especially the behavior of the line managers who actually make the deals into desirable, consistent, and mutually reinforcing patterns. The sogo shosha's lack of such a control system is a matter of choice not of ignorance. We found officials in charge of administering planning and control systems to be quite knowledgeable about advanced techniques. We suspect that these officials would like the firm to adopt such advanced techniques, for this would enhance the importance of their own role in the company. All of this suggests that a sogo shosha's business is not easily managed via formal controls.

Resource Allocation

The planning process performs the very important function of allocating resources among the various parts of the organization.[5] The process by which resources get allocated is commonly referred to as "capital budgeting," and a great deal of business and academic effort has been put into developing the process into a more "rational" mechanism. Space does not permit even a cursory review of the techniques that have been developed for analyzing proposed expenditures, but the general principles can be set forth.

Basically a "rational" capital budgeting process is one that creates a common denominator ranking for each proposed expenditure, so that limited resources can be applied to only the highest ranking projects. The magnitude and timing of expenditures and of receipts of a project are incorporated mathematically into a series of formulas that also adjust for the risks inherent in each phase of the subject. Naturally the judging of risk is partly subjective, but refined techniques have been developed for calculating risk judgments. An appropriate "cost of capital" for each firm must be calculated, and this too is a complex problem. As an end result a number, such as the "internal rate of return" or the "net present value," is calculated for each project, and the available investment opportunities can then be ranked according to this numerical criterion.

Most large American firms use a similar process for analyzing the investment opportunities they want to consider seriously, but very few firms apply it totally uncritically. Typically, after the single-scale ranking of alternative uses of funds is accomplished, a firm will consider strategic and political questions. For instance, perhaps the number-one ranked project is in a business line the firm is not really interested in or committed to over the long term. But no matter how the final decision is made, the input of the capital budgeting analysis constitutes a very significant and widely relied-on objective and rational standard.

In a sogo shosha these capital budgeting techniques are not known, but they find only very limited application, such as for evaluating an equity investment in a fairly capital-intensive subsidiary. For many allocations of capital funds, no mathematical analysis of disbursements, income streams, and risks is undertaken. The process is described as one of "negotiations" based on the perceived general levels of opportunity for the individual geographic regions and product units. In more colloquial language it is much more of a "gut feel" or "seat-of-the-pants" process. It relies on collective judgments and perceptions of the long-term outlook and of the firm's strategy and opportunities. Compared to American firms, there is less attention to analysis of predictable income streams, and more to the strategic implications of various fund allocation alternatives. Experience in a new line of business is thought of as valuable, and an unprofitable business may be handled for a period of time as an investment in experience.

Given the nature of a sogo shosha's business, it is not difficult to understand why complex capital budgeting procedures are not widely used. A large portion of capital resource use goes for the extension of credit to customers, the financing of inventories, and the purchase of equities. These investments are different from either an investment in a factory or an investment in a security, in which cases there are roughly predictable flows that will result from the investment: either products that can be sold for money or money itself in the form of interest or dividends.

In the case of most of sogo shosha investments, credit is extended to solidify customer ties and gain access to the client's business, not simply to earn a direct return as an investor normally would. So, the return on the investment will come not so much in the form of interest received from a borrower or dividends, or the sale of output, as in the form of increased trading business from the client over the life of the client relationship. The amount of increased business and its marginal profitability depends less on the investment itself than it does on the ability of the sogo shosha to provide new services, to help its client's business expand, and to come up with new opportunities. In other words, at the time the credit is extended and the investment made, it is terribly difficult to predict with any precision just what the returns will be. With ownership of a factory, at least, one knows what the output will be and what price one is likely to get.

A second barrier to complex capital budgeting is that the time span involved in many investments, especially extensions of credit or purchases of inventory, is quite short. The interval between the opportunity arising and a decision being required is often not enough to permit a committee to review it, much less to make a complex analysis. In many cases something approaching a snap decision must be made by the person on the spot. Also the amount of money involved in any particular deal may be relatively small, even over a period of six months or a year. Thus, although there are many exceptions, much of the money that the sogo shosha commits to its business is not in a form that lends itself to capital budgeting analysis. Rather than specifying the final uses of the money, the company can give the sections or branches a budget, combined with a credit limiting and checking system, which is left up to their discretion to use. In the final analysis an individual credit decision for a customer has to be based primarily on that customer's value as a continuing source of business, though excessive risk is to be avoided. The people involved in dealing with that customer are usually the ones best able to assess the value of the relationship.

As a formal part of the planning process, allocation of resources among the product groups and regions are usually considered by committees consisting of staff units from finance, corporate planning, and representatives from the product groups. These committees have the final say in matching the allocations of resources with the priorities and needs of the firm as a whole as well as with the product group's particular needs.

Normally one would anticipate that each group would fight fiercely at these meetings to obtain a larger share of resources for itself. However, these meetings are not usually stormy affairs, and in fact relatively few and minor changes are made. A number of factors can be pointed out to explain this seemingly peculiar harmony:

1. Each product group is charged for the resources it uses. The financial staff can calculate the cost of capital to the firm as a whole, largely based on what it costs the sogo shosha to borrow money. The finance department can charge slightly more than this to the line operating departments, functioning as an internal bank. Thus, unless the operating department can earn a good return, allocation of extra resources will hurt its profits.

2. There is some elasticity in the amount of funds available to a sogo shosha. Much of its borrowing is in the form of letters of credit for foreign trade, secured by the goods in transit. If trade increases, this source of funds automatically increases. Banks also generally look upon sogo shosha as good customers and will loan money if business opportunities suddenly turn up.

3. Relative priorities among product lines have already been decided by other parties, at a very high level. Although the sogo shosha strives to keep this important question of priorities oriented toward the overall good of the firm, inevitably it has political implications. These are normally played out in complex ways. The planning system enters late in the game. Usually the issue is decided among the top directors, who formally identify the areas of priority for all to see. The informal system, to be discussed later, provides constant reinforcement to follow the priorities determined at high levels of the firm. It is notable that these committees assigned to iron out resource allocations—what would normally be high-level issues in an American firm—are composed of personnel several levels below top management.

4. Unless a department has business opportunities available, extra resources will hurt its profits. Unlike a manufacturer a trading firm realizes gross margins of usually only a percent or two. Therefore extra business "bought" via price reductions (often the only way to get extra business quickly) can easily become unprofitable.

This resource allocation process concerns primarily the product side of the matrix. The geographic side may not even be a part of the formal allocation process. In form, the overseas trading subsidiaries are free to finance themselves locally and to establish their own presence in overseas credit markets. But in practice, this seemingly broad area of discretion is rather narrow, for the following reasons:

1. The procurement of funds by overseas subsidiaries is primarily to finance trade—that is, the funds will be in the form of letters of credit, which do not raise complex financial issues, due to their short duration and relative security.*

* They are, as just mentioned, collateralized by the goods in transit.

2. Overseas trading subsidiaries have little or no real autonomy in the matter of investing money in affiliates and subsidiaries. This type of resource allocation is usually handled by the product side of the matrix, which has the perspective of an entire product system. An apparel manufacturing subsidiary in a foreign country may be legally a subsidiary of the locally incorporated trading arm, but administratively it is a subsidiary of the textile product group.

3. Overseas trading subsidiaries sometimes have very little formal authority in the granting of credit. Only relatively small amounts of credit can be approved by overseas traders acting solely on their own authority. Others require approval from regional heads for medium-size sums and from Tokyo-based product groups for large sums. This feature of the organization has two significant facets. One is that the regional operations, regardless of whether or not they are locally incorporated, lack operating autonomy in some of their most critical functions for all but relatively small-scale decisions. This lack of autonomy can be interpreted as a reflection of the integrated nature of Japanese and overseas operations. The second notable facet of the procedure for large credit lines is that the regional managers get approval from the product groups, not from senior management or from a centralized credit department. This is a very clear expression of the dominance of the product axis of the organization over the geographic axis. The credit department acts as a check, to see that unusually large or risky credits are not extended, but it is not heavily involved in most decisions. In difficult economic times, when credit risks increase, the credit department's role can easily expand, however.

4. A large portion of the borrowings undertaken by overseas trading subsidiaries is from the local offices of Japanese banks. It would be a safe assumption that these banks do not consider local subsidiaries to be entirely separate credit risks from the parent in Japan. For its part, the sogo shosha usually assumes that the banks consolidate the borrowings of overseas subsidiaries into one corporate line of credit. Because it relies so heavily on banks as a source of capital, banking relations are very important. There is good reason for a sogo shosha to wish to centralize borrowing policy. Although they are legally able to borrow their own money, the overseas subsidiaries in prac-

tice have only limited financial independence. Probably the best way for a subsidiary overseas to enhance its financial independence is to generate a strong cash flow from its investments and its operations. When net resources are being added to the firm, it is much easier to keep some to use than when resources are being diverted from others. This phenomenon is by no means limited to the sogo shosha.

Matrix Coordination

Finance is only one of the dimensions on which the product and geographic sides of the matrix must be coordinated. Planning and the implementation of operations must also be coordinated. To a surprising degree, there is a lack of elaborate formal mechanisms for accomplishing this, for most of it takes place via an informal process of negotiation. An example may help illustrate this. When a sogo shosha's industrial machinery division sells a machine to a customer in Houston, it is a sale by both the division's section and by the Houston branch's machinery department. During the planning process there should be coordination and consistency between the plans submitted by the product side and the geographic side of the matrix, so that both agree on how much machinery will be sold in Houston over the next planning period. But there may be no formal occasion for the reconciling of the two plans for the two sides of the matrix. Only the fact that the head of the Houston machinery department reports to *both* a machinery person in Tokyo (who reports up the product hierarchy) and to a machinery person in New York (who reports up the geographic hierarchy) keeps the two sides consistent with each other. Coordination between the two sides of the matrix is thus dependent on the ability of managers in overseas offices to negotiate and bargain successfully with two different sets of bosses in two different hierarchies. This may require great skill in interpersonal communication and a high level of knowledge of the priorities and orientations of two very different organizational subunits.

Satisfactory progress in meeting planned goals depends on an atmosphere of cooperation existing between the geographic and product sides of the matrix. For example, the Houston branch, reflecting its region's booming economy, may want to get the product-line divisions to agree to budget large sales increases in Houston. But perhaps the machinery department is pessimistic and does not want to be bound to sales goals that would require a large increase in sales. Or else the machinery department might not be able to obtain enough machinery of certain types for all its customers. Selling extra machinery in Houston may require cutting off important customers elsewhere, such as Brazilian steel mills.

At this point the role of the section chief of the Houston machinery department, and his ability to mobilize informal support, may be crucial. With the backing of the Houston branch manager, he may discuss the plan with the regional head for machinery in New York. With the backing of the regional head for machinery, an approach may be made to divisional or even product-group management in Tokyo, asking them to increase their goals to take account of business anticipated in Houston.

Authority Limits

The formal system provides one other major form of coordination and control via the allocation of specific types of authority to specific individuals and subunits within the firm. Although firms vary in their exact methods of assigning formal power, three basic categories of authority for various decisions can be distinguished:

1. Authority to render the final decision, which implies responsibility for the outcome of the decision.

2. Authority to approve a decision, which implies a veto power, though it may not often be used. Approval does not connote the same degree of responsibility as the decision making.

3. Authority to be informed of a decision, which implies no power or authority, other than that which is inherent in knowledge.

The sogo shosha allocates authority among various classes of officers for decisions of almost every sort. Areas where limits of authority are specified may include policymaking, organizational changes, personnel questions, credit decisions, trading deals, finance, management of subsidiaries, project management, insurance coverage, routing of goods, legal questions, investments, foreign exchange, liquidation of goods, accounting, labor relations, communications, research, and the catchall category of general affairs, which includes everything from golf club memberships to the management of office supplies.

The sogo shosha specifies channels for each class of decision, indicating who has what category of authority for each matter. Most areas have different patterns of authority depending on the amount of money that might be involved. The more money involved in a decision, the higher the level of person who must give approval, or be kept informed.

In our judgment, the sogo shosha appears to be a very centralized formal organization. As we mentioned earlier, the number of items that must be decided or approved by the executive committee is staggering. Executives just below this level also must approve huge numbers of items coming from below them in the hierarchy. Credit limits alone require high-level executives to approve quite small sums. It is clear that much decision-making authority must be actually in the hands of persons lower in the organization, or else the company could not function effectively. An emergent system of delegation of formal authority is required in order to get decisions made with the requisite speed and accuracy.

Committees and Task Forces

One other formal organizational mechanism must be mentioned before the examination of the ways in which a sogo shosha structurally coordinates its business can be completed. This mechanism is the standing or temporary committee, which works as a special coordinating organ to bring people together across product or geographical lines and which can also include relevant staff personnel. Such committees exist at the sogo shosha, with some firms using them more extensively than others.

There are three basic types of committees:

1. *Special committees* are fairly high-level, regular meetings to determine strategy or policy toward important topics. For example, there might be for the Brazil market a high-level special committee that has the responsibility of formulating strategy to maximize a sogo shosha's potential in a rapidly growing, large country.

2. *Project committees* are set up to coordinate activities for special projects. A good example is a committee set up to handle the computerization of accounting functions.

3. *Task forces* are purely implementation-oriented groups. Very frequently they are set up under special committees or project committees to implement whatever has been decided.

The Formal Administrative System in Overview

The sogo shosha's business strategy requires that very extensive, but selective and often intermittent, coordination take place among many types of business units. Within the trading network these units are categorized along two dimensions of geography and product, forming a matrix organization. Coordination up and down these two hierarchies, as well as across units in both of them, must take place quickly. With 20,000 or more products and markets in scores of countries, the questions of who should process information and make decisions are formidable.

The complexity of the required integration contrasts sharply with the relative paucity of formal structure to facilitate it. Compared with organizations of similar size, the formal administrative system of the sogo shosha is minimal. A further striking factor is the absence of individual job slots below the level of section chief. Even the job descriptions that do exist are vague and subject to great interpretation.

The sogo shosha employs a management control system that is capable of generating monthly profit and loss and other data for its basic business units, the sections. But the formal system does not always regularly review or emphasize these data. Only in the long run, or in cases of trouble, are these data the keystone to formal administrative procedures. And even then, such data are not directly tied into the reward system.

Formal allocations of authority do exist, and documents are published internally that attempt to specify the authority and communications channels for all types of decisions. However, any one of these documents reveals an organization that is extremely centralized. From the many decisions that are formally the prerogative of top and upper management, it is clear that informal delegation must be the rule, not the exception.

All of these point to the inescapable conclusion that the sogo shosha's formal system of management alone is inadequate to the organizational tasks it faces. We must therefore turn to the emergent system of management as a likely source of the integration required for organizational survival. But before doing so, we must examine the human resource or personnel structures that create the "living environment" of sogo shosha managers. It is within this environment of formal structures that the emergent system develops.

8

Human Resource Systems

"Human resource management" is rapidly becoming a catchall term for a broad set of organizational policies and practices. Anything that influences the ways in which members acquire, develop, and use their potential skills can be included under this rubric. Everything from the criteria for recruitment of potential members, to job or rank changes over the span of a career, to reward, retirement, and firing policies can be included.

An older term that covers much, but not all, of the same ground is "personnel." Most of what will be described in this chapter could simply be described as personnel issues. However, human resources is a more desirable term, for it directs attention not just to a set of policies and practices undertaken by particular departments at a particular time but to those factors that over long periods of time shape the development of the individual and collective skills, perspectives, and limitations of an organization's membership.

External Influences

The choices of the basic employment, recruitment, reward, rank, and evaluation structures that make up the human resource system of the sogo shosha have been shaped by two primary forces. One of these is the managerial labor market in Japan. The sogo shosha must take account of the expectations that are strongly conditioned by what they know other employees of other companies experience in their jobs. Japanese employment markets are the result of a complex historical process, and they also have been strongly conditioned by Japanese culture. It is not our intention to explore these influences in depth.

Nevertheless, we shall occasionally make reference to both in order to place the sogo shosha's practices in meaningful context.

The other major influence on human resource structures is adaptation. As is the case in the administrative structures, companies retain practices that they perceive to be effective and discard those that seem ineffective. For this reason we must temper any urge to explain the sogo shosha's personnel structure as being a simple consequence of Japanese culture, market conditions, or any other single explanatory factor. The human resource structures are one more piece of a complex social system of management. An important question to keep in mind is: What kind of responses are likely to be evoked from people who live in a setting such as this?

The Core Staff

The sogo shosha, following the practice of virtually all large Japanese employers, hires those destined for its managerial staff with the implicit understanding of a career-long commitment. In practice, this means that employment will continue until retirement, or permanent transfer to a nontrading subsidiary. This group of career employees does not include all personnel, so we shall call it the "core staff" (*shain*, in Japanese) to distinguish it. The sogo shosha hires its core staff only from the ranks of recently graduated male college students, and only core staff members can rise to managerial responsibility. There are only a very few exceptions to this rule. Women are openly relegated to clerical status, which is the dominant practice in Japan.

The core staff numbers from about four to over six thousand in the six major sogo shosha. Its members are the product of a careful selection, training, and development process. They are conscious and proud of being a special breed of businessman, what they call being a "shosha-man."* They also learn and carry a deep identity of the particular firm they have joined.

* This is a common phrase (combining a Japanese word with an English word). It connotes a certain flavor of hard-driving commercial practice, as well as an international sophistication, even worldliness, among those who have devoted their careers to being the middlemen of Japan's international commerce.

The mutual career commitment of employer and employee heightens the importance and the depth of the socialization process.

The Career Commitment

The career commitment is not, precisely speaking, a commitment to lifetime employment, for there are circumstances in which core staff members permanently lose their jobs in the sogo shosha. And there are circumstances in which core staff members voluntarily leave the firm. But for most core staff members in most circumstances, the guarantee of employment and the career-long commitment of employee to the company are lifetime in nature.

There is no legal requirement on either employer or employee to enforce the commitment. But, in practice, a handful of core staff employees are involuntarily terminated in a year (company regulations typically list crime, insanity, and physical incapacity as virtually the only reasons for dismissal). Each year as many as twenty to forty core staff members might leave a firm before retirement. Most leave for personal or health reasons. After a few months or years of experience a few new recruits may even be among those who decide to leave. But for those who stay, unilateral midcareer exit is quite rare. Many factors, including the social and economic structures of Japan as well as the human resource policies of the sogo shosha, help to reinforce the strength of the career commitment. Wages rise with seniority at a rather steep rate so that the employee is part of a de facto deferred compensation scheme. To collect the major part of his career-long compensation package, the employee must remain with the company until retirement age, when his wages will be at their peak.

The "carrot" of deferred compensation is also complemented by a "stick" of sorts. Japanese managerial labor markets do not provide many opportunities of comparable prestige, security, or remuneration for the core staff member who might contemplate making his fortune elsewhere. Among most large companies there is a norm of not hiring away the managers of a rival firm. This is particularly true among the larger, older, "establishment" firms, who tend to be concentrated in the basic industries. This is an important constituency for the sogo shosha. A sogo shosha manager's primary work contacts are likely to be with a set of firms that will not generate alternative job offers.

Japan also lacks a highly developed infrastructure of executive recruitment firms, employment agencies, and other channels of managerial mobility. There are few, if any, opportunities to move upward or even laterally by job-hopping as far as a sogo shosha manager is concerned. The best external opportunities that a shosha-man can usually find are with smaller, less prestigious, and less secure firms. The core staff member who might wish to consider leaving the permanent employee system he has joined thus encounters substantial "barriers to exit" that arise out of powerful norms in the structure of employment markets in Japan. The two factors are related, of course. Various cultural factors have conditioned managerial employment markets in their present form and the particular human resource supply and demand situations which have existed over the course of Japan's industrialization have encouraged companies to adapt and build on older, sometimes latent traditions. In particular, the present-day structure of employment among large firms has drawn on a set of cultural attitudes that hold group membership and loyalty to be very important to the individual.

The commitment of core staff members to the sogo shosha as their primary group affiliation is very powerful. Virtually all scholarly observers of employer-employee relations in Japan have noted how strong the commitment of employees is to their company, as compared to the situation in the United States or other countries. In Japan the permanent employees of the top sogo shosha are considered to be among the hardest working and most dedicated of all employees, for reasons we shall soon explore.

Women

The men in the core staff are assisted by about half as many women, working under the status of *joshi shain* (literally, "female employee"). They are recruited after graduation from junior college or sometimes college. Female staffers are paid less and have no real hope of significant advancement. The likeliest fate that awaits them is retirement or, in their midtwenties, marriage. For those who stay on, retirement may not come until age fifty-five, the same as for men, but chances for advancement to management are small.

It is sometimes possible for clerical staff members to take an examination and join the core staff after several years of work. However, only a handful ever do so. Moreover, given the importance of age cohorts, career path experience, and other factors to be described later, as well as the current norms of Japanese society, it is highly unlikely that many women would find it possible to have a career in the core staff comparable to that of a successful male. Thus, for all intents and purposes, the executive management of the sogo shosha is properly thought of as exclusively male.

There are also a few hundred people in other miscellaneous work categories, such as driver specialists on loan from other companies and retirees hired back on a yearly basis. The core staff, however, is preeminent in the sogo shosha organization, and therefore the analysis to follow will deal primarily with that group.

Recruitment

The sogo shosha's core staff is literally an elite group drawn from an elite group. The firms recruit only from a limited number of universities, all of which are highly selective institutions. In Japan, much more so than in the United States, for a variety of reasons, there is a widely accepted prestige ranking of universities. In part this is because universities use "objective" competitive examinations as virtually the only criterion for selection.* It is also partly due to the fact that most large employers, including the sogo shosha, use the schools as screening devices for recruitment.[1] The employers who are regarded as most prestigious—a few ministries in the national government, the biggest banks, airlines, large newspapers, some high-technology firms and the large sogo shosha—recruit only from the very top-ranking schools. Since most of the professions, other than medicine, are less developed and less prestigious in Japan than in the United States (e.g., recall the small number

* These examinations largely emphasize rote learning. If a student fails an examination, he or she may take it again the following year. It may be fair to say that persistence and memorization are at least as important as creative intelligence in succeeding on them.

of lawyers), for an ambitious young person the predominant image of success is entry to a top school and recruitment into a top government ministry or elite private firm.

Competition for entrance to the handful of prestigious universities is fierce. The university one enters influences one's future career in a most fundamental and decisive manner. Every year there are numerous reports of suicides by students who failed to pass the examinations for the prestigious schools. There are literally hundreds of private full-time schools that do nothing but prepare failed applicants for next year's examinations. This intense competition ensures that the entering classes at the top universities are perceived as a meritocratic elite, qualified to be elite because they have studied for and passed difficult examinations.

Recruitment takes on an understandable importance for Japanese firms whose only source of capable personnel is young, untested college graduates. The sogo shosha has occupied an extremely privileged position in this regard, for survey research has consistently shown that, among graduating college students, the six sogo shosha have been considered virtually the most desirable private employers in Japan. Among the reasons why this has been true might be the glamor of work in international trade, the prestige and long history of the sogo shosha, and the presumably unusually interesting work in these somewhat mysterious, but large and prominent, organizations. Whatever the reasons, the sogo shosha traditionally has had little trouble in attracting what is considered to be the cream of the crop of Japanese college graduates to its recruitment process.

Very recently, as the sogo shosha has been perceived as a mature institution facing difficult times, its relative popularity as an employer, though still very high, has slipped. More important, the sogo shosha is beginning to recruit heavily from the pool of graduates with technical and scientific training in high-technology fields. In doing so, it is competing with firms such as Hitachi, Fujitsu, and others, which enjoy very great glamour as well. Although still able to draw an elite work force (in these new fields, as well as in more traditional ones), the sogo shosha must prove itself able to perform well in new fields if it is to continue to enjoy its preferential access to high-quality human resources.

The applicants must be considered to be hard working and intelligent, for earning a place in a top university in Japan requires these characteristics. But they are also fairly homogenous in several other important ways. Japan's educational system is centralized under the Ministry of Education. It is said by critics of this centralization that on any given day, students in a particular grade all over Japan will be studying the same pages of the same textbooks. This is an exaggeration, to be sure, but there is certainly far greater uniformity of content and quality of education in Japan than in the United States.

The mass media are also far more centralized and uniform in Japan than in the United States. Three national newspapers have circulations of several millions each and are read daily in all parts of the country. The government-operated radio and television networks, supplemented by private networks, also reach everyone in the country. The media have played a prime role in eliminating regional dialects or accents. A standardized accent and vocabulary is used on virtually all broadcasts; and this speech pattern becomes the language of all educated persons, outside of their homes, at least.

Even more fundamental is the fact that there are no major divisions of Japanese society along the lines of race, religion, or ethnic background. Furthermore class differences are surprisingly minimal. The peerage was abolished in 1945, and noble ancestry is not usually a matter of any importance. Perhaps more than any other people, the Japanese are overwhelmingly middle class. In a 1967 nationwide survey 88 percent of the respondents identified themselves as middle class, with 1 percent identifying as upper class, 7 percent as lower class, and 4 percent not knowing their class.

Thus the entrants into the core staff are fairly homogeneous in many important ways. Their educational process has both selected and trained them for hard work, persistence, and success. Throughout their educational careers, they become inculcated with a strong sense of motivation, discipline, and achievement. Because they share so much in social outlook, background, and education, they can form strong ties with each other and can work together closely, even when separated by vast distances.

Prior to the slowdown of sogo shosha growth that followed the 1973 oil crisis, the sogo shosha had each been recruiting large entering classes of two hundred or more each year. Since then recruitment has slowed down to a replacement level of one to two hundred or less. Though the exact number of recruits fluctuates with the economic condition and outlook, at least some must be recruited every year to ensure the availability of senior staff in several decades.

A mix of backgrounds and personality types is sought: athletes, student activists, and very studious graduates in different fields of study, from business and economics to literature. Recently there has been a marked increase in the number of engineering and scientific graduates hired, for the sogo shosha has diversified into sophisticated chemicals, electronics, construction, and other fields requiring technical expertise. But a variety of backgrounds is always sought.

All sogo shosha organizations place a special emphasis on seeking recruits who will be compatible with their own corporate culture. There are many subtle differences among the sogo shosha companies. In general, however, their corporate cultures stress initiative—such as is needed to develop new businesses—cooperation, and teamwork. There is no question that each firm has a strong sense of identity and values. Some people in fact claim to be able to distinguish employees of one firm from those of another without being told, so pervasive are the differences. There is certainly some truth to this, for along dimensions such as aggressiveness and independence there are noticeable stylistic tendencies. But the sogo shosha cultures also have much in common, as distinguished from other Japanese firms. For one thing, their members' life-styles are quite similar as compared with employees of non-sogo shosha companies.

Colleges graduate their students in March in Japan, and April 1 is the standard day for inducting new recruits into the firm. The Ministry of Labor has a policy that prevents large employers from beginning formal recruitment before October 1 of the previous year. This is because there is fierce competition among even the most prestigious employers to obtain what they view as the best human resources. In earlier years this had led to companies attempting to beat others to the best candidates by contacting them early and obtaining their commitment before they were approached by other firms. Despite the regulation informal contacts between promising candidates and the sogo shosha do occur before October 1, some through the intermediation of individual professors who are anxious to find appropriate positions for all their students and have established relationships with certain firms.

The formal selection process gradually eliminates most candidates. Only a small percentage of those who inquire about employment are ever hired. The largest sogo shosha firms receive thousands of inquiries a year. Both standardized testing and interviewing are used as part of the elimination process. The standardized tests often include both achievement and psychological personality tests.

The interviewing process is multistage as well. Candidates are usually exposed to three groups within the company: top management, which devotes an impressive amount of time to interviewing candidates, professionals from the personnel function, who are experts at recruiting, and members of line management, especially those with several years' experience but not yet of executive rank. Thus it is necessary for a cross section of the firm to approve someone's hiring before he will be taken on.

Candidates must choose fairly rapidly which firms they want to pursue seriously. Many of the most prestigious firms in Japan schedule their entrance examinations for November 1, so the decision to take one sogo shosha's examination virtually precludes the possibility of employment in a comparably prestigious organization. Although less than ideal from the applicant's perspective, this arrangement ensures that only those who are strongly interested in the firm will go through the entire recruitment process. This strong desire and commitment is highly prized by the companies. It also enables the firm to reduce its expenditure of manpower during the interview process, focusing only on the most serious candidates.

Joining the Firm

Each year new employees enter the company on April 1, so each age cohort has precisely the same seniority. Fairly elaborate entrance rituals symbolize the importance Japanese attach to group membership. It is the usual practice that all members of top management who are in Japan are present at this April 1 ceremony. This is considered a key function, and attendance takes precedence over almost any other activity for the company's board members. The president personally greets all recruits and gives a major speech. It is a big event for the company and for the new individuals, for the company's future is indeed in their hands.[2]

Since the commitment made to the company is for an entire career, and since Japan's culture increases the importance to the recruit's self-identity of that group commitment, it is easy to understand why the entrance ceremony has such high symbolic significance. Perhaps a wedding is not a wholly inappropriate analogy.

All recruits gather in Tokyo, and an entire day typically is devoted to entrance ceremonies and lectures on company history and philosophy. Top management attends these meetings every year. Particular emphasis is given to the concept that the recruits are entering an entire new life: no longer are they students, they are members of adult society and part of the "family" of the sogo shosha. At the end of the first day, only after membership in the firm *as a whole* has been symbolically confirmed, are specific job assignments revealed.

Up until that moment, recruits have little or no idea which part of the company they will work in or what their actual first job will be. Their preference, they know, will be only one factor considered in making assignments. To an American, it would be rather surprising to join a company without even knowing whether one would be in accounting or in lumber sales, for example. For sogo shosha recruits, the reason such uncertainty is tolerable, is that simple membership in the group of the company's employees is initially by far the most important fact of one's identity, and this is a highly prized reward in itself, the very basis of one's new social status. Common group membership outweighs the very considerable differences among the specialized units of the company, especially in the earlier years of an employee's career.

After the initiation day ceremonies, more days may be spent at headquarters learning about company policies, organization, employee benefits, and other such basic information. Following this, in one representative firm the recruits spend a week together at a conference retreat located in a relatively remote and isolated area. They live, barracks style in groups of about eight, with each group assigned a *sempai* (literally, a "forward companion") about thirty years old, who plays something of an older brother role and provides his perspective on what being a member of the firm means.*

Team sports and group discussions are the major features of the orientation at this firm. The discussions are on general topics, such as the major issues facing the world, and gradually narrow down to the role of the sogo shosha and of the company itself. Nothing specifically job-related is touched on. The emphasis is completely on building spirit and rapport among members of the class of recruits. They will be colleagues for thirty-five years, and it is important that they know each other well.

Following orientation, the recruits report to their assigned sections, which are almost always in a headquarters unit. The company wants new recruits to be exposed to as many areas of the firm's activity as possible, and only a headquarters location can provide this scope. Management training departments offer several kinds of courses on a regular basis. During the first year new members are allowed or required to attend management education courses in such basic business skills as accounting, commercial law, and international trade practices. After the first year optional continuing education courses are offered and are usually well attended. But the real training takes place on the job.

The sogo shosha operates dormitories for unmarried managers who are not living with their parents. These are subsidized operations, and access is usually restricted to those who do not have parents living in the Tokyo area. The dormitories provide a small room, meals, and laundry service. They will hold a meal until late for those who are working late at the office, as frequently happens.

From the standpoint of the young manager, the dormitories offer not only economy and convenience, they also may offer a career advantage. Many managers report that they were able to form friendships with young people from other parts of the country, which turn out to be of considerable value. In this setting they can interact with those of a similar age more informally than is possible on the job. Seniority and age grading are most strictly observed in formal settings, but in informal situa-

* The image of the *sempai* is that of an older and more experienced model of what the recruit will become. The term connotes a relatively warm, yet hierarchical relationship.

tions, they may be somewhat relaxed. Thus the dormitory settings provide a way of getting to know others from different age brackets as well as from different product or functional groups.

All are conscious of the fact that they will be colleagues for the rest of their professional lives and that their personal success is closely bound up with the success of their company. Furthermore in these early years differences of interest are not as strong as they will be later. In time the people assigned to accounting will develop into rather different types than the people assigned to rubber trading, due to the great dissimilarity of their work; the degree of homogeneity they displayed as recruits will be less evident.

Competition among younger employees is strongly discouraged, even though members of the same age group ultimately will be competitors for the limited number of top management positions. Promotion for approximately the first decade and a half of a core staff member's career is virtually automatic; in fact every effort is made to minimize overt recognition of individual differences in achievement. This permits a growth of solidarity among young employees, which tends to overcome the long-run fact that they are indeed competitors. It also allows time for a broad consensus to form as to who is most capable and deserving of promotion. Yet, though friendships can be made through dormitory contacts, some younger core staff members have reported that they spent so many hours on the job and with colleagues from their sections that they spent little more than their sleeping hours at the dormitory. It is remarkable that not one informant mentioned a need to "get away from the office" when speaking of the pros and cons of dormitory living. Group domination of one's activities is the norm, and a need for privacy is not.

Transfer and Promotion Policies

Work assignments within the section are fluid and at the discretion of the *kachō*. Promotions out of the section and transfers or rotation of personnel among sections require personnel department approval. The exact procedure and the balance of influence between the personnel officials and the line department officials in transferring and promoting traders among line units vary from firm to firm.

In practice, the lower the level of the employee, the greater is the discretion left to the line managers and departments. They are not only most familiar with the capabilities of individual staff members, they also understand the needs of product system management. For instance, at a certain time it may be necessary for someone with a strong background in agricultural machinery, good command of English, and good bargaining skills to go to Australia to develop a particular market. This type of decision usually is best made at the operating level.

But each firm also places some systemwide constraints on personnel decisions for junior managers. These rules may require at least two formal rotations to different sections in the first ten years or prevent an employee from working more than seven consecutive years in a domestic branch, for example. Such rules prevent anyone from being "buried" in one situation for too long. This is not only a protection against working under one particular boss who might not be ideally suited to develop all aspects of an employee's talents, it also ensures that the employee's performance will be closely observed and evaluated by more than one superior. Another effort at preserving fairness is the requirement that the personnel department formally review performance every few years during the first half of a career. In these reviews personnel department employees at various levels solicit both oral and written evaluations of multiple aspects of an employee's performance. An effort is thus made to tap a wide variety of opinions in a wide variety of contexts. This is again to ensure that multiple evaluations of performance and potential take place.

Finally, each firm applies age constraints on employers' promotions through the company hierarchy. For each level there is a minimum age that must be reached before a promotion can be considered. This infuses a strong component of seniority into the hierarchy.

The Rank System

The sogo shosha's hierarchy system bears some resemblance to that of a military bureaucracy. Except in dire necessity, the only way to enter is to start at the bottom. Rank determines salary, benefits, and a large component of prestige. Rank belongs to a person, not to a job. The rank does not necessarily directly determine the level of the job; it is possible to have two people of different ranks performing equivalent jobs, but receiving different compensation. However, in both the sogo shosha and the military, there is usually a flexible coupling of rank and job, so that certain positions usually have a person of at least a certain rank filling them. In the military not all colonels are equal; in the sogo shosha neither are all department heads (*buchō*) equal.

Each firm has about eight to ten ranks below that of a director. These eight to ten ranks are further divided into two categories: ordinary class and manager class (see table 8.1 for the percentage of staff at each rank in one firm). The ordinary class comprises the first three or four grades. During the time a manager is in these grades he is automatically promoted through them, every four years or so.

The philosophical premise underlying automatic promotions for the first twelve years is that since the company has acquired human raw material of a specified quality, it is the company's responsibility to check this quality and to utilize this raw material effectively. If a person is misassigned, so that he finds himself in an environment where his best efforts are not called forth, it is the company's responsibility. It is presumed that the

Table 8.1
Percentage of managers in each status rank at a major firm

Executive class	
Directors (*yakuin*)	0.9
Senior managers (*sanyō, sanji*)	2.1
Department chief (*buchō*)	4.4
Assistant department chief (*bucho-hō, ji-chō*)	8.8
Section chief (*kachō*)	16.1
Assistant section chief (*kachō-hō* *kachō-hosa* *kakari-chō*)	19.3
Ordinary class	
Grade one	14.0
Grade two	18.2
Grade three	16.3
	100.1

Source: Various company records.
Note: The total is more than 100 percent due to rounding.

basic will to work is present, or can at least be brought out by effective leadership. Therefore, if an employee is not functioning properly. it is considered primarily the company's fault.

The ordinary class comprises about half the membership of the core staff. It takes twelve to sixteen or more years after hiring to rise through to the top of the ordinary class. This period can almost be considered an apprenticeship. Promotion out of the class is considered to be a significant recognition, and its timing is an important signal of the direction a managerial career is taking. Those who are promoted into the managerial class as soon as the required four years have elapsed at the top of the ordinary class are clearly marked as the ones who are on their way up much further. Only a small portion of those who entered the company on the same April 1, a dozen or more years ago, are recognized this way. Each subsequent year more and more of the cohorts are promoted, until those few stragglers left behind in the ordinary class are clearly, but only implicitly, singled out as lacking in ability. Although there are cases of people retiring without having made manager class, they are fortunately few. Life must be uncomfortable for them in such an achievement-oriented environment.

The lowest rank of manager class is either assistant section chief or section chief, depending on where the firm chooses to draw the line. The key to being in the manager class is that one is formally responsible for the work of others, as well as for one's own work. Promotion up the six or so ranks of the manager class is also a slow process, with each successive step up the hierarchy being harder to surmount. For those who were late in being promoted, section chief may be their rank on retirement. Ofen such people will only be given the rank but will not actually be put in charge of a functioning section. They may also be promoted to the rank and posted to a subsidiary or affiliated company.

The ranks narrow sharply above section chief. Promotion to *buchō* ("department head") rarely occurs before the midforties. Managers at this level typically have the responsibility for formulating and implementing strategies for several related sections, whose combined sales may total several hundred million dollars, or even in excess of a billion dollars annually. With the slowing of sogo shosha growth, the percentage of core staff members who will ever rise to this level of responsibility is decreasing. For new recruits, the odds against rising this high must appear long—perhaps one in ten.

For the higher levels of senior manager (*sanyō* or *sanji*) and director (*yakuin*), the gates are even narrower. The personnel department of one major firm estimated that at best only 1 to 2 percent of recruits could hope to become members of the board of directors. For a group of individuals as talented and ambitious as the sogo shosha's core staff, this is a severe competitive struggle.

The minimum time span for promotion to a particular executive rank is determined in practice by the conviction that no one should formally report to someone younger than he. For seniority-conscious Japanese, the idea of having a boss who is younger is intolerable. The minimum seniority for promotion to section chief at one firm is fifteen years; for department chief, the figure is twenty-two years. At another the figures are fourteen years and twenty-four, respectively. But, if the form of rank is determined by seniority, the substance of power and responsibility is not. Older employees may indirectly defer to the judgment of lower-ranking, but more competent, juniors without great embarrassment as long as the form of seniority is preserved and the junior pays proper formal deference to his senior.

As noted, usually the employee's division effectively manages the promotion and transfer process at lower levels. The personnel department mainly conducts reviews and keeps records. The required reviews conducted by personnel officials are aimed at finding employees who might do better if transferred to other divisions. Of course an employee who is genuinely unhappy and wants to be transferred out of his section or even division will be accommodated eventually. The universal principle that an unhappy employee is not able to work to full potential applies in Japan as elsewhere. A similar midcareer review is often scheduled when a manager is in his midforties and is aimed at identifying those with potential for advancement to top management, and at finding suitable positions for those without such potential.

Compensation Systems

Core staff compensation follows common Japanese corporate practices, which are considerably different from American patterns and assumptions. Each compensation system is the product of the tradition, philosophy, and history of its homeland. Neither system is particularly universal, for compenstion patterns show a great variety all over the world. Each tends to be generally regarded as fair and appropriate in its homeland, for the concept of fairness is closely related to culture and is therefore a relative term.

To put the Japanese system of the sogo shosha in perspective, we shall first draw a simplified general model of American practices and their underlying assumptions. There are three elements that are most important in determining the level of compensation in the American system:

1. *Job content,* or the demands the job makes on the employee, including such factors as the necessary know-how, job-specific problem-solving abilities, level of responsibility, and accountability. In theory, each factor can be assigned a weight, and job slots can be arranged in a hierarchy. Generally, the higher the job rank, the more direct should be the impact of individual effort on overall results.

2. *The market* that exists for the particular skills necessary for the job slot. A corporate lawyer's and an accountant's slots may be rated the same on the job slot scale, but if corporate lawyers are in short supply, their salaries will be higher.

3. *The level of performance* of the employee. High performers should be paid better than low performers, within a given position. Eighty to 120 percent of base pay is common in large bureaucracies.

Bonus payments are typically limited to employees whose performances contribute greatly to the particular business of a division, branch, or the company as a whole.

There are three characteristics of this model worth noting. One is that the reward structure strongly emphasizes financial compensation. Although there are certainly many situations where an individual may be given a title instead of a raise in salary, the major emphasis is on financial reward as the ultimate source of motivation. Second, rewards are immediate and directly related to individual effort. A substantial delay in rewarding desired behavior is thought to decrease the reinforcing impact that the reward has on that behavior. Third, the system reflects a strong free market orientation. Even after a person is hired by a company, the value of his or her services continues to be measured against a market standard for supposedly comparable services from others. All three of these characteristics contrast sharply with the Japanese-style systems of the sogo shosha.

Based as it is on the concept of the job slot, the American system has essentially a static image of the unit. It also presumes that the necessary tasks can be broken down and specified. In practice, this is easiest to do for positions that are routine and require little discretion or judgment. Under this system a change in job content should potentially require a change in salary.

Promotion should be based on "merit," although the definition of that term is often elusive. Seniority may have some applicability. Underlying it all is the presumption that equal pay should be given for equal work. The personal needs of the employee do not enter into the determination of compensation.

The Sogo Shosha Compensation System

The sogo shosha's compensation system contrasts sharply with American practices in a number of ways, some of which are by now familiar. A person is hired for lifetime potential, not for specific skills or a particular job slot. The compensation model is based on the amount and pattern of compensation to be received over an entire career. Equal pay for equal work applies to a career but not necessarily at any given point. A younger person and an older person doing the same specific tasks will receive very different salaries, due to the emphasis on seniority; but over their career lifetimes they could receive comparable compensation (adjusted for inflation, changes in the standard of living, the rank reached by retirement, etc.). This pattern of compensation appears to be quite well accepted among sogo shosha employees. The work forces below the managerial ranks are unionized, but this seniority-influenced system which penalizes precisely these ranks is not a serious issue in union-management relations.

Base salary is the largest determinant of overall compensation. It accounts for about three-quarters of monthly compensation on average. By U.S. standards, pay levels are not terribly high. For example, in 1982, the average starting salaries for college graduates was about six hundred dollars per month.

This figure applied not only to the sogo shosha but to most large prestigious employers in Japan.

For approximately the first fifteen years, age, position in the hierarchy, and base salary ascend in virtual lockstep. An employee with ten years' seniority will receive approximately two times the base salary of a new recruit. By the time the employee has reached sixteen years of experience, and is poised at the threshold of the managerial ranks, he will be receiving about 250 percent of the base pay of a starting recruit.

The onset of competitive, merit-based promotion has no dramatic immediate effect on compensation differentials among employees of the same age cohort. The salary calculation formulas used by the sogo shosha still place heavy emphasis on age, at least into the midforties. For example, in one firm the maximum differential between the fastest rising and the slowest rising forty-five-year-olds is 20 percent. In other words, after 23 years of service, an employee still stuck in a section as an ordinary section member will be receiving 80 percent of the salary of a fast-rising star, poised to take over the management of an entire department comprised of several sections, as a *buchō*.

Although this fairly egalitarian system is designed to ensure the maintenance of smooth relations among members of the same cohort, by preventing excessive income differentials, it is currently being questioned seriously by personnel managers and top managements. One key factor is the "demographic bulge" that the sogo shosha, like all large mature Japanese companies, is experiencing. In the pre-1973 oil crisis days of heady, almost automatic growth, large entering classes of managers were recruited, on the assumption of continued expansion. The oil shock, which lowered growth and sparked structural adjustment in the Japanese economy away from the sogo shosha's traditional business base in heavy, commodity processing industries, caused the sogo shosha companies to reduce drastically the size of the entering classes.

Today these pre-1973 classes are in, or are about to enter, the middle management ranks. One organization planner lamented: "Our organization is no longer shaped like a pyramid, it's a diamond. Middle management and above rankings now account for 46 percent of our managerial and staff members, and we fully expect it to reach 50 percent. Because we recruited very large classes of 250 or more during the 1960 era of high growth, we now have the inevitable demographic consequences to face."[3]

Important consequences follow from the demographic bulge of the sogo shosha. One is that competition for promotion to senior and top management ranks is becoming much more severe. In the high-growth era the base of the management pyramid was expanding, so at the top there were always more positions being created. When the base begins shrinking, obviously there can be little hope for the creation of more new posts at the top of the hierarchy.

This has already forced a lowering of expectations on the part of those at the middle management ranks and below. Whereas previously it was not unreasonable for a manager whose work was of good quality to hope for promotion to the level of *buchō* ("department chief"), today it is recognized that only a fraction of those in a lower middle management cohort will attain this post. The post of senior manager (*sanyō* or *sanji*), which accommodates those who supervise several departments or those engaged in policy formation, is likely to be achieved by only a small percentage. And membership on the board of directors, which really defines top management, can only be expected for 1 or 2 percent of the typical class.

A second consequence is that there is considerable pressure to reduce the influence of seniority on compensation. Today seniority after the midforties plays little or no role in compensation. In other words, after this age promotion is the only way for base salary to increase. Managers who have "peaked out" in their career potential thus face the prospect of no increase in their real incomes after this age. Some firms have already announced their intention to lower this age at which seniority ends as a salary factor to the early forties or lower. It would not be surprising to see in the future that this age would be pushed down even further. This would mean a severe heightening of differentiation among managers as soon as the first merit-based promotions occur at the bottom of the managerial ranks. A clear message would be sent: competition among managers for limited rewards is the key to individual success.

The richest rewards accrue to the ranks above *buchō*. Not only do the base salary differentials increase more rapidly, but the pace of potential promotions also accelerates, for those marked for the top. Promotions may occur every three years or even more rapidly. Several grades of director exist, and pay increases with each rank. Moreover the perquisites of office, such as expense accounts and the ability to borrow money at low interest rates, increase. In addition a very significant factor is that the mandatory retirement age is raised from the late fifties into the sixties for those who rise to the most senior levels. This allows many more years of service at the highest paid levels, greatly expanding the total career compensation package.

Additional Compensation

A range of fringe benefits exists, which typically is somewhat broader than is common in the United States. These can include the dormitories for single staff, athletic facilities, subsidized lunchrooms, subsidized health insurance, low-cost company-owned vacation and retreat lodges, death benefits paid to survivors, and low-interest loans for housing and emergencies.

The housing loans are the most significant monetarily. Interest rates are usually a few points below market rates, which help to ease the burden of purchasing a home in Japan, where real estate prices are much higher than in the United States. Typically there is a limit to the amount that can be borrowed, though this limit is adjusted upward with status rank. In addition to company-underwritten housing loans, there may also be company-guaranteed bank loans, also limited in their amount, made available for housing purchases. Naturally these carry market-level rates of interest. It should be noted that repayment of these loans is made automatically out of the employee's salary and bonuses. The only security the company has is the employee's commitment to stay with the company. In the Japanese value system, however, "benevolence" of this nature tends to strike an emotional response, increasing the employee's commitment.

Provision of extensive fringe benefits is consistent with Japanese views of the employment relationship, which emphasizes the heavy involvement of the employee and the company in each other's welfare. For the employee the benefits have great symbolic value as a tangible manifestation of the company's concern for his *total* life. In contrast, American employees, with their less intensive commitment to a single firm, apparently would rather have cash to spend at their own discretion than fringe benefits, although for tax and other reasons fringe benefits have greatly multiplied in recent years.

Overtime is paid only to the ordinary, not executive, class (see Table 8.1) of employees. In other words, about half of the core staff does not receive overtime pay, despite the fact that they often work more than sixty hours a week. As members of management, it is officially presumed that those above assistant section chief status will put forth whatever efforts are necessary without extra pay. The fact that overtime is put in without extra pay bespeaks a very high level of motivation. The overtime rates are usually 125 percent of base pay until 10 pm and 150 percent thereafter. According to company statistics employees in this category typically average almost thirty hours a month of overtime. We strongly suspect that there is a great deal of unrecorded overtime in addition to this.

One other form of compensation to be discussed is the retirement allowance. We will cover this in the following chapter discussing exit from the firm.

9

Career Outcomes

The competition for advancement, so important to the aspirations of sogo shosha managers, ultimately results in a variety of career outcomes. In order to understand how competition for advancement affects managerial behavior, it is first necessary to understand the general range of possibilities offered by the system.

This chapter examines the overall career patterns in the sogo shosha. But competition among managers will remain a continuing focus of analysis as the workings of the emergent organization are described.

Retirement

The career-long employment commitment of company and core staff members means that in a majority of cases, retirement is the way managerial employees leave the organization. For most, retirement occurs in their mid- to late fifties, which is quite early considering that Japanese life expectancy now reaches into the seventies for males. As we noted earlier, promotion to the rank of senior manager defers retirement a few years; a further rise in the hierarchy, into the ranks of the directors adds a few more years with each step, so that it is possible for the presidents and chairmen of the sogo shosha to retire well into their midsixties. This early retirement is considered a holdover from earlier days, in which Japanese life expectancy was much lower.

Recently most sogo shosha have raised the basic retirement age from fifty-five to fifty-eight, responding to both governmental policy and popular sentiment. However, it is extremely difficult to raise the retirement age rapidly. Such a move would virtually block most promotion opportunities for those in the lower ranks, since exit at the top is the primary source of senior-level vacancies, given the lack of growth in recent years. Those at the middle and upper-middle ranks of the organization thus face something of a paradox in their self-interested view of retirement regulations: on the one hand, they do not wish themseles to be forced to retire when still relatively young and vigorous, and, on the other hand, both the speed and the very possibility of their further promotion depends greatly on those above them in the hierarchy leaving at a younger age.

From the corporate perspective, raising the universal retirement age requires keeping on for further service the most expensive group of employees, those with the most seniority. Since those with exceptional capabilities will have presumably been promoted to rank levels that defer the retirement age a few years, those whose expensive tenure is being prolonged are assumed to be the less capable. It is perhaps then not so surprising that the raising of the mandatory retirement age, which everyone agrees would avoid much individual discomfort and waste of qualified human resource, is being accomplished only very slowly.

On retirement, a core staff member receives a substantial retirement allowance, which is a multiple of his yearly salary. The precise multiple used varies with the firm and with the rank of the employee. Usually the amount would be six figures if translated into dollars. If wisely invested in starting or purchasing a small business, it may be enough to sustain an adequate, though perhaps lower, standard of living. Some firms also subsidize a contributory annuity plan for employees, to supplement their retirement allowances.

Secondary Exit: Shukkō

Besides retirement another major form of exit from the core staff is the posting or forwarding of core staff members to other corporations, either temporarily for a period of a few months or years or indefinitely. In Japanese this practice is known as *shukkō,* or "sending out."

Most of those sent out are posted to subsidiaries and affiliates (see chapters 6 and 13) engaged in tasks closely related to product systems in which the parent sogo shosha is active. Table 9.1 presents data from one firm showing the percentage of managers at each level of the hierarchy being externally posted at one given point.

Relatively few staff members of the most junior levels are sent out. Their early training and evaluation requires their presence in the trading operations. For the younger middle levels of the core staff, the major purpose of *shukkō* is usually familiarization and training. Someone working in the ferrous metals area might be sent to a coal dock facility managed by an affiliate. There he would not only learn to manage the technicalities of loading and unloading coal, he would also become familiar with the people carrying out this important step in the product system. This knowledge and these contacts would then become a valuable resource for the balance of his career.

Middle-level managers are also posted to subsidiaries and affiliates. In this case the purpose is often not just the accumulation of knowledge and contacts but also the testing and development of managerial and administrative skills. Managers in the middle ranks may find themselves given a senior operating position in a subsidiary or affiliate. There they will be responsible for potentially large amounts of money and large numbers of people. When a major problem or issue is involved, such as the turnaround of a money-losing operation or the development of a new product or service, the posting may be the gateway to a significant career advance on return to the core staff.

For older managers a posting to a subsidiary or affiliate may have a much more ambiguous, even threatening, character. Unless the challenge or opportunity at the new assignment is a significant one, the posting may implicitly be a way of removing the manager from the core staff, so as to open his position

Table 9.1
Percentage of staff sent out on *shukkō* to nontrading subsidiaries and affiliates in one major firm

Senior manager	29.5
Department chief	22.5
Assistant department chief	21.6
Section chief	16.4
Assistant section chief	12.7
Ordinary class top grade	7.0

Source: Company records.

there for others. Although none of the sogo shosha companies wishes to admit it, there are clearly instances of postings to subsidiaries being used as a way of clearing deadwood out of the core staff. Since most subsidiaries are engaged in work that has less variety, uncertainty, and challenge to it than the task of managing the product system, it may be that such a posting is a more effective utilization of the talents of core staff members who are perceived as less promotable than others of their peer group.

A posting that lasts until retirement is not necessarily an unmitigated loss of status, however. The core staff member usually occupies a higher relative position in his new post than in his old core staff position. Instead of the continual competition for a limited number of posts higher in the organizational pyramid, he is usually comfortably close to the apex of a hierarchy, albeit a smaller and less prestigious one. His title and the formal deference paid to him by those among whom he works will usually be markedly superior to his old situation. His salary and benefits may be smaller than before, though this is not always the case.

The biggest loss, however, is in security and prestige. Once permanently posted to the subsidiary or affiliate, he no longer has the assurance that the parent's size and economic clout will protect his livelihood. If his new company should encounter financial difficulties or go bankrupt, he may well be left with no recourse to the parent. Once permanently sent out to the subsidiary, his fate rests with it. It is up to him and his new fellow employees to make it into a successful enterprise, capable of rewarding them adequately. It is especially for this reason that not all *shukkō* postings are regarded equally. A posting to a prosperous affiliate located in a growing and lucrative market may resemble a sinecure, whereas a posting to a struggling company may be seen by some as a virtual exile or death sentence.

For the career-long employees of the subsidiary, the arrival of older managers from the sogo shosha may be a mixed blessing. On the one hand, the ex-core staffer may bring valuable knowledge, experience, and influence. But, on the other hand, he will certainly be seen as blocking promotions and eating up resources that might well have gone to career managers otherwise. Again, much depends on the character of the firm as well as the character of the individual being posted.

On returning to the parent from a *shukkō* assignment, the core staff member customarily loses no seniority or benefits including cumulative benefits. This is to ensure that a temporary posting not be a financial burden to the manager affected. Since many such postings are indeed for the purpose of career enhancement, it is important to make them as comfortable as possible for those sent out.

Shukkō *to Trading Subsidiaries*

Transfer to the overseas wholly owned trading subsidiaries, which effectively function as part of the global product system management network, is also, in form at least, a matter of *shukkō*.[1] These corporations are after all incorporated under the laws of their host governments, so that their employment terms and conditions may be required to be different from those in Japan. For example, Mitsubishi International Corporation, the U.S. trading subsidiary of Mitsubishi Corporation, has recently moved to implement a requirement that core staff members transferred from Japan formally resign from their position in the parent.

Even with a formal requirement of this nature, experience proves that a posting to a trading subsidiary is quite different in character from one to a nontrading subsidiary or affiliate. For one thing, the content of the work is much more similar to operations in the parent. The daily work flow has staff members continually interacting electronically with other core staffers. Moreover core staff members posted to a trading subsidiary eventually can be expected to rejoin the parent.

Overseas Postings for the Core Staff

The sogo shosha firms are anxious to limit the number of core staff members working overseas in their trading subsidiaries. Clearly it is a very expensive matter to maintain an expatriate family overseas. At a minimum the companies must provide at least a comparable standard of living for employees stationed overseas as that enjoyed by those based in Japan. Since this usually means providing funds for private Japanese-language schools and for the purchase of often expensive Japanese foodstuffs, among a variety of other expenses, the costs quickly mount up. As is generally the case in U.S. and European multinational corporations, a standard of living model is created based on items typically consumed in the home country. This model is then priced in various locations around the world and used as the basis of expatriate salaries and allowances.

Compensation for employees overseas is a highly sensitive issue. The fundamental issue is that of equity. When the core staff member joins the firm and implicitly agrees to go anywhere in the world, the firm incurs a reciprocal obligation to cushion the disruptive impact of transfer to a foreign land by providing an adequate level of compensation. It is not so much a matter of giving employees an extra financial incentive to go overseas as it is a question of ensuring that no unreasonable sacrifices are demanded. In other words, a comparably comfortable standard of living should be guaranteed for the employee no matter where he goes. In addition as representatives of the firm to a country's business community, the employees must be able to maintain respectable standards.

To maintain the feeling among the core staff that equity is being upheld, a very careful process is undertaken to set up and revise continuously the compensation scheme for overseas core staff. The firm is always vulnerable, and therefore sensitive, to charges that inequities have developd. Core staff members form a highly homogeneous group, in frequent contact with each other across national boundaries. Besides conducting business, core staff members frequently have opportunities to compare their relative living situations in various countries. Core staff members are in continuous circulation: typically the overseas stay is limited to five years. If an especially good situation—or worse, an especially bad situation—develops in one locale, due to currency fluctuations, inflation, or other economic changes, core staff members throughout the worldwide system are likely to hear about it rather quickly.

The employment system maintains continuity for core staff members wherever they are assigned. Seniority accumulates at the same rate wherever the core staff member is assigned, as do retirement benefits. A core staff member's semiannual bonus is based on the corporate results of the parent in Japan, and he receives the same bonus he would get if he were stationed in Japan. His compensation is unaffected by the profits of the office or subsidiary where he works.

By far the greatest single fear among staff sent overseas is educational disruption of the children. Because Japanese schools follow a uniform curriculum nationwide, and because rigorously competitive entrance examinations determine university admission and subsequent career opportunities, the possibility of chidren overseas falling behind their classmates in Japan is worrisome. Progress in the arduous and long task of learning the 1856 characters necessary to write the modern Japanese language is especially important. But in addition to this, children's progress in mathematics is also crucial. Japanese school children consistently score as the most advanced in worldwide standardized mathematics tests, so that attendance in foreign schools is increasingly seen as penalizing both linguistic and mathematical progress.

In cities such as New York, London, São Paulo, and Dusseldorf, where large expatriate Japanese communities exist, there are Japanese schools, so these worries are mitigated. However, outside of this limited number of cities, the educational options diminish. In the case of the harshest or remotest postings, such as New Caledonia (an important source of nickel), there is a tendency to assign young, unmarried staff members, if possible. When this is not possible, or when children are at a particularly sensitive age, such as the years immediately preceding high school or college entrance examinations, it is not at all unusual for married staff members to leave their families behind for a period of years. In these cases their families usually receive a living allowance, in addition to the salary paid overseas to the manager.

There is usually no formal requirement that a core staff member have a specific number of years of experience before going overseas. In practice, however, the necessity of having a knowledge or expertise base, and of knowing and working closely with a group of colleagues in Japan, dictates that three or four years' experience in a main office is a practical minimum. There are a few exceptions, though. Some units, especially those actively trading basic commodities, send recruits with even less than a year's experience overseas as trainees, to get first-hand experience of commodities exchanges, such as the London Metals Exchange or the Chicago Board of Trade.

Table 9.2 shows the percentage of managers at each rank level serving overseas in one firm. The pattern here is clear: the highest peak occurs at the top of the premanagerial, or apprenticeship, years. This rank typically has about twelve years of experience, enough to accumulate knowledge and expertise but prior to holding formal administrative authority over other core staff members. An assignment overseas can tap functional skills while testing and developing administrative ones.

Once overseas, there is the likelihood of having significant authority and responsibility in the handling of local staff members. There can also be a larger scope for independent business development and decision making than would be possible in Japan, where many other core staff eyes and ears are watching one's activities. Finally, one of the most important skills in a firm as international as a sogo shosha is the ability to work effectively in a non-Japanese business environment. An assignment to an overseas office may often be regarded as a proving ground or rite of initiation prior to the all-important appointment to the managerial ranks.

The middle management ranks are also well represented overseas. Typically such managers occupy somewhat greater positions of responsibility than they would hold in Japan. Thus they usually hold a title overseas one full step higher than their title in Japan. Section chiefs become department chiefs, and department chiefs become division managers, for instance. Partly this is because they are a relatively scarcer, more expensive resource overseas than in Japan. But it also reflects the fact that the scale of organizational units in Japan are usually much larger than comparably titled units overseas.

Those members of top management working overseas are usually heading important offices and trading subsidiaries. These positions are usually considered quite demanding, not

Table 9.2
Percentage of members at each status rank assigned overseas in one major sogo shosha

Director	8.9%
Senior manager	12.4
Department chief	13.8
Assistant department chief	12.4
Section chief	15.8
Assistant section chief	15.1
Grade one	21.7
Grade two	11.7
Grade three	4.5

least because there are so many issues that affect both the parent organization and the local organization's interest and thus require extensive liaison work. Running an important overseas office or subsidiary is an important opportunity to manage beyond the boundaries of the product system of one's origin. These positions are therefore both preparation and testing for the truly corporate responsibilities incumbent on the very pinnacle of the sogo shosha hierarchy.

Local Staff and Localization Issues

In the largest of the sogo shosha approximately one thousand core staff members work overseas in the trading network. In addition from three to four thousand locally hired employees also staff the overseas branches and subsidiaries. This ratio of three- or four-to-one local staff to core staff is also characteristic of the smaller of the big six firms, where the overseas contingent of core staff members is limited to several hundred.

But this systemwide similarity among firms masks considerable variation in the same ratio among the offices of any one firm. Offices in the developing countries, with low wages prevalent, often have a higher ratio of local employees to core staff members. In these locations there will often be a number of drivers, porters, and other strictly manual workers employed. In high-wage countries few if any such workers may be employed by an office.

Even in strictly white-collar functions there will be a higher ratio of local to Japanese employees in the poorer countries. To some degree lower-priced local labor can substitute for higher-priced core staff labor. Simple economics dictates that the degree to which substitution occurs will be a function of the differential between local and core staff wages. Where this differential is higher (as in low-wage countries), the degree of substitution will be higher.

There are other factors that contribute to the higher ratio of locals in developing countries. One set is internal to the sogo shosha firms. Most of the largest overseas offices of the sogo shosha, particularly those offices that serve as the administrative headquarters for overseas geographic regions, are in the developed world. These offices naturally attract the largest numbers of core staff members. The work of these offices is most often either handling the biggest deals or coordinating deals worked out by the smaller branches. Both sets of tasks tend to require the presence of a critical mass of core staff members, particularly the more senior ones. This in turn makes the offices all the more attractive to others in the core staff who wish to have their own work visible to others in the core staff and who wish to enjoy the momentum and comfort of working with a larger number of their familiar compatriots.

But not all of the internal pressures are purely work related. As previously discussed, family concerns weigh heavily on those transferred overseas. Because as many sogo shosha employees and their families feel that public safety, health, and other living condition variables are superior in the developed world, there is a greater willingness to accept transfer to these outposts. Thus do large Japanese business communities (not just the representatives of the sogo shosha, but those of many manufacturing firms as well) tend to proliferate in a few key business centers, largely in the developed countries.*

External pressures also affect the staffing ratios of overseas offices. Currently these are the most intensely felt in the developing world.[2] In some countries the sogo shosha are regarded suspiciously, their functions are not always well understood, and the intentions of large Japanese companies are generally held to be suspect. Such countries may impose restrictions on the activities of the sogo shosha within their borders. Exports may be permitted, but import restricted, for example. Or the authority of the local office to borrow money, enter into contractual relationships, or undertake other business procedures may be limited. In such cases quite naturally the number of core staff members assigned may be held to a minimum.

Other countries, particularly those quite concerned about their unemployment problems, may impose requirements on the number of local people who must be employed for every

* Perhaps the most notable example of this phenomenon is to be found in Dusseldorf. Although by no means the principal business center of the Federal Republic of Germany, Dusseldorf has become the overwhelming center for Japanese business in that country. The initial importance of the metals industry (centered in and around Dusseldorf) in German-Japanese trade led a critical mass of Japanese business offices to accumulate there. Susequently schools, restaurants, and other business and social support services proliferated there. Today even Japanese businesses unconnected to the metals trade often make Dusseldorf their German or even European headquarters for this reason.

expatriate Japanese let into the country. This is most common in Latin America. For instance, in Colombia, 90 percent of the employees must be local citizens, and in Chile and Venezuela, the required figures are 85 and 75 percent, respectively. Other countries set their requirements in terms of the percentage of the local payroll that must go to their own nationals. In Peru 80 percent of the payroll must go to locals, and in Brazil, the portion is two-thirds.

Ensuring that local citizens get "a piece of the action" is a concern that is no longer exclusively that of the developing world, however. Though formal regulation is more advanced in the third world, "localization," or the developing of increasing amounts of managerial responsibility into local hands overseas, is now a global concern, and in some cases a formal policy of the sogo shosha. In the United States, for example, two groups of non-Japanese employees of two different sogo shosha have launched separate Equal Employment Opportunity actions in court against their employers, one alleging discrimination against white males. These actions are currently pending court rulings and, due to their complexity, may continue in the court systems for many years before achieving resolution.

We believe that the issue of localization is one of the most fundamental challenges facing the sogo shosha, for it raises fundamental and complex questions in the realms of both business strategy and organization. For that reason, we will defer further discussion of it until the end of the book.

Evaluation Systems

An elaborate system for employee evaluation exists in the sogo shosha, but its application is limited by two factors:

1. For all but high-level executives functional promotion is determined within the employee's division, usually by people who are intimately familiar with his daily performance. Status rank promotion involves the personnel department but for most ranks discretion rests in the division, if guidelines are followed.

2. Performance evaluation has relatively little direct effect on compensation.

Therefore the evaluation system is best regarded as a way of formalizing the process of daily evaluation that occurs in the physically close environment of the office, where daily business requires close interaction and contact. It provides standards and hints as to how such informal evaluation should be conceptualized, indicating what the company expects of its employees.

Two types of evaluation usually take place: performance evaluation and evaluation of employee potential or ability. This dual system gives explicit recognition to the notion that the current posting may not be an adequate or fair test of the employee's actual capacities or potential contribution. The performance rating is an attempt merely to assess the actual job content performance in the short term. Due to its short-term nature it is carried out more frequently than the career potential rating, often semiannually.

In order to ensure equity in cross-unit comparisons, usually each division, department, and section must meet an imposed average performance rating. In other words, the leader can vary the ratings among the individuals under him, but their average rating must be some corporatewide figure. This is particularly important because of the short-term performance ratings sometimes used to allocate the merit-based adjustments to compensation. Most often this involves increasing slightly the semiannual bonuses of those with high-performance ratings, and sometimes decreasing the bonuses of those with low ratings. The monetary amounts are not very large—a maximum of 10 to 15 percent of total compensation—but the symbolism is unmistakably important.

The longer-term employee potential assessments happen less frequently and have less direct impact on the employee. However, the longer-term impact may be more important, for these ratings can be quite influential in determining the rotation patterns and promotions the employee receives over the course of his career. Both forms of evaluation tend to involve considerable care and work on the part of the unit leader holding formal responsibility for them.

Assignment and Rotation Patterns

Rotation from posting to posting, traveling over the contours of a product system, is inherent to the careers as well as to the very concept of the core staff. One of the most fundamental distinctions that separates the core staff from all other sogo shosha employees is that core staff members are hired as employees of the company system as a whole and agree to work wherever the company might assign them, in Japan or overseas. The others (including locally hired employees overseas) are employees of the particular office into which they were hired and cannot change work sites. They are not obligated to accept an assignment in another locale. The maintenance of the sogo shosha's worldwide operations as a system is the responsibility of the core staff. The maintenance of local offices as places where the core staff can work effectively is the responsibility, broadly speaking, of the other categories.

Despite increasing sogo shosha responsiveness to heightening overseas demands for localization, in many ways core staff members remain within the same employment system, regardless of where they work. In the long run, which is all that really matters to most, they anticipate being transferred back to the parent in Japan. Individually, core staff members, particularly those involved in line trading functions, tend to see themselves as part of a global system and are not particularly concerned with the formal niceties of the legal status of their own current office or subsidiary or the details of the local personnel system. In contrast, the administrators who are concerned with functions such as finance, legal affairs, taxation, and human resources, as well as top management on the local scene, spend much of their time and energy working on these affairs.

There are few fixed policies on the term of rotation from one section to another, other than the earlier noted mandatory personnel reviews and transfers typically conducted twice in a career. Within a section of course a manager may be constantly changing the content of his job, for the section chief is constantly assigning new duties in order to develop fully the skills of section members. But rotation from one unit to another is a function of the needs of the units involved and the development of the individual manager. As a rule of thumb, however, assignments to a particular unit tend to run from three to six years. But there are numerous exceptions to this.

For a younger manager a transfer of sections usually involves moving to a new section dealing primarily in the same product system as his first. Until rather late in a career, rotations are mostly within the same division. Managers tend to learn the contours and dynamics of a product system through this kind of rotation. But again there are no rigid rules prescribing this pattern. One possible reason is that transfers across product systems and divisions can lead to innovative ideas, which are a source of major innovations in structuring or modifying systems. The managers involved in proposing and approving transfers routinely take a case-by-case perspective on their decisions.

The sogo shosha's relative lack of systematic career development policies does not indicate a lack of interest in career development as a process. On the contrary, as we shall see, career development through transfers is a vital part of its management system. It is the nature of the structure of job assignments that brings about this attitude. Because job slots as formal assignments of sets of duties do not exist, managers are able in effect to "rotate" their job duties from one function to another without ever changing their formal position. In U.S. firms, in contrast, a change in duties usually involves a change in formal position. But the sogo shosha and many American firms see the virtue of having employees perform a variety of closely related functions over the course of their careers. The sogo shosha, however, is able to achieve this without going to the bother of as many formal transfers as such.

As years accumulate, however, identifiable patterns of career rotation appear.[3] As abilities, interests, and potentials become clearer, certain individuals may be broadly recognized as being groomed for higher responsibility, while others are seen as on their way to less stellar heights. But it is not simply a matter of who is going to be promoted higher, for there are alternative paths to progress up the hierarchy. The sogo shosha needs more than one type of manager, and so it is not surprising that a variety of patterns exist. Five of the most common can be given labels.

Generalist stars are those who demonstrate a capacity for quick learning, for seeing the broader implications of developments and thinking strategically, for being able to interact skillfully with senior managers as well as peers and subordinates, and for showing a voracious appetite for work. They are the true "fair-haired boys" of the organization. Their career path rotations are marked by relatively frequent transfers among the largest offices. They may go from one product system to another, gradually expanding the range of experience. They may also rotate into a particularly important staff function, such as finance, personnel, legal affairs, or accounting and control. Sometimes they are given large projects or serious problems to work on at a young age. They will not be formally in charge but will be expected to generate ideas and implement them under the supervision of a seasoned senior official.

Their rapid transfers and broad range make it difficult to build deep roots in a particular business area, and this may be a serious problem in obtaining future promotion if they cannot take credit for visible major accomplishments in business development. But at its top levels the sogo shosha needs managers of experience that transcends product system and line/staff divisions. The relatively broad exposure given to those who are seen as having the requisite capabilities helps build a talent pool suitable for top-level corporate responsibilities.

System specialists rotate throughout a product system, building deep knowledge and experience, as well as personal contacts within and outside the firm. The steady accumulation of technical knowledge, experience, and solid business relationships prepares system specialists for the task of managing ongoing flows of business, and for the development of new business opportunities. Because the system specialists are in a position to take responsibility for creating the profit-producing transactions that are the heart of the sogo shosha's business, the most successful among them wield considerable power within the firm.

Periphery controllers are those managers who gravitate over time toward management of subsidiaries and affiliates, or whose rotations become less frequent as they specialize in particular products or markets. They serve to oversee a more limited set of business flows and link these with the overall product system operations. For this reason their career rotations may take them through *shukkō* transfers out of the firm to subsidiary management and back in one or more times. If they have the good fortune to be located in a profitable and growing business area, their promotion opportunities may be substantial. But if they become stuck in a more marginal area of the firm, their progress up the status hierarchy becomes uncertain.

Staffers are those who become fixed in support staff functions and have little or no opportunity to earn money for the firm by managing a line function. Although some support staff functions are very important to the sogo shosha's operations, and some staff members accumulate considerable influence, in general, they have less prestige and power than line managers. Vladimir Pucik of the University of Michigan has studied aggregate promotion data at one sogo shosha and found that promotion opportunities for support staff members overall are much more limited than for line managers.

Locals and administrators are those who permanently leave the core staff to run specific business operations in the network of subsidiaries and affiliates, or who stay within the core staff but are given well-structured responsibilities. Some may have shown a particular knack for handling one type of product, set of relationships, or type of function. But others may have proved unable to handle the demands of the less structured coordination functions of system management. For whatever reason, this group tends to remain within a narrower sphere of rotation and job functions.

These patterns must be applied with extreme caution when viewing any individual career path, for they do not represent corporate policies. Individual promotions and transfers tend to be made opportunistically, to fill a need rather than to fit a model of career development. The career histories of many sogo shosha managers would not fit easily into any of these types. Moreover, though we have listed them in the approximate order of their prestige, there is considerable variation in ultimate promotion among those who would fit into any particular pattern. The firm quite clearly needs capable managers in each category, and rewards exist for those who perform well in each.

The Sogo Shosha as Professional Service Organizations

The sogo shosha's general practices for hiring, training, promoting via seniority, and employing until retirement a white-collar managerial group are common in Japan. But two aspects of a sogo shosha make it unusual when compared to most Japanese companies:

1. The managerial class of employees constitutes a far larger percentage of the total employees than in almost any other business. There are very few blue-collar employees, who would make up a majority of the work force in most manufacturing firms; there are relatively small numbers of clerks exclusively

concerned with routine work compared to banks, insurance companies, or other "service industry" firms. In terms of the percentage of employees called on to exercise managerial and operational decisions, the sogo shosha resembles nothing so much as professional service organizations, such as law firms, accounting firms, or management consultants. However, few firms in these categories come close to a sogo shosha in overall size.

2. There is very little in the way of capital-intensive machinery, brand names, proprietary technology, or captive markets that provides an automatic basis for continuing operations. As is the case for a professional service organization, a sogo shosha's continuing operations are dependent on the active initiative of its core staff in making the firm's services useful to its clients.

In addition to the similarities noted, it is interesting that professional firms often take a similar approach to training and promotion. It is usually felt that it is necessary to work one's way up the organization, starting with relatively humble tasks such as case research in law firms or field auditing in accounting firms. Only after gaining experience by performing such relatively routine tasks is one ready to assume higher responsibilities. Typically in such firms a modified seniority principle also operates, with senior partners being the oldest people in the firms.

But differences also exist and are instructive. For one thing, most professions require specialized education prior to entry, at the undergraduate level, at least, and often at the graduate level. In the case of the sogo shosha the entire burden of training must be met by the firm itself. Furthermore in the United States there is often mobility among professional firms. One can sometimes enter law firms, accounting firms, or management consulting firms at the partner level. In contrast, the sogo shosha only promotes from within.

In this chapter we have seen an overview of the formal policies and practices that shape the human resources of the sogo shosha. We have also seen that these systems alone do not provide a full enough framework for understanding how the organization is actually able to administer the complex product systems it deals with. To examine this, we will turn next to an analysis of the informal but systematic features that make up the emergent organization of the sogo shosha.

10

The Context of the Section

The Emergent Managerial Organization

Now we will look inside the social universe of the sogo shosha at its operating level, the section. There we will be able to examine the forces that shape the performance of work. The formal system presented thus far is the context in which the emergent system of management has grown. The emergent system of management refers to the sum of practices and activities regularly performed by members of the organization but not formally required or codified in its formal system of organization. We have already seen that there is little precise guidance for activity in the sogo shosha's formal system. So the residual, to be explained by the emergent system, is correspondingly important. It is this emergent system that produces the actual behavior of managers as they react to the social, cultural, financial, organizational, and other forces in their daily working environment.

The dynamics at work inside the section, in this most fundamental unit of the sogo shosha organization, derive from the business strategy of the firm, from the influence of formal structures, and from the effects of Japanese and corporate cultures on the human beings who comprise the managerial work force. Understanding the emergent systems of management within a section is the first step in building an understanding of how the organization as a whole functions.

The Section as a Unit of Analysis

As we explained earlier, a sogo shosha's organization chart reveals multiple levels of operating units. At the bottom are sections, with departments, divisions. and product groups rising above them. In fact over 80 percent of the managers work in a section. The bottom five or so grades of the status system work primarily in sections, although they do occasionally rotate through other types of work groups in such settings as affiliates and subsidiaries. These five groups include over four-fifths of managerial personnel.

All members of management, regardless of their rank, share the common experience of entering the firm and working in a section for most of the first two decades of their careers. Patterns learned in this setting become deeply ingrained, so as to become almost second nature. Attitudes toward problem solving, authority, one's peers, other units in the firm, corporate culture, and virtually all other aspects of the managerial world view tend to be formed and fixed during this long and fundamental socialization process.

The section is the setting within which the overwhelming majority of operations is undertaken. The units that stand above the section on the organization chart exist primarily to control and coordinate its work. Most trading decisions are usually assigned to a section, not to the other types of units. However, sections are by no means autonomous. The interconnectedness of the business of different sections, plus the formal centralization of authority common to most of the firms, make the section very dependent on higher units for this control and coordination function.

The Group Context of Training and Development

After undergoing the entrance ceremony and orientation, a new recruit returns to headquarters to enter the section to which he has been initially assigned. Though mandatory formal training courses are offered during the first year of employment, the really important education occurs on the job, within the section. Since job slots do not exist, the *kachō* ("section chief") has the responsibility for allocating specific duties to specific individuals. It is expected that the division of labor within the section will be fluid, according to the work load and individual abilities of the section members.

Despite the diversity of products and tasks assigned to sections, there is a remarkable uniformity in office layout (see figure 10.1). The section members sit in two rows of desks,

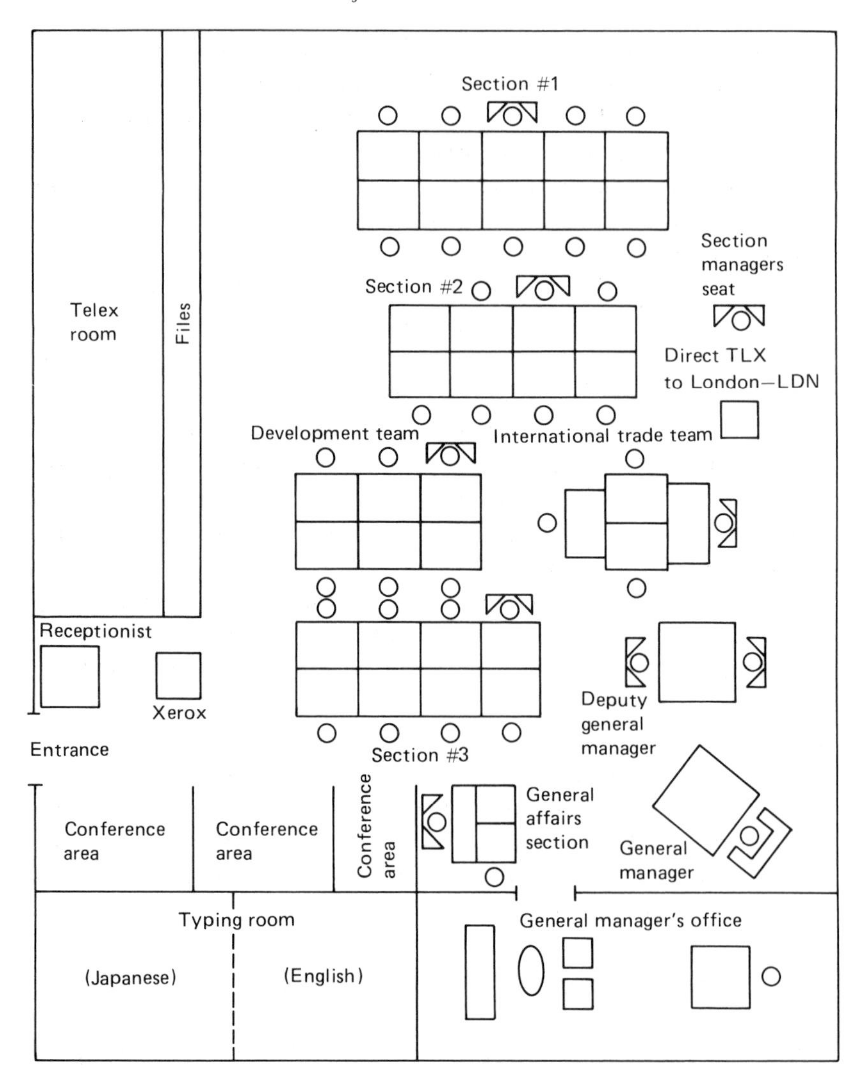

Figure 10.1
Floor plan of a typical department (*bu*)

pushed together and facing each other. This arrangement puts section members in close contact with the activities of the others; it is impossible not to overhear what is being said or not to see what is being written. Younger members are expected to observe and learn from their seniors' activities. As anthropologist Thomas Rohlen has commented on this type of floor plan, "one will never see a section arranged so that people are looking at the backs of others in the same group. Invariably there is a sense of an inward-looking circle. . . ."[1]

The *buchō* ("department chief") sits behind the *kachō* (usually at a desk in front of a window), facing inward to observe the sections he supervises. Both the section chief and the department chief can readily see, and even hear, the activities of those they supervise. They are in a position to know what every person in the office is doing. Having risen slowly within the constraints of seniority, through a variety of positions within a product system, the department chief has probably performed nearly every task each of his subordinates is working on. He literally knows what it feels like to sit at their desks. Conversely, each section member can observe the section chief and department chief. They learn their personal characteristics and also come to form an understanding of leadership as a process. Since the seniority system means that almost everyone will someday rise at least to the level of a section chief, the training provided by this long-term observation is important.

Ties among members of a section are deliberately fostered in many ways. After-hours socializing is particularly important. These nocturnal sojourns are seldom purely for fun. There are certain elements of recreation, to be sure, but these occasions also provide a setting in which the superior can provide informal, but important, advice or counsel to subordinates, softened or mediated by the effects of alcohol, sports, food, or other diversions. Training goes on even in social activities. Weekend outings are encouraged, and the companies provide inexpensive lodgings a convenient distance from the major offices in Tokyo and Osaka. In the somewhat formal, ceremonial Japanese manner there are also nearly always special parties to welcome new members or to say good-bye to departing members of the section. The importance of the group receives constant reinforcement.

The section is an excellent example of a primary work group: a stable set of people and roles within which the members work most of the time. Membership in a section implies joining a group of people who interact closely, frequently, and intensely. Over time, primary work groups evolve informal rules and operating procedures. Individuals take on their own peculiar roles and standing within the tight social microcosm. Because of physical proximity, the collective nature of the work assignment, the relative stability of membership, and the general importance of groups in Japanese life, the section is a particularly powerful and important aspect of the sogo shosha.

Social life for members of a section usually revolves around the work group. Rather than visiting each others' houses and being hosted by husband and wife, such occasions are usually held at an eating or drinking establishment, and spouses are not invited. By this very position the *kachō* is expected to play the role of host more often than not. At the level of *kachō* and above there is usually an increment added to salary scales to pay for such outings as well as other expenses involved in playing a role in the external life of subordinates.

The importance of deep personal relationships between *kachō* and section members in providing individual motivation helps explain how the *kachō* can be effective while lacking any control over the financial reward of his subordinates. But the lack of formally specified tools and powers of the kacho also derives from the rather different concept of leadership in Japan compared to the United States.

In the United States a leader is often thought of as one who blazes new trails, a virtuoso whose example inspires awe, respect, and emulation. If any individual characterizes this pattern, it is surely John Wayne, whose image reached epic proportions in his own lifetime as an embodiment of something uniquely American.

A Japanese leader, rather than being an authority, is more of a communications channel, a mediator, a facilitator, and most of all, a symbol and embodiment of group unity. Consensus building is necessary to decision making, and this requires patience and an ability to use carefully cultivated relationships to get all to agree for the good of the unit. A John Wayne in this situation might succeed temporarily by virtue of charisma, but eventually the inability to build strong emotion-laden relationships and use these as a tool of motivation and consensus building would prove fatal.

Vertical Ties and Work Relationships

In Japan relationships within work groups are usually between individuals whose status or rank is disparate. In other words, hierarchical or vertical relations predominate over peer or horizontal relationships. Naturally horizontal relations do exist, but they are relatively less important than in the United States. For Japanese people relationships among equals are inherently ambiguous. Emotional ambiguity is very difficult for Japanese people to cope with. Peers are potential competitors in the seniority-based systems of Japanese firms, yet they should also be friends. Nevertheless, all are conscious of the fact that they are lifetime members of a competitive system. There are only a few positions at the top of the pyramid, so it is clear that rivalry is a genuine aspect of peer relationships no matter how deeply people might wish to ignore this uncomfortable fact.

It is quite unusual for a section to have two members of the same age and seniority. Rather, the section members form an age and seniority hierarchy or continuum. Relations among members are thus predominately vertical, not horizontal in nature. This helps foster solidarity among members by removing a major source of ambiguity. Emphasis on the vertical nature of ties among section members is given by the use of the terms *sempai* ("forward companion") and *kōhai* ("follower companion") among section members in referring to each other.

Vertical ties bear the major load of organizational integration. Although horizontal ties are generally uneasy in work organizations, vertical ties are elaborated and used. Japanese culture abounds in rituals, myths, and models of hierarchical relationships. A rich and vast etiquette exists so that emotional ambiguity is minimized, and predictability, hence comfort, in hierarchical relationships is maximized.

One leading social theorist in Japan, Professor Nakane Chie of the University of Tokyo, has elaborated the predominance of vertical ties among Japanese into a general theory of Japanese society which has gained wide currency within Japan and abroad.[2] Whether or not one accepts the contention that vertical ties form the very basis of all Japanese social organization, the inner character of hierarchical work relations at the sogo shosha, and their importance as part of the emergent administrative system can be seen to be worth some considerable attention.

The importance of hierarchical vertical relations, particularly those between a *kachō* and his subordinates, is enhanced by a fundamental psychic characteristic of the Japanese people: a need for secure dependence on another. Psychoanalyst Doi Takeo has posited that this need for *amae,* "a passive feeling of dependence," underlies the importance of vertical ties in the structure of Japanese society.[3] He explains this need to receive active psychological and other kinds of support without actually soliciting it, and he traces its origins to Japanese child-rearing practices. There is widespread agreement among social scientists and psychiatric researchers that family structure and child-rearing techniques are a fundamental source for patterns of personality and interpersonal behavior in any culture.

Amae, Doi explains, is an essential function in Japanese small groups. For this reason groups develop elaborate vertical structures, whose hierarchical relationship can provide *amae* for the subordinates. If the need for *amae* cannot be satisfied within the group, it is unlikely that the group will be meaningful. The commitment and self-identity, of which we spoke earlier in describing the importance of groups, will go to another primary affiliation, and the motivation level of the group members consequently will fall drastically.

Exactly what goes into satisfying a subordinate's need for *amae* is a question that goes vastly beyond the scope of this work. However, in general, it consists of being able to read feelings and provide carefully balanced doses of support in situations where it is needed. *Amae* is definitely more of an intuitive sense than a rational concept for most Japanese, and it is likely that successful filling of a subordinate's *amae* need is primarily learned over the course of one's life in a Japanese social environment. In any event a leader who cannot fill this need is a leader who cannot be effective.

A leader who does manage to fulfill the *amae* need of a subordinate gains a reciprocal level of dedication and energy put at his service. Achieving this requires a relationship and a commitment that transcends the workplace setting and involves the leader in the entire life of the subordinate. Providing advice on personal matters is only the preliminary aspect; active involvement is often expected. For example, employees often rely on a company superior to find a suitable marriage partner for them and to act as ceremonial go-between in an arranged marriage (which is still quite common in contemporary Japan). Having arranged the marriage, the superior often becomes something of a family counselor and may even be asked to mediate important disputes between husband and wife.

Section Leadership: The Kachō*'s Mandate*

Because often the task assigned to a section is defined only in very broad terms, the *kachō* has the responsibility of translating the task into meaningful directions. He must then distribute the various duties involved in executing the task among the members of his unit. In this matter there are few formal guidelines or constraints, such as written job descriptions. It is up to the leader to identify the abilities, strengths, weaknesses, and aptitudes of each member so that each can be assigned appropriate duties. He must also monitor their performances, and reevaluate and redistribute the loads, as members develop their abilities.

According to at least two models of leadership, the magnitude of the leadership task in the sogo shosha section is tremendous. If, as some students of leadership believe, the essence of leadership is the influential increment over and above mechanical compliance with routine directives of the organization and if leadership declines in importance as the formal structure approaches complete determination of behavior, then the *kachō* has an important and formidable task. Not only does the organization *not* provide a regular stream of routine directives that determine behavior (not even job slots for section members), the leader does not have a large arsenal of short-range penalties and rewards to use in influencing behavior. Salary and bonus are out of his hands, except for his long-term influence on promotions. He even lacks the ability to fire subordinates. As leader, he has only his personal leadership to rely on. He must develop the "influential increment" into a daily working tool.

In carrying out his multifaceted role, the leader's primary concern is naturally the effective discharge of the unit's mission. However, in addition to this consideration, the leader must also take care to provide opportunities for members to develop as managers. At the sogo shosha the management development responsibilities of the section chief are taken very seriously. A sogo shosha's major asset is its human resources which it purchases in career-long units, so the development of this asset is seen as a vital role. Balancing the two goals of task accomplishment and management development is often a matter of very fine judgment.

A sogo shosha's operations provide a regular supply of situations requiring concerted unit effort. Because the business lines of many units are seasonal or may fluctuate, it is not unusual for overtime demands to be extreme. Trading requires that the unit be able to react quickly to opportunities that may appear without warning. In many cases it is simply impossible for the unit to plan ahead to minimize overtime.

Members must be prepared to be available on short notice to perform long hours under pressure. Sixty or seventy hours of overtime a month at busy times were figures quoted by many people we interviewed. It should be remembered that the work of a sogo shosha depends on the active initiative of its employees; overtime has a very different character from that in a factory where workers may simply be tending machinery, physically demanding though that may be. Overtime in the sogo shosha is also somewhat different from that put in by most professionals in that sogo shosha overtime usually requires tight coordination among members of the unit, as opposed to the more solitary or individualistic work of many lawyers or accountants.

Learning Product Systems

In the line sections that trade in products most often the recruit's first assignment is to arrange for delivery of the product—a seemingly simple, but actually complicated, process.[4] This is done for several reasons. The new member learns the importance of the *flow* of goods and the interdependency of each party that handles it. Also, by working in delivery he can observe firsthand how goods physically move from one owner to another. It puts the young core staff member in physical proximity to the commodity he will be trading.

Many of the products handled are intermediate goods to be used for a further stage of manufacturing within the system coordinated by the sogo shosha. The contours of the product system, and the sogo shosha's role as coordinator and expeditor of a flow of goods throughout its various stages, gradually become tangible and clearer to the novice over the course of work with different customers.

The importance of maintaining flow in the product system is rapidly brought home to the new recruits through this work. In their delivery work they can see or hear about the consequences of running out of materials at various stages of the system. Clients are very conscious of such costs, and look to the sogo shosha for help. The sogo shosha in part sells its services on the basis of its ability to remove or respond to uncertainties in supply, so it is anxious that its youngest members visit clients and hear their views on the importance of timely and secure delivery.

Costly errors can and do take place when young career staffers make mistakes. Of course everyone wants to minimize errors. Yet company managers are aware that they are an inevitable cost of the training and socialization process. Several managers recalled that mistakes they had made on delivery assignments had taught them that even small errors on seemingly trivial assignments would cause inconvenience to clients and would make the jobs of others in the company much harder. Responsibility to others and the importance of the flow of goods are the major lessons to be learned at this point in a manager's career.

In delivery work feedback is immediate. The recruit learns that all is not routine, people make mistakes, and various contingencies affect the success of his work. His job ceases to be abstract; he becomes "in touch" with his product's world.

Delivery work also puts the recruit into direct contact with client organizations. He learns the peculiar characteristics and needs of the clients. He learns to deal personally with all the people involved in the systemic flows—from truck drivers to steel mill superintendents; he is introduced to the people who can influence the flow of his product. He is afforded many opportunities to build personal ties with members of these organizations who will also likely be rising in a seniority-based hierarchy parallel to the one at his sogo shosha. Figure 10.2 shows the principal lines of coordination in a delivery assignment.

In addition delivery teaches the employee about the characteristics of the products the section handles, so he learns to

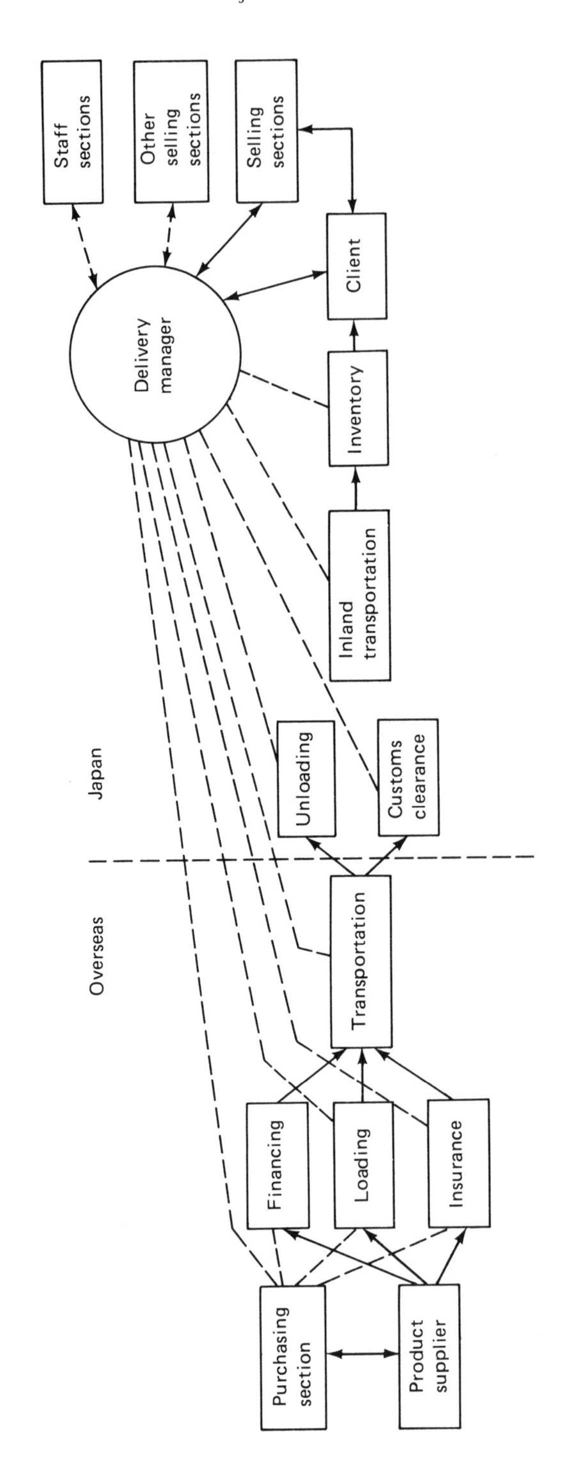

Figure 10.2
Principal lines of coordination affecting delivery

distinguish among the varieties of soybeans, or of marine turbines, for example. Naturally it teaches him about the intricacies of transportation, insurance, and the other details that make up the distribution chain. When working on delivery, a recruit rapidly becomes accustomed to taking responsibility for perhaps millions of dollars worth of products, and thus dealing with very large amounts of money.

Besides delivery new recruits may also be assigned to other detail work, such as billing, bookkeeping, and filling out reporting forms. This is particularly true in staff sections, but it is common in line sections as well. If they have an intimate familiarity with the "nuts and bolts" of the business, it is felt that everyone will eventually be able to understand it and to make better decisions when seniority places them in more responsible positions. In a real sense everyone must work his way up from the bottom.

Because of the interdependencies among work units in the sogo shosha the younger manager frequently must work with representatives of other units of the firm. He interacts with both superiors and peers on these missions. With the superiors, he can form vertical ties. With peers, the horizontal relationships are somewhat more ambiguous. However, the fact that they work in different units and share in the same socialization process tends to suppress rivalry.

Over time the younger manager has an opportunity to observe the manner in which routine operations yield possibilities for developmental activity. He can understand which kinds of data to be sensitive to and know which other subunits of the firm would be interested in learning about the types of information that could come into his hands in the course of operations.

During this initial period the younger manager also learns the jargon of the trade he is dealing with. An industry develops verbal shorthand to enable those familiar with it to communicate rapidly and accurately about matters of importance. The sogo shosha manager must pick up not only those terms used by the trade at large but also the special language that develops within the firm to refer to ideas, clients, methods, objects, places, and the other things which managers habitually deal with and communicate about.

Since most of the functions cannot be routinized or standardized, the period of training is quite long. The young manager must be exposed to a wide variety of situations and customers because he must learn not only techniques of trading but also product characteristics, industry structure, product flow, and vagaries of customers. But, most important, he must acquire judgment and an almost intuitive understanding of the business.

Rather than telling people what to do, the process emphasizes watching and assisting; it especially encourages employees to figure things out for themselves. Many managers, at all levels of responsibility, emphasized that this method builds self-confidence and credibility. It results in a series of screening or testing occasions, but it also requires an atmosphere in which the employee knows that the company will forgive or back up any mistakes that are produced by this method. When an employee who makes an error observes that his boss or colleagues forgives him and unites in overcoming the consequences of his mistake, his need for *amae* is gratified, and he incurs a feeling of obligation. This serves as a very powerful motivating factor for hard work in the future.

This policy makes great demands on the section chief, for he must monitor the work of everyone assigned to new tasks, lest the unnoticed consequences of a mistake grow too expensive. He must also know when the employee has adequately mastered his task and needs to be assigned a new challenge. The *kachō* must then reallocate the tasks of the section among its members. He is a doer, a trainer, a manager, a mediator, and a counselor. Figure 10.3 is an attempt to diagram the relationship of *kachō* to section members, showing how closely the *kachō* must selectively monitor the work.

In the sogo shosha there appears to be a greater willingness than in a typical American company to bear the cost of mistakes made in the process of training. For example, the head of a soybean section estimated that the mistakes made by a soybean commodity trader in the training may cumulatively cost as much as $200,000. But, given the assurance that the employee will stay with the company, and that a mistake especially in the earlier stages of an employee's career will make him very strongly motivated and also more seasoned and self-confident, the cost of a mistake may well appear to be a justifiable investment.

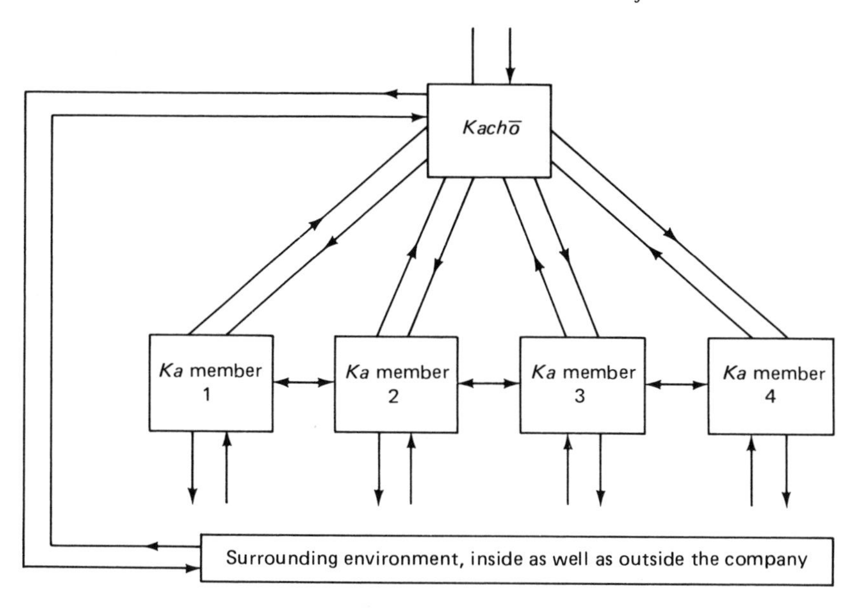

Figure 10.3
The flow of work in a typical section (*ka*)

Increasing Responsibilities

At first the new member of the core staff may do the same tasks as some members of the secretarial-clerical staff. But he is on a very different career path, and the intent of assigning him these tasks is very different. He is performing tasks to learn about them, to have experience that will be valuable to him in the future. Equally important, he absorbs the methodology of training and management development. Later in his career, when he has his own subordinates to develop, he will know how to handle trainees and will also from his own experience be able to empathize with them. Also he is expected to learn how to delegate, coordinate, and manage interpersonal relations with the female secretarial-clerical staff who are subordinate to him, regardless of age or experience. These are the key skills of management in Japan, particularly in a sogo shosha; inculcating and refining them is a central theme in the development of career paths for all core staff members.

Thus, although at first glance it may seem a waste of valuable time to have mundane tasks performed by recruits who have been selected from the top graduates of the most elite universities, the training (especially given the opportunity for observation inherent in the office layout) and seasoning (especially the opportunity to make mistakes whose consequences are not too severe) are the real objectives. These top-level recruits accept assignments to such tasks because their perspective is a long-range one. They have their career paths in mind and see beyond their immediate duties. Clerks could after all perform many of the tasks more economically. But, for the future success of the system, the sogo shosha must expose its eventual top management to these tasks for from one to three years.

The Individual Career and the Structure of Work

There is a certain element of "dues paying" during these initial years of a career. The relationship with the *kachō* and with more senior members of the section does provide a counterpoint of hope. The young manager sees in them his own future and hears stories of how they dealt with the same problems he faces. Moreover, because a good *kachō* is continually changing the mix of tasks performed by a section member as soon as he has mastered them, boredom is minimized, even though the tasks themselves may be routine. Client contact, with its emphasis on learning the client organizations and building relationships, also denotes this period of a recruit's life.

Both the seniority system and the lifetime commitment of a job make it imperative to the company that core staff people be hired and developed more for their long-term potential than for the particular job skills they happen to possess at the time of university graduation. Since everyone will rise to at least some level of executive responsibility, such long-term potential is obviously important. About thirty-five years are available for training and experience, and since an employee is very unlikely to quit and take his company-provided education with him, the company can safely invest in expensive training to develop in its employees whatever skills or abilities may be required.

By contrast, in the United States it often makes better sense for a company to hire people for specific skills, since internally developed (at company expense) human resources can and often do quit for a better offer elsewhere. This in turn has contributed to the development of the concept of job slots, into which it is presumed people can be inserted interchangeably.

The attaining of the skills necessary for a job slot is seen as largely an individual responsibility, although company-sponsored training programs for them may exist. For management positions the United States has used the concept of graduate business education. The MBA degree is usually acquired at the student's initiative and expense, and it is thought by some to be relevant preparation for work in almost any field or company.

Since in the sogo shosha a promotion is to some extent inevitable for every core staff member, an important part of an employee's job at any given point is his preparation for future responsibilities. In other words, there are two separate aspects to the duties being performed by any employee: the accomplishment of the task itself, and the training of the employee for future duties. This parallels the duality of the *kachō*'s responsibility.

The training for higher responsibilities occurs primarily in the form of on-the-job experience, under the watchful guidance of a senior and more experienced fellow worker. Because of the nature of a sogo shosha's business, there is no other way to provide training as effectively. The bulk of trading activity takes place under time pressure, with thin margins but familiar products and actors. Under such circumstances many decisions must be made on the basis of "gut feel." There is no time to use standard management analysis techniques, and too many unquantifiable variables for elaborate analysis to be effective.

A manager must, in other words, be trained to have an instinctive understanding of every process that makes up a complex deal and to know and consider in his decision making the characteristics and behavior of every actor on the market. The only way to develop such an almost reflex level understanding is to have worked one's way up through every step of every operation that a sogo shosha performs in a given commodity area. Starting with routine tasks, the sogo shosha employee is assigned progressively harder and more complex tasks. As old tasks are mastered, the employee begins teaching them to employees younger than he. He also begins to learn new tasks from senior employees.

The overall picture of the organization that emerges is one of people simultaneously learning new tasks from superiors, performing certain tasks on their own, and supervising their subordinates' performance of other simpler tasks. Each person goes through three stages in performing every task: learning from superior, performing it himself, and teaching it to subordinates. The process can be labeled "learning chains," for it links members to one another through the process of teaching, learning, and delegating.

If we try to visualize the overall flow of work, and we assume that the tasks are arranged in a static hierarchy, then people flow *upward,* performing more and more difficult tasks. If we focus on the people in the organization and assume that they are arranged in a static hierarchy, then tasks flow *downward,* as everyone is constantly learning new and more complex tasks. In reality of course neither the tasks of the organization nor its people are static. Over time the tasks performed by the organization grow in diversity and complexity, as new people enter at the bottom, move their way up the hierarchy, and then exit at the upper levels.

The initial assignment to a particular section provides a flexible yet well-structured environment for this learning. The organic nature of work division and the strong elements of emotional support among section members promote a very thorough socialization into a complex role system. Over time contacts with other units of the firm, and rotation of section mates to other assignments provide the young manager with a larger organizational horizon than his first section.

Eventually the young section member will be rotated himself. There is no set period of time for this first transfer. It can vary from six months to several years after entry, depending on organizational needs, the nature of the section's business, and personal readiness. Typically rotation is to a section in a line of business closely associated with the first assignment. The new assignment will usually have a few familiar faces, perhaps one or two people who have worked closely with the young manager previously.

The process of rotation into related units of the company thus functions progressively to widen the organizational perspective of the manager, simultaneously widening his set of contacts, or his network. At the same time, however, assignments into totally unfamiliar units tend to be avoided, though they do occur. For most managers a new assignment combines familiar and unfamiliar people, functions, and clients. A continuity of human relations is seen as desirable.

Although any organization faces the problems of preparing its members for their future responsibilities, it is clear that the sogo shosha's organization is particularly dependent on effective on-the-job training. The only way a person can be prepared for senior levels of responsibility is to have had the experience of starting at the bottom and working his way up to more complex tasks through the process of learning-performing-teaching.

The Functional Logic of Seniority

Nowhere is the contrast between the sogo shosha's managerial system and American models more vivid than in attitudes toward seniority. For upwardly mobile Americans seniority is almost universally experienced as an impediment to their own careers in particular and meritocracy in general. In contrast, capable young managers in a sogo shosha, though they too may experience some personal frustrations with the pace of their own progress, tend to see major personal benefits in the seniority system besides the costs.

One important dimension centers around the delicate issue of peer relations. As a manager is developed and personally deals with more complexities of the product system within which he works, he comes into contact with more and more peers in other units. Though his section remains a stronghold of vertical relations, interunit coordination tends to rely a bit more on horizontal ties, which inevitably raise suppressed competitiveness. The fact that these horizontal ties are with people in different units helps suppress the competitive aspects somewhat. But in the long run all managers within the same age cohort are still competitors. However, the fact that the first decade and a half features automatic promotion allows this competitiveness to be at least deferred. Competence and personality of one's peers can be thoroughly evaluated, and alliances and rivalries entered into carefully.

The extended respite from differential promotion also reassures managers that they will have ample time to be assessed fairly before any binding decisions about their fate are made. If they should make a mistake, they will have time to atone. If a particular superior does not appreciate their talents adequately, they will have time to demonstrate to others and to him the error of his perceptions.

Almost counterintuitively, seniority can create flexibility as well as rigidity within the sogo shosha managerial system. There is no doubt that a seniority system does lead to certain kinds of rigidities in the organization. Yet such rigidities can be kept to a minimum by skillfully managing the degree of coupling between rank and responsibility.[5] For example, although two people may have the identical title of section chief, one may be merely a functionary, whereas the other may be given actual control encompassing far more territory than his formal title indicates.

A supervisor can assign difficult tasks to his more competent subordinates with relatively little regard to their ranks. Significantly the subordinate given a difficult task would consider this as a recognition of his ability and would be motivated to perform the task without extra compensation. He sees it as a chance to prove himself and enhance his credibility and reputation in the organization. Excellent performance will lead to even more difficult tasks. Over time his *kachō* and others with whom he works become convinced of his suitability for promotion. In the end, in part because the company is committed to him for his entire career, he is certain that his outstanding performance will be rewarded with status promotion. He obviously has been molded to take a very long-range view of his career progress and reward.

Note that in the American corporate ethos there must be direct linkage between responsibility, status, and reward. A person can be promoted and rewarded without reference to seniority. However, if a supervisor wishes to reallocate duties among subordinates, job descriptions must be rewritten and promotions and demotions made, with reward changes following suit. This involves rigidities of a different order from those entailed in the sogo shosha system.

A related consequence of groupism, seniority, and other aspects of the sogo shosha management system is that most superiors show little discomfort when a subordinate proves himself more capable than the superior himself. This is because the subordinate is really more of an asset than a threat to the boss's job. Seniority assures the superior of his formal status rank as superior, so there is not the kind of fear of being replaced by an aggressive subordinate that might be the case in an American company. The leader is protected from the formal embarrassment of being upstaged. Indeed, the Japanese concept of management places much more emphasis on developing and facilitating the work of others than on making solitary decisions, as being the function of leaders, so the emergence of an outstanding subordinate tends to prove the worth of a superior, rather than to threaten it.

Because the form of seniority provides a stability that enables the superior to deal emotionally with a subordinate whose competence might exceed his, it is not very unusual in Japan to find units in which actual decision-making power on various measures has been delegated by the formal leader to a more competent subordinate. Real authority and power are thus not severely constrained by the formal hierarchy of status.

This kind of flexibility serves the organization well, especially if we consider the inflexibility inherent in the contrasting American system. In an organization in the United States, if a junior seems more competent than his or her leader, a common reaction on the leader's part is fear for his or her own job. Whether or not the leader actually hampers the subordinate or conceals his/her good work from others, it is almost certain that the leader will not make full use of the subordinate's talents at the expense of his/her own prerogatives. The organization is thus denied maximum access to the full talents of capable subordinates as leaders seek to protect themselves from being upstaged.

Authority and Its Delegation

In the sogo shosha, as in most large Japanese bureaucracies, the form of hierarchy is rather rigidly adhered to. This is consistent with the comfort with vertical relations and discomfort with horizontal relations experienced by most Japanese people. A tightly defined hierarchy characterizes not only compensation, promotion, and other aspects of the formal organization but extends to such matters as always addressing a superior by his title and showing proper formal deference. However, though the *form* is understood and followed, the *substance* of authority can be actually quite vague and ad hoc in nature.

As we have discussed, there is no formal definition of the authority of a section chief, other than to take responsibility for the fulfillment of the section's mission, itself defined only in the broadest of terms. Of course, in theory, a section chief can order any member of his section to do anything he wants; however, such an absolute type of power really doesn't exist and wouldn't be useful if it did. As we have seen, the business of a sogo shosha depends largely on the initiative of core staff members in seeking out and structuring transactions.

In fact the substance of authority is something that each leader must earn by demonstrating his superior knowledge and judgment. Of course most unit leaders are given the benefit of the doubt, but they must also demonstrate their abilities to their subordinates. In an organization where someone can be promoted solely on the basis of seniority, a superior must often prove himself to those whom he supervises. This process takes place using a symbolic language that draws on many Japanese concepts and values. Both leader and subordinate start with a culturally determined notion of what a leader can and ought to be. Much of the real division of labor springs from this notion. Within the context of this notion it is up to the leader to prove his worth, by meeting employees' emotional needs, by correcting their mistakes without humiliating them, and by giving able employees increased discretion over time.

The job assignment function of a leader is particularly important in earning credibility with his subordinates. His ability to judge subordinates' contributions, as well as their potential, is something on which they can in turn judge his effectiveness. If he withholds credit where it is due, this will be particularly damaging. Often the subordinates have opportunity to learn data about each other that remain hidden from the *kachō*. To the extent to which he misjudges them, his credibility and authority are eroded.

Decisions on credit extension are formally rather centralized, even though traders "in the field" rely on the ability to grant credit as a key part of their trading operations. In the heat of negotiation, when faced with competition and associated time pressures, it may often be necessary to extend credit on the spot. There may in many cases simply be no time to go through the formal channels, so the authority to grant credit must be informally delegated. This reflects the very nature of the organization's top-down delegation of authority to lower-level managers who are closer to the realities of decisions to be made.

At the level of the section this pattern finds its most basic expression. *All* of the authority in the section formally lies in the section chief's hands. The lack of individual job slots means that the *kachō* actually informally delegates some of his duties to each of his subordinates. The only basis on which he can do this is his own assessment of their abilities. He must therefore keep close watch on their performance, knowing exactly who is capable of what tasks and who ought to be tested by being assigned a new task. No structure of defined responsibilities aids (or hinders) him in doing this. It is all subjective. But the *kachō* knows that he is being evaluated by his superiors to a great extent on his ability to develop the skills of his section members, without allowing them to make very many serious mistakes. Accountability remains with him for the mistakes committed by his subordinates.

Such informal delegation of authority is not limited to Japanese organizations of course. Everywhere there are occasions when rules are circumvented to cope with the complexities of real life. However, such sanctioned informality often sets off a rather different kind of dynamic, particularly in the United States, where the principle of rule of law influences attitudes toward formal rules of all kinds. In the United States, as examined by Melville Dalton, superiors often seek ways to remain officially ignorant of subordinates' actions in order to preserve "deniability."[6] The ultimate extension of this is the pattern of issuing "orders for the record" which an official knows will be violated but which will protect him or her in the event of an official inquiry.

These two approaches differ fundamentally in their distribution of accountability. The pattern in the United States forces accountability downward, to the level of the organization that must take the action. The "fall guy" is the one who was forced to take action by the superior, who is protected by the formal record. In contrast, when accountability is forced upward, basic security is provided for those who actually take action, compelling those who authorized it to monitor it closely. Of course a subordinate must take some responsibility for the outcome of his decisions and actions. But he knows he will not become a scapegoat and is guaranteed job security. So his perceived risk may be diminished compared to that of a subordinate in Dalton's example.

This pattern in the sogo shosha rests on a general expectation within the organization that (1) rules concerning official authority will have to be violated and (2) in such cases the manager granting discretion must retain responsibility. The sogo shosha system, in other words, accepts that rules are only one source of influence on behavior and thus has developed alternative mechanisms to ensure senior-level accountability and control in instances where rules are inadequate.

Informal Evaluation Patterns

Because of the heavy responsibility he holds for their actions, a section chief must reach an accurate assessment of his subordinates' abilities. He is therefore compelled to seek as wide a range of opinions as possible. Not only do others in the organization bring different perspectives to this job of evaluation, they also can provide a kind of insurance for the section chief. Should one of his subordinates make a major error, and the section chief be brought to account for his misplaced confidence, his case would be strengthened if he had come to his opinion by a consensus process involving other people in the firm who share his view of the subordinate's abilities and in fact provided some of the data he used to evaluate him.

During young section members' direct contacts with other young managers in the firm, they are closely observed by the section chiefs of these other general class managers. Because section chiefs all need to get outside evaluations of their own section members' performance and seek to promote consensuses that can protect them against harsh criticism in the event of a large mistake by a subordinate, they take care to observe and evaluate the performances of subordinates of other section chiefs. They can then trade evaluations of each others' subordinates, spreading some of the accountability for evaluation of their own section members among their own status peers, other section chiefs. The accountability for granted departures is forced upward and then spread horizontally via this social mechanism.

Outside evaluation of subordinates is only one of the ways in which section chiefs come to depend on one another. The flow of goods and services inevitably makes sections depend heavily on other sections of the firm. The following two chapters will examine the ways in which the sections and other units of the sogo shosha are coordinated within the formal structure of the organization.

The Section in Overview

A section's task requires that its members work together in a coordinated and cohesive fashion. Even a simple transaction can require shipping, insurance, credit, pricing, delivery, inspection, and a wide variety of other subtasks to be packaged into a single deal. Often these aspects will be handled by several different members of the unit who must be prepared to closely work together and make complex trade-offs. Thus a *kachō* must build a strong sense of identity for the unit. The necessity of coordinating with other sections on more complex deals only magnifies this need for the section to have a sense of self.

A section manifests an organic structure. Tasks are not assigned to one particular person, nor is authority for particular decisions. The division of labor and relations among members are constantly evolving in response to the unit's internal and external conditions.

Under these conditions the maintenance of the unit's identity, morale, internalized understandings, its collective memories, myths, and unity vis-à-vis other units becomes a critical matter. As we noted in our discussion of leadership, it is the making of the group *as a whole* capable of meeting the demands made on it *as a group*, rather than the inspirational performance of the most difficult tasks on his own, which is the greatest challenge to a section chief. The importance and prestige of a leader derives from this function of being the custodian of group effectiveness, not from his abilities as an individual.

Because the knowledge, skills, networks, and other resources of the individual members of a unit change gradually in time, the leader must be frequently reallocating duties and responsibilities, exposing members to all aspects of a job, and giving them a base of shared experience. The personal growth and the professional development of unit members depend on this. If unit members' assigned tasks remain stagnant, they will be deprived of the breadth of experience crucial to their career development. They must continually be prodded to see their future in the organization as a continuing growth process. They come to incorporate this growth into their very identities.

The nature of this training and managerial development process fits well with the demands of sogo shosha strategy. Daily operations require many buying and selling decisions to be made rapidly, if not spontaneously. It is therefore necessary that managers have internalized a consistent "instinct" for business judgments. Because these buying and selling decisions are not made purely on their own individual merit but are related to a whole complex of other business factors, such as long-term relationships with various clients, they are not subject to "rational" quantitative analysis.

It is not enough for a manager to know how much profit his trade will generate; he must also know how that trade will influence other business the firm wishes to conduct with the same client, or with the client's competitors or supplier. Most of these relationships are long term and are governed by mutual commitment and trust rather than by contracts. Many of them are primarily managed by other subunits of the firm. Thus the relevant knowledge for a manager includes a knowledge of the human personalities involved in the relationship between the sogo shosha and its clients. He must have a feel for how they would react to various contingencies he might present and how his unit would respond to contingencies posed by the client.

The young manager thus faces a long, uncertain process of learning. The section chief and the older members of the section provide a rich and generally supportive environment for this to take place. Rivalry among members is discouraged by both formal and informal patterns of authority and promotion. The flexibility inherent in the lack of structured job slots and the "organic" approach to unit work allows a well-paced progression on increasingly sophisticated and judgmentally demanding tasks to be offered over the course of years.

11

Administrative Networks

This chapter begins our examination of the central aspect of the emergent organization of the sogo shosha: its use of interpersonal networks as a primary channel and tool of management. We believe that these networks are the single most important aspect of the management systems of the sogo shosha, and that they account for much of the institution's capacity to cope with diversity, complexity and change. Because they are most usefully analyzed as a part of the management system, we call these networks "administrative networks."

Administrative Networks

The concept of networks is a familiar one to sociologists, social anthropologists, and indeed the general public. It is easy to see in many situations that "whom you know does make a difference." Recording who knows whom—that is, tracing networks—is an obvious method of finding out how things get done and who has what kinds of power.[1]

But despite all their underlying importance, networks as a theoretical tool in the study of organizations are in their infancy. Two broad avenues of investigation exists. One is the sociometric approach.[2] It looks at the patterns and and at pairs of relationships within networks, trying to account for structural positions and specific ties between pairs of individuals according to easily measurable characteristics. As one might suspect, this approach tends to be heavily mathematical. The other approach is known as the ethnographic.[3] This method looks closely as specific sets of ties among people in a particular setting and tries to understand the nature and functions of the patterns of relationships observed. The little attention paid to networks as an aspect of management has largely been confined to governmental and quasi-public organizations, particularly in planning and social welfare.

Our treatment of networks in this chapter will fall within the ethnographic mode of investigation. Rather than attempt to map or otherwise measure specific networks, we will explain the genesis and utility of networks as administrative tools. Some of these administrative networks could also be called ego networks. That is, the relationship linking a manager (ego) with others (alters) in the organization are the point of departure. The sum of the ego networks of all members of a sogo shosha constitutes the overall structure of administrative networks. For the purpose of clarity, we will call ego "Mr. Tanaka" and alter "Mr. Sato" in our discussions here.

The defining characteristic of the relationships that make up an administrative network is that in the course of business, the managers are able to exchange contingent obligations with each other.[4] This means that a specific favor by Mr. Tanaka for Mr. Sato, performed in the present, is exchanged for the obligation to perform a reciprocal favor or favors in the future. The magnitude of the future reciprocal favor is contingent on the outcome engendered by the first favor. Figure 11.1 presents a schematic representation of this basic process.

We maintain that the systematic sharing and use of administrative networks underlies the ability of the sogo shosha to integrate its highly diverse and complex organization. Though the basic mechanism is simple, the practice is highly complex and primarily intuitively, and not consciously understood by the managers themselves. The abstract analytical construct of networks is entirely our own; never in the course of our interviews did a manager employ the same kind of terminology we use to describe the way in which information was channeled,

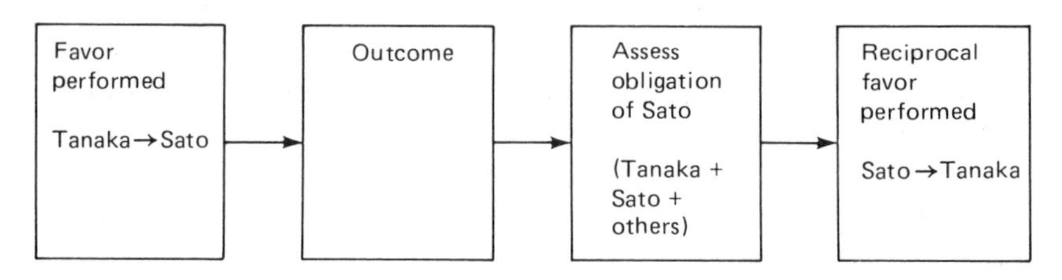

Figure 11.1
Schematic of a basic contingent obligation exchange

understanding created, or trade-offs made. The managers would at most speak of relationships and understandings. Nevertheless, we have found networks persuasive and useful as a way of understanding the otherwise inexplicable ability of the sogo shosha organization to act coherently. Managers in the sogo shosha to whom we have presented the scheme have also found it persuasive.

In order for contingent obligation exchange to work reliably as a component of administration, a number of conditions must be present. Commitment must exist between managers in an administrative network so that Tanaka believes Sato will try to reciprocate Tanaka's favor. Credibility must adhere to Sato, so that Tanaka will know Sato is capable of reciprocating, and to Tanaka, so that Sato will be sure he is participating in a worthy venture. There must be a mutual basis of understanding the nature and potential of the favor being performed. Finally, there must be agreement on standards of fairness in assessing obligation so that both parties can agree on what constitutes full reciprocation in the contingent future.

Commitment and understanding are the relatively static elements of the system.[5] They are preconditions for the system of exchange to operate, and as long as they are present at the minimally acceptable level, the system will operate. Credibility and obligation are the more dynamic elements. According to the outcomes of the particular exchanges these two elements increase or decrease, affecting future use and potential of the network.

Credibility may be defined as the ability to persuade another manager to enter into a contingent obligation exchange of a particular magnitude. Obligation is either positive or negative in nature. Positive obligation is a call on the energies and resources of another manager. Negative obligation is the liability to have one's own energies and resources called on by another manager.

An administrative network relationship is really an ongoing process made up of a series of transactions of the type pictured in figure 11.1. In most instances a perfect balance of positive and negative obligations is rarely obtained. Rather, a running account is kept of positive and negative obligations between a pair of managers. Similarly, as they interact, more data are generated which increase or decrease the credibility of each manager. Outcomes that go according to plan enhance credibility, and those that don't detract from it.

When these minimum conditions are present, managers can overcome the differentiation and conflicts of interest that impede unified coordinated action of subunits of the firm. This improves the ability of one unit to subordinate temporarily its immediate interest to the interest of another subunit, in order to enhance overall organizational interests in the longer run. Depending on the degree to which these overall interests are realized, the obligation owed to the first unit can be measured.

Subunit Interest

Two levels of analysis are involved: the individual manager and the subunit. In theory, the distinction is important; in practice, it tends to be blurred. Nearly all exchanges of obligation are between managers acting in behalf of their respective subunit's interests. Tanaka identifies his own benefit with that of the subunit in which he works. The lack of job slots, the heavy dependence on the unit leader for guidance and evaluation, and the strong cultural links between unit and group contribute to this. Morever, when Tanaka incurs an obligation to Sato, who works in another unit, the corporate culture strongly supports his unit's backing it up, or making good on it. The individual thus seems submerged in this subunit.

Yet, despite this blurring of the distinction between unit and individual, managers are very conscious of dealing with each other as individuals. One key to understanding this apparent contradiction is the time frame. In the short run Tanaka is a member of a particular subunit and can be regarded as a virtual extension of it in many ways. But in the longer run he will move on from the particular subunit to other assignments. In this longer run too he will carry with him the relationships and reputation he has built with Sato and all others with whom he has had obligation exchanges. Thus in the longer run he operates as an individual, though always in behalf of organizational subunits.

A second key to understanding the relationship between the interunit and interpersonal levels of analysis lies in the kind of discretion the *kachō* possesses. The structure of responsibilities give broad but vague charges to section chiefs and others running business. They must delegate discretion to section members. Moreover the nature of a sogo shosha's business, requiring on-the-spot decisions to be made quickly, also reinforces the discretion of an individual manager.

Thus, although he strongly identifies with and acts in behalf of his unit, Tanaka has some personal discretion which enables him to act as an individual in giving and collecting on obligation. Whether or not to research a request for a particular piece of information from an alter in another unit is basically a personal decision a manager makes. It is up to him to structure his use of time in a way that will best serve his own and the unit's interests. Despite the very strong relationship between unit and individual, individuality is not lost at a sogo shosha. Managers see themselves and others as individuals, and the exchange of obligation is primarily an affair between individuals who act as members of subunits.

Stable Framework

The career-long employment system is a major element in the ability of the administrative networks to work. In all cases sogo shosha managers are aware that they can expect to be dealing with each other as members of the same firm for the rest of their careers. They know that no one who owes them an obligation will unexpectedly leave the firm, leaving behind an unfulfilled debt that will have to go uncollected.

They also know that they will have to learn in detail about the individual characteristics, abilities, and judgments of the other managers with whom they deal. So many business operations in the sogo shosha require quick decisions based on partial knowledge and intuition that these individual attributes are of the greatest possible interest. The perspective of a thirty-five-year career stretching before a new manager offers the possibility of real depth of understanding between managers.

The building of networks into effective managerial tools is a long process, and many elements of the organizational structure, business activity, and cultural setting of the sogo shosha contribute to this development. We shall begin our examination of the network mechanism with a look at the origins of the network building process in the early stages of a managerial career.

The Emergence of Administrative Networks

As we have discussed earlier, most managers entering their first assignment in a section are put to work handling delivery of products to client organizations. In addition to teaching the young manager the characteristics of the product involved, this also puts him into direct contact with client personnel. His first business experience involves him in managing aspects of a domestic client relationship.

Business transactions between the sogo shosha and its Japanese clients are rarely primarily governed by contract but instead by long-term mutually beneficial transactions. The expectation of future benefit to be derived from such relationships and extensive contact between members of the respective firms at several levels of their hierarchies work to create pressures toward compromise on any dispute.

Delivery is a complex process. Activities of different parties in different locations must be closely coordinated. Loading, shipping, unloading, customs clearance, inland freight, inventory and storage, and other physical operations must occur in sequence. Insurance, financing, and other paperwork operations must also take place according to plan. The weather, human error, and countless other recurring factors insure that disruptions will occur. When disruption happens, the activities of the various parties must be recoordinated.

Delivery thus immerses Tanaka in a situation where he quickly faces the task of coordinating activity undertaken by clients, other subunits of the firm, and the firms working as suppliers of services, such as trucking companies. Of course Tanaka does not have the primary responsibility for the original decisions, nor does he have any real authority. But he is the one who must help handle rescheduling of unloading when ships are delayed at sea, who must help file insurance claims when goods are lost or damaged, or who must help client personnel find space to store excess inventory that piles up when shipments accidentally converge.

These activities place Tanaka in contact with staff sections of the sogo shosha that handle financing, insurance, shipping, and other services. The staff sections coordinate the buying of services to ensure that the firm uses its volume purchasing power as effectively as possible. They maintain ongoing relationships with providers of these services and are a reservoir of expertise.

Tanaka must ask them for advice and help in his coordinating activity when adjustments must be made. This is a situation in which network contracting becomes useful.

It is very often possible for these staff section alters to be of great service to Tanaka, enabling him better to serve his client. They can instruct him in the ways business is done, they can tell him who the key people are for him to contact in order to accomplish something, and they can use their own influence in his behalf. Since the staff section personnel have far greater expertise than he in their own field of specialization, he finds it easy and productive to consult them. Their help usually works out to his advantage.

But Tanaka soon finds that in return for this kind of help he accumulates obligations. There are many ways a young manager can make things easier for the other managers working in staff sections. Perhaps Mr. Sato of the shipping staff requests that he delay a subsequent shipment for a few days, in order to be able to consolidate it with the shipment of a different product out of the same port, so as to receive a lower shipping rate on a higher volume of cargo. If the cost in terms of inconvenience to the client is not too high, Tanaka will more than likely cooperate, even if it means extra work for him, involving rescheduling of a number of operations subsequent to unloading. He learns that he is paying off a contingent obligation. Directly and indirectly, the corporate culture encourages this behavior.

Other line sections of the firm also may become involved. Frequently clients deal with a sogo shosha for more than one product. If coal shipments to a steelmaker are subject to change, then iron ore shipments are also affected. At the delivery level there are numerous opportunities for young managers in related line sections to exchange small favors with each other. They often use the same transportation and other facilities, deal with the same or related client personnel, and affect each other directly in countless small and large ways. Once again a pattern of exchange is established whereby a favor is performed and the obligation collected later, whenever the opportunity or reciprocity arises.

Older *sempai* in the section and the *kachō* all play a major role in introducing a young manager to this use of a network of acquaintances throughout the firm. The "testing" of cadet managers encouraged by the corporate culture leads to frequent requests by them to more senior members of the section for help.[6] A frequent response is for the *sempai* to suggest talking with a particular person in another subunit of the firm who could be of help. In other words, the *sempai* shares a network relationship with his junior *kōhai*. It does not take the *kōhai* very long to figure out that he now owes an obligation to the person recommended by the *sempai* who helped him. The *sempai* rarely has to explain that a failure to live up to this obligation will injure the *sempai* as well as the *kōhai*.

Understanding Obligation[7]

In order for this early pattern of mutual favors, with payment deferred, to flourish and establish itself, it must rest on a foundation of agreement on the nature of obligation. The Japanese have developed a high level of awareness and sensitivity to implicit but bidding obligations, and they tend to measure them with care and exactness. This cultural raw material provides sogo shosha managers with concepts and rituals that help in using obligation as a medium of exchange among each other. Two concepts, *on* and *giri*, are essential to understanding the very large role a strongly internalized sense of obligation plays in determining interpersonal behavior in Japan.

On may be very roughly translated as "benevolence," for it is a favor extended by a superior toward an inferior without direct expectation of a repayment.[8] To some extent the extension of *on* by a superior justifies the superior's status. To carry out properly the role of superior, and meet the expectations of subordinates, one must know how to pass out *on*-producing favors.

A subordinate who regularly receives such benevolence from his or her superior, on the other hand, comes to owe an obligation that is difficult, if not impossible to repay. The only way to cope psychologically with the obligation is to offer utter devotion and loyalty. The perennially most popular traditional story for novels, plays, movies, and other artistic expression in Japan is "The Tale of the Forty-Seven Ronin," a legend based on an eighteenth-century fact, about forty-seven warriors whose lord was unjustly killed. To repay the *on* they owed to their superior, they spent years sacrificing everything, including their families, in order eventually to carry out a suicidal mission of revenge, killing the person responsible for their lord's death. The tremendous popularity of this tale is directly related to the Japanese fascination with the problem of repaying the obligation of *on* and with the dilemmas that arise when that obligation conflicts with other obligations, such as those to one's family.

On can be thought of as part of the cement that holds together important vertical relations. It binds superior and subordinate together in a web of emotionally tinged mutual obligations. Because the bonds are not susceptible to precise measurement, they are difficult to discharge, and therefore relatively enduring. The *on* a subordinate feels toward his superior can be a powerful source of motivation in work situations.

Giri is a much more mundane and measurable category of obligation. *Giri* is subject to precise calculation and repayment. In many senses it resembles the implicit trading of favors that goes on in any organization in any culture. What makes it distinctively Japanese, however, is the widely held agreement about the necessity of repayment, and the common understanding about what degree of obligation is produced by a particular act. In other words, all sides have a fairly precise sense of the implications of favors given and received. Repayment thus becomes virtually certain, as failure to live up to obligations is regarded extremely severely. Since group life is so important to the Japanese, few are willing to violate the commonly held sense of propriety by failing to discharge an obligation. In the business context this means that even informal bargains or trade-offs can occur with regularity and with certainty of repayment of favors rendered.

Career Progress and Selectivity: Rising Responsibilities and Rising Use and Selectivity of Networks

It becomes necessary for a manager to choose carefully, from among all those he does business with, those people with whom he will develop relationships capable of bearing the burden of a contingent obligation exchange. He must to some extent design his administrative network.

As Tanaka gains seniority and competence, his work is increasingly of a substantive deal-making nature, putting him in contact with ever-broader circles of management within the firm and its clients. His discretion, the range of uncertainty with which he must deal, and the time horizon within which he sees his goals achieved increase. The use of and need for administrative networks grow in parallel with this progress. As his discretion increases, so does his credibility. This increases the amount of obligation he can bargain for with others. As uncertainty increases, the importance of the contingent nature of the exchange also grows. As the magnitude, complexity, and scope of his activity increases and the time horizon in which results are achieved expands, the need for standards of fairness and the assurance that his alter will have the commitment become more pressing.

Network ties must bear an increasing burden as magnitude, complexity, and time horizon increase. Only those ties that are strong and growing stronger are capable of meeting the increasing challenge. A manager finds it ever more important to choose carefully which alters he will include in his emerging administrative network. He must, in other words, begin to design his own network.

A number of circumstances work to foster concentrated network ties among a limited group of managers. The Japanese language itself contributes to this tendency at the very earliest stage of relationship formation. The importance of nuance, the elliptical nature of the language, the richness of nonverbal cues, and the need to establish relative position, all require intensive groundwork to be laid before effective interpersonal communication can take place between two Japanese persons with no history of interaction. The sunk costs of establishing such relationships means that once this groundwork has been laid, there is a tendency to continue interaction with that person. It is simply easier than going out and establishing the groundwork for interactions with others. This contributes to an impulse to establish and use a network of persons with whom the ego shares an attribute that gives them an occasion for knowing one another.

As Tanaka experiences the daily give-and-take of delivery and other early assignments, he builds a social, linguistic, and business understanding of the managers in staff and line sections and also in client organizations. Familiarity builds rapport. Instead of deference, a secure relationship with each other allows the expression of frank opinions and disagreements to take place without disruption of the basic relationship. Verbal shorthands also develop. Relatively complex meanings can be described and understood quickly. The elliptical nature of the language is, used to a good effect, as special words, gestures, postures, tones, and the like, convey richness in a few words.

Most important, shared experience allows Mr. Tanaka and Mr. Sato a common base of reference for communications purposes and a history of testing each other to make the behavior of the other more predictable. Through this process they work out an understanding of the capabilities and limits of each other and define for themselves the meaning of obligation and the form of its discharge. They can test each other's mettle and learn how much value to place on the other's opinion or promise. They gain a sense of what the other will be capable of doing to discharge the various kinds of obligation that might be incurred in a career-long relationship.

This process also leads to a mutual commitment. Commitment has been conceptualized as a bet that promotes trust by making it disproportionately disadvantageous for one person to violate an agreement.[9] That is, the losses that would be incurred by reneging are seen as greater than the benefits to be gained by doing so. For two sogo shosha managers with an investment of time and energy accumulating in their mutual relationship, the costs of reneging continuously mount as the relationship continues over time. This is particularly true because time devoted to an existing relationship has as its opportunity cost the relative neglect of development of other relationships. The stronger a relationship is, the fewer and weaker the alternative relationships.

Moreover an obligation exchange relationship between two managers is a public one centered around the achievement of organizational tasks in which others are involved. This greatly increases the perceived costs of failure to live up to the other party's expectations of obligation fulfillment. Others become aware of the fact that a manager has failed to discharge an expectation that was created in another manager's mind. This alerts them to be cautious in dealing with him.

Both operations and development aspects of a sogo shosha require that managers from diverse parts of the firm be able to work together harmoniously without a formal system of administration to regulate allocation of profits, determine individual responsibilities, and the like. Under these circumstances the only way managers can work together with confidence is to rely on the credibility of each others' obligation to achieve long-term equity in the relationship. If word spreads that a manager does not live up to the expectations he has created, then others will be reluctant to compromise their own or their unit's interests in order to achieve a pressing goal that would benefit the entire firm. A manager who allows his own exchange relations with network members to deteriorate to the point where the others' lack of satisfaction becomes public, risks losing the ability to induce others in the firm to work with him in the future. Since he is committed to the firm for life and since his ability to produce new development opportunities is crippled by such a lack of ability to exchange obligation with others, the cost is very high indeed.

Thus two related but analytically distinct processes operate to reinforce the use of social contracting as an effective and reliable functional equivalent to formal administrative control systems as a means of regulating relationships. On the one hand, the individual exchange relationship becomes increasingly valuable as sunk costs rise and the potential opportunities to form other relationships decrease. Both parties' commitment to it ensures their adherence to its preservation. On the other hand, the nature of such relationships is ultimately public, and public disharmony in an obligation exchange warns others to be cautious about dealing with the disputees and increases the difficulty of their forming new exchange relationships or utilizing other established relationships. Thus both parties have an additional incentive to protect the harmony of the relationship.

It is also worth noting that when disharmony in an exchange relationship becomes public, both accuser and accused suffer. This is because the accuser is felt to bear responsibility for not having made his expectations clearer or managed the relationship smoothly. He can easily become known as someone who has "trouble" in his relationships and is therefore a risky person with whom to do business.

The mutual nature of blame in cases of disharmony acts as a powerful discipline to force any two parties to an exchange to work out their obligations between themselves. It tends to prevent managers from engaging in forms of blackmail and instead directs them to work out their problems within a very private sphere: if not alone with the other party, then with a third party who mediates.

Sogo shosha managers are vitally concerned with knowing the degree to which other managers are capable of working harmoniously with members of their own network. They want to know whose obligation can be relied on and who is likely to be difficult to deal with. Their business requires them to contact and work with others in order to produce the development opportunities that build the firm's business. It is not a matter of idle gossip; it is a practical necessity to learn of others' business experiences.

Managers are in continuous contact with each other around the world via telex, travel, and telephone. They use these opportunities to accumulate data about the character of various managers they may never have even met or know only superficially. Thus, what we call a "credibility rating" for each manager tends to emerge and become diffused as that manager's cumulative activities with other managers increase over time.

These credibility ratings receive an early start in the process by which a section chief seeks out opinions as to the capabilities of his section members. Recall that the section chief must bear responsibility for his delegation of authority to section members. This causes him to seek the opinions of the section chiefs of sections with which his subordinate has dealt. The section chiefs of these sections naturally rely on their own observations but are likely to supplement them with inquiries among the associates of the young manager in question. These associates, after all, are the ones dealing most intimately with him. A fairly widespread discussion of the capabilities of the young manager is likely to result.

This discussion involves section chiefs and their own subordinates in the evaluation of members of other sections. This process serves to teach the young section members the methodologies of evaluating other members of the organization. It also socializes them into the process of sharing their intimate opinions of other managers with members of their network.

The combination of a practical necessity for knowing the personal characteristics of other managers in the firm and an internalized shared process for reaching collective opinions on others' capabilities and trustworthiness leads to managers spending a great deal of time recounting their experiences with one another. Often these exchanges take place outside the office in a relaxed social setting, such as an eating or drinking establishment. Managers report, with few exceptions, that their social life centers around workplace acquaintances. When they travel of course they have many opportunities to meet other managers of the companies with whom they can share information.

Of course the impulse to utilize general assessments of credibility based on past performance is by no means limited to Japan or to the sogo shosha. A study of the capital budgeting systems of American firms reveals that "track record" may often play a significant role in the granting of funds for capital expenditures despite the existence of fully "rational" standards.[10] What is striking about the case of the sogo shosha, however, is the degree to which continuous informal evaluations of credibility are systematically produced and used as a means of control and decision making at all levels of the firm. Capital budgeting decisions after all are usually the province of a small group of managers near the top of a firm. Credibility can be taken into account because there is usually a long history of face-to-face interaction. In the sogo shosha the informal process of credibility analysis covers more people and becomes the substance of control and decision making, not just a supplement to formal systems.

This overall pattern is a system that requires broad subjective decisions about subordinates to be made by superiors in the hierarchy. But the superiors, in order to enhance and protect the subjective judgments being made about them by *their* superiors, must submit these judgments to the scrutiny of others before staking their own personal credibility on them. This process depends on the manager's initiative. The selection of the "reference group" which evaluations are traded is also up to the manager. He must act in whatever way he determines will enhance his own credibility in the long run.

Recalling that the sogo shosha business strategy requires managers to act on personal initiative, as entrepreneurs who must make difficult commercial judgments daily in behalf of the entire firm, there is an evident parallel between the credibility assessment and commercial transaction categories of decision. In both cases the decision criteria often are broad and never fully subject to rational analysis. These subjective decisions are often checked with a reference group chosen by the manager himself. In this reference group, managers face similar categories of decision, and as a result they exchange observations, both to deepen their understanding and to protect their own interests. As a result common analytical frameworks and standards of fairness in an obligation can emerge, further reinforcing the formation of a common corporate culture conducive to effective administrative networks.

12

Interunit Coordination

We have seen that the sogo shosha's distinctive activity is the building and managing of product systems. This involves coordinating the numerous clients and institutions that are in contact with different subunits of the sogo shosha. Vast amounts of information must be gathered and channeled to the appropriate persons within the sogo shosha. Complex trade-offs must be made under uncertain conditions. All of this means that the sogo shosha must develop its own ability to integrate itself to a high degree.

The mere fact that two subunits belong to the same overall organization is no guarantee that they can work together effectively. For any complex organization there is a tendency for subunits in contact with different portions of the external environment to develop their own distinctive styles, vocabularies, time horizons, values, and other differences. This process impedes their working smoothly with each other. Moreover different parts of an organization, as is the case in a sogo shosha, may often have interests that diverge or directly conflict.

Formal management control systems have the potential to impede as well as facilitate interunit coordination. Disputes over transfer pricing are one potentially serious source of interunit conflict in a sogo shosha.

The computerized accounting systems of the sogo shosha produce monthly profit-and-loss statements for the sections. These are arrived at by treating the sections for accounting purposes as if they were actually buying and selling to one another even if, as is often the case, the firm actually does not even take title to the goods it is handling. One section "buys" a product from its client, and another "sells" the same goods to its client. The difference between the two prices creates the gross margin of the firm, which can be split among the sections involved.

The split of the gross margin is a potential source of conflict among sections. It is after all a zero-sum game, where one section's gain comes at another section's expense. Usually there are transfer price rules or accepted practices that seem reasonable to all concerned. But problems develop, particularly where the division of labor among sections changes over time.

For this reason, as well as others, the accounting control system is not the primary governing mechanism of interunit coordination. These data are but only one input into the evaluation and coordination of section activity. These profits are watched by senior management as a concrete indicator of trends and activity. But the artificiality and the assumptions underlying profits are also acknowledged. There are numerous other considerations in understanding the total impact of what a section is doing. Just because they can't readily be quantified doesn't cause them to be ignored. Section profit-and-loss statements are not as important an element of the managerial system as they would be in many American firms.

Many other subtler problems also attend interunit coordination. Putting together a deal requires a series of very fine judgments. When a selling section negotiates a price with a buying client, it must have a good sense of how much in the way of price cutting, servicing, financing, or other concessions can be given to the buyer. The judgment of the selling client as well as the buying section serving that client must be understood. A poor decision could cause the other section much trouble in dealing with its client. Often there is no time to check, for an on-the-spot offer must be made while bargaining with the client.

Information is the basis for such judgments. Information gathering itself is a major activity of a sogo shosha. But deciding what kind of information would be useful and allocating the resources to go out and gather it requires another set of fine judgments. The kinds of information that are of greatest value require both initiative and time. Sometimes one subunit of the sogo shosha will request another subunit to uncover a certain piece of desired information. Other times a subunit will on its own uncover a piece of information that it knows would be of value to another part of the firm. Making sure that the most valuable requests are honored, and the less valuable ones ignored, and creating a situation where productive initiatives benefiting other subunits will be taken is a formidable challenge.

Forging a viable business entity out of the diversity of activities, orientations, and interests of its constituent parts requires a sogo shosha to find ways of channeling information, creating common understandings of the profit potential, and making the internal trade-offs necessary to take action. These all require close interunit coordination.

But our examination of the formal organization has revealed very few robust formal integrating mechanisms. Such decision channels and formal communications routes that do exist clearly play a subordinate role, functioning as checks and balances rather than as primary administative tools. The emergent system, the sum total of informal interactions created by the social system of the firm, has been spotlighted as the source of integration. As yet, however, we have no way of understanding how this emergent administrative system works to coordinate the subunits of the sogo shosha. Administative networks are produced by the interaction of the business strategy and task of a sogo shosha, the human resource policies and structures of the firm, and the culture shared by the managers. This managerial culture is a complex mix of ingredients. It is derived from Japanese culture, and from the particular organizational experiences of the firm.

Networks and Communications

Channeling information is one of the major problems facing the sogo shosha. With so many people generating so much information of potential importance to so many others, information overload becomes as serious a danger as lack of information. To be sure, there are regular patterns of information need in the operations side of business that can be handled by formal or informal established communications channels. A fairly predictable group of managers and subunits in the sogo shosha would have a continuing need to follow price and volume trends in metals trading in London, for example.

But for development of new business, on which sogo shosha profitability ultimately depends, formal communications structures would be counterproductive. Development requires, as its first step, creative juxtaposition of information and resources from different subunits of the firm, each dealing with its own unique product and geographic environments. The challenge to the organization is thus to provide a system that reinforces existing linkages necessary to operations while avoiding overloads, without precluding the creative urge to seek new combinations of data and resources.

Every manager in a trading section theoretically faces virtually infinite possibilities for gathering information and transmitting it to other units of the firm that might be able to use it. Every manager therefore must deal with the question of how to allocate his limited information-gathering and transmission capacity. Similarly every manager has a virtually infinite number of options in deciding what kinds of information requests to make of other units of the firm.

These concerns are not purely theoretical. Each of the sogo shosha spends tens of millions of dollars a year for communications. Each section and overseas branch receives far more inquiries seeking information and expertise than it could possibly handle completely. Some of these are purely routine of course, but it is precisely the nonroutine ones, often related to development opportunities, that call for special effort and extra time.

Each manager undertakes two types of information gathering for transmission to other segments of the firm: one is in response to specific requests from other units; the other is self-initiated. Networks are fundamental to both types.

Inquiries from other managers with whom a network relationship is established generally receive priority over other inquiries.[1] This is so for two reasons. First, a response involves an expenditure of a number of limited resources, particularly the manager's time. Managers prefer to receive a return on such a resource expenditure, and an established network relationship ensures that a return will be forthcoming, as well as substantial agreement on the fairness of the return. Exchanges with non-network members are much more problematical.

Second, the process of establishing a network relationship involves creating shared understandings. Two managers in a network relationship have previously discussed their business activities fairly extensively and are likely to understand the thinking and plans that might underlie a seemingly trivial request. For those communications that take place via telex, this background of shared understanding is especially important. Telex systems involve an economical form of wording that runs counter to the tendency of the Japanese language toward indirectness. Furthermore telex systems must be phonetic, and not use ideographic characters in their transmissions. Since the Japanese language has relatively few basic sounds, and abounds in homonyms, the very mechanics of the process can lead to confusion.* In these circumstances a telex is much more meaningful if the receiving party can "imagine the face of the sending party" (a recurring phrase heard in field interviews). Put at its simplest level a telex from a network member is likely to receive priority because it is more likely to be fully understood. The words and the thinking behind them are clearer than they would be coming from a stranger.

Networks and Interunit Coordination

Communication among different subunits is the first step in the process of developing and operating the systems of product flows that a sogo shosha coordinates. But these systems, particularly when they are being developed or when they must cope with environmental changes, require trade-offs to be made among the interests of clients and the sogo shosha subunits that deal with those clients. Networks play a key role in facilitating this coordination.

The overall interests of the firm lie in maintaining these systems, in enhancing its role within them, and in maximizing long-term profits to the firm from its role. As we have stressed throughout, it is extremely difficult to conceive of a formal or "rational" managerial system that could provide automatic guidance to managers in resolving the inevitable conflicts of interest that rise in these systems. There are simply too many contingencies, interdependencies, unquantifiable elements, and unknowns to allow for a formal analysis and decision based on the quantifiable results of that analysis.

But the very success of the sogo shosha as a institution indicates that the trade-offs involved in managing these systems

* The use of ideographs of course allows distinctions to be made among homonyms. Telex systems are not, however, usually equipped for 2,000 characters. Facsimile transmission, much more expensive and slower but coming into increasing usage, is a promising communications aid.

are not left to whim or chance. It is the use of obligation exchange among network members that is the structural basis for these trade-offs. Rather than describe the operations in abstract language, an example of obligation exchange in making a moderately complex trade-off in an established system subject to environmental change may be more useful. The following example is drawn from commodities trade. The example is hypothetical but is based on interview data.

Sogo shosha play an active role in the coffee trade, originally as a purchaser of beans overseas and a seller of beans to roasters and distributors in Japan. The drinking of coffee in Japan is a relatively recent phenomenon, as the traditional beverage has always been locally grown green tea. However, in the postwar era coffee houses, offering various distinctive blends of coffee and a relaxed atmosphere for conversation, have become popular. These coffee houses, buying their supplies from coffee roasters and distributors in Japan, depend on the quality of their coffee bean supply for much of their competitive appeal. Coffee is still somewhat a luxury commodity, and Japanese consumers are discriminating in its blend and brewing. Nearly all coffee houses offer at least five to ten different coffee blends and varieties for their customers to choose from.

In recent years a similar phenomenon has appeared in Taiwan, also traditionally a tea-drinking country. As in Japan this market has had to be carefully nurtured to take root and grow in the face of the traditional preference for tea. The sogo shosha sell coffee beans to customers in Taiwan. This trade is obviously part of what was earlier labeled third-country trade—that is, trade not involving Japan.

However, when coffee prices started spiraling in the 1970s and supplies from some areas became quite short or unavailable due to a severe frost in Brazil, the personnel involved in the coffee trade faced many problems surrounding the issue of where to sell the supplies of coffee they were able to obtain. On the one hand, the world market established prices on various coffee exchanges that from time to time offered opportunities for large trading profits on coffee inventory. But, on the other hand, the sogo shosha, the coffee roasters and distributors, and coffee houses in Japan and Taiwan have all made a considerable investment in cultivating a coffee-drinking public in those countries. Competition from tea, the traditional beverage, limits to some extent their ability to raise or hold down prices by cutting quality. How then is the sogo shosha to decide where to sell the coffee supplies it obtains, and at what prices?

The answer to this question lies in the ties of mutual understanding that the sogo shosha has built up among its personnel involved in the coffee trade, principally via the careful structuring of career paths. A manager in Brazil, for example, with a limited inventory of high-quality coffee, might face three basic alternatives: (1) selling to Taiwan at one price, (2) selling to Japan at another price, and (3) selling on the world market for an even higher price. His own trading unit would obviously show the highest profits if he selects alternative 3.

But the coffee manager in Brazil would have worked in Japan earlier in his career. In fact he most likely began his career in coffee by working on delivery of coffee to wholesalers, who in turn supply a myriad of coffee houses. In that capacity he very likely accompanied some of the sogo shosha's distributors as they delivered coffee to individual coffee houses, listened to the concerns of the coffee house operators, and heard their observations about the characteristics and preferences of the coffee-drinking public. There is also an excellent chance that he is still in regular contact with large coffee distributors in Japan. To them developments in key coffee-producing countries such as Brazil have a strategic importance. They therefore expect to receive a regular supply of data from their sogo shosha representatives in those countries.

Furthermore the coffee manager in Brazil knows that he will eventually be returning to Japan to work. There he will have to face the consequences if his decision is to cut off the Japanese customers that he and the sogo shosha have so carefully cultivated for so long and with whom the firm hopes to continue doing business well into the future.

A similar set of understandings applies to Taiwan, although since Taiwan is not home base, the coffee manager in Brazil may never have worked there. Nevertheless, the cultivation of the Taiwan market has been established as a priority by the headquarters section with worldwide responsibility for coffee. Compared to Japan, its growth prospects may be better, as the market is at an earlier stage of development. The manager for coffee in Taiwan is also a veteran of coffee operations in Japan and will eventually return to Japan to work, perhaps alongside the coffee manager from Brazil. He must therefore respect the priorities established by the headquarters section.

Thus, when the coffee manager in Brazil considers options 1 and 2, and weighs them against 3, his mind must weigh many other factors besides the short-term profit of his unit in Brazil. He will undoubtedly receive communications from the coffee managers in Taiwan and Japan, stating the importance of supplying the steady customers in those two countries. The fact that all these people share not only a common national and corporate cultural background but have had similar work experience and training in Japan enables the various dimensions of the problems to be communicated with relative precision. All share a similar undersanding of the importance of short-term profits versus care of customers who are dependent on supplies from the sogo shosha's carefully cultivated distribution network. It is up to the Brazil manager to handle the trade-off in such a way as to maintain a smooth working relationship among all the parties. The fact that all three managers expect to rotate through a variety of assignments to various geographical units helps them to think first of the welfare of the total system, rather than the narrow interest of their own geographic unit. Also personal contact in their travels and transfers provide many social opportunities to smooth over rough edges.

Implicit or explicit bargaining may also go on. If the Taiwan manager, for example, feels it is crucial to supply his customers or else risk losing them, he may be willing to incur a relatively high debt of obligation to persuade the manager in Brazil to send supplies to him. The manager in Japan might also make the same offer. In effect they both make bids in an internal auction. However, the terms of this auction will, for the most part, be unquantifiable. The measure of a bid is not necessarily money but rather the credibility of the manager making the bid. A manager whose credibility is high is assumed to know the objective importance of his goal, compared to the importance of the goals of the others whom he is bidding against. Furthermore, if his bid is successful, he possesses the personal and organizational resources to make a full payment, in the future, of the favor done to him. Because he must make a repayment, each manager has an incentive not to overstate the importance of the immediate goal at hand. Furthermore, since all the managers share a career-long commitment to the firm and will likely to be working in the coffee (and related products) trade for many years to come, they all share an interest in seeing the long-term profits of the coffee-trading business rise. A manager who insists on getting his way, and is ultimately seen to have done so at the expense of overall profitability, will incur a particularly heavy obligation and will have diminished credibility with which to discharge his obligations. The precise nature of the obligation incurred thus changes over time, according to the perceived results of the outcome of the bidding.

In the end the decision reached, whether option 1, 2, or 3, will be one that has been carefully considered and weighed as to the overall benefits to the firm. Each manager serves as an advocate for his own unit's interest, but each also shares a set of intuitive understandings about the general interests of the firm. Only by having this decision made by a group of managers who share a common cultural base, a similar set of work experiences, and the expectation that all will eventually return to Japan to work together could such delicate trade-offs occur rapidly and precisely without damaging their working relationship.

This example well illustrates the routine nature of many of the problems in which networks and exchange of obligation can be put to use. The process of bidding is an extremely subtle one, for the actors involved know each other well and have a history of making many such trade-offs. The process of settling accounts is likewise drawn out. The person whose activities contribute to overall, longer-range goals has less obligation to repay for getting his view favored than does the person whose activities hurt overall profits. Overall profits in the commodity or geographic unit are a shared priority. If overall profits of the unit are high, all unit members receive some credit from other units of the firm. The person within the unit whose actions are perceived to have led to high profits thus is able to repay out of the resources so created the obligation he incurred in the process of getting his views accepted. In this way some managers can accumulate much greater stocks of others' obligation than most managers. This accumulation translates into an even higher credibility rating, and a consequent ability to get others to follow one's wishes.

Second-Level Access to Networks and Intermediation

The transactions of which we have spoken so far have all required face-to-face interactions between two managers, in order for credibility to exist, so that the contingent nature of the exchange can be faced with equanimity. But with 5,000 career managers scattered about the globe, working in different industry environments, it is obviously impossible for a manager to have network relationships with every other manager with whom he might profitably exchange obligation. Career paths are structured so that network relationships can be established with those managers in areas with which interactions are likely to be relatively frequent. But the innovative linking of units, which produces the new business on which the firm's long-term prosperity depends, requires new connections to be made among formerly unrelated units of the organization.

One way in which these links (involving information initially, but interest trade-offs eventually) are forged is by what we term "second-level access" to networks. This simply means that when two managers need to be linked together for the first time, a third manager, who is linked to both by networks, can stand as an intermediary. It may be necessary to use two or three more managers before a specific pair can be linked, but given a universe of 5,000 lifetime members, most linkages should require only one or two intermediaries.

In becoming an intermediary a manager may perform some duty as an interpreter of meaning, but his primary function is to offer assurance that any obligation incurred will be repaid. He stands as a guarantor of the relationship, substituting his own credibility for the lack of mutual credibility between the two managers who would link up. He can do this because each of the two parties already has a stake in an established relationship with him, and each knows that the other party stands to lose this valued relationship if he fails to repay any obligation.

It is not essential that the guarantor be a superior of the parties he links together, but there are good reasons why a superior is especially qualified for this role. First, by definition, in a seniority-based system a superior has longer experience in the firm. Therefore the superior has had more opportunities for network building and is likely to have a more extensive network. When searching for a "linking pin,[2] one is more likely to be found located at a higher level of the hierarchy. Furthermore the hierarchical pyramid is narrower at higher levels, so a superior has more direct access to broader segments of the pyramid.

Second, a superior, because of his access to greater organizational resources via his formal authority and his networks, is likely to have a higher level of individual credibility. This means that he is perceived as being able to repay higher levels of obligation. Such a person is obviously more desirable as a guarantor than one who may not be able to readily pay back a "bad debt."

Third, because relationships among status equals are inherently less defined and somewhat uneasy in Japan's "vertical society," it is relatively easier and less threatening to use a pair of vertical hierarchical relationships as the intervening link when establishing a new "horizontal" relationship between two status equals. There are many analogues to this in traditional Japanese culture, such as the custom of using a person of superior status as ritual intermediary (*nakōdo*) when bringing together two prospective marriage partners.

But intermediation is not limited exclusively to superiors. There are strong incentives encouraging everyone with the requisite network linkages to act as intermediary in the facilitation of second-level access. Both of the parties so linked realize that the intermediary has placed his own credibility at risk to enable them to work together. At a minimum, if the intermediary should someday require access to someone in either of their networks, they would be duty-bound to reciprocate and put their own credibility at risk in order to facilitate the linkage. Note that in return for one such facilitation, the intermediary receives a counterpart obligation from *two* others. The intermediary can ask both the ego and the alter to use their networks on his behalf. Access to his one network is "traded" for access to two other networks.

The intermediation function is capable of producing large amounts of positive obligation for the intermediary, if the relationships and transactions facilitated prove to be fruitful. More often than not, the intermediary's initiative and judgment play an active and important part in the development of the business possibilities inherent in the new linkage. This increases the obligation owed to him beyond mere access and credibility-guaranteeing to include initiative and energy in the subsequent reciprocity.

Although an ego may sometimes approach an intermediary and ask to be introduced to a specific alter in the intermediary's network, this is not the only pattern. It is likely that the ego often approaches the intermediary and asks if he knows anyone who could use a specific piece of information, join a specific transaction, or otherwise link with the ego in a useful business relationship. This requires an intermediary to use considerable knowledge and judgment in knowing who has the requisite information, capabilities, and position. It also requires him to gamble that the two, the ego and the alter he proposes, are capable of working together effectively. For if the relationship he suggests comes to naught, the ego and the alter will likely think less than highly of his intermediation skills. Depending on his role, they may even feel that their time has been wasted by the intermediary. At a minimum the intermediary's credibility would suffer, and fewer managers could be expected to approach him in the future in search of intermediation.

But if the intermediary has a network that includes capable managers in key positions, if his knowledge of them and their capabilities is deep, and if he is creative in understanding innovative business possibilities, then he can effectively link managers and realize rich returns for his intermediation. The number of managers he has future access to expands geometrically through the doubling effect. The net positive obligation owed to him also expands due to the doubling effect.

Intermediation is attraction enough that many managers can be expected to use their own initiative in approaching two other managers to suggest that the intermediary facilitate a linkage that has occurred to neither of them. If such active intermediation is to be successful, both of the other managers must share a high personal opinion of the intermediary's credibility. The successful intermediary must also be knowledgeable and creative enough to see possibilities that had not occurred to the persons most directly involved in the contemplated deal. If the intermediary meets these requirements, and if the relationship proves successful, the obligation owed to him by both becomes correspondingly higher.

An intermediary is not necessarily restricted to bringing together just two managers. If his network and capabilities are great enough, he can link three or even more managers together in more complex relationships. This type of activity lies at the very heart of the sogo shosha's ability to perform its most complex entrepreneurial activity: systems development.

Intermediation and Development

In chapter 4 we distinguished two aspects of a sogo shosha's activities: operations, the facilitation of exchanges within existing product systems, and development, the modification or creation of product systems. Intermediation, which brings together managers who previously did not have network relationships with each other, allows new patterns of linkage to be explored, which can lead to the innovative combinations of resources constituting development activity.

For example, a modification of the broiler chicken production system discussed in chapter 4 might occur as follows. Mr. Suzuki learns of the availability of underutilized Canadian feed-mixing facilities from Mr. Tanaka, a member of his network. He learns from Mr. Sato in his network that a need for reasonably priced feed-mixing capacity exists within the current broiler production system. He puts Tanaka and Sato in touch and urges them to explore an arrangement, to see if it makes economic sense. If it does, Mr. Suzuki then may have to contact Mr. Yamamura and Mr. Nakamura, grain-buying and shipping experts, respectively, to explore the impact on them of a switch to Canadian facilities. Mr. Kato, who handles the relationship with Japanese feed mixers, will certainly also have to be involved.

As this group explores the impact of the contemplated change on themselves, their units, and their clients, the long-term and short-term effects will become clearer. Some of the managers will find that their shorter-range interests suffer. For example, Mr. Kato might lose both business and goodwill with his Japanese feed-mixing clients. Kato will have to be compensated. It may be possible to structure the deal so that compensating profits will flow to Kato's unit out of the new arrangements. But if this is not the case, then Kato will probably be given a call on the obligation of the person(s) who benefits most from the new situation. This would most likely include Mr. Suzuki.

But Mr. Kato may not wish to wait for his compensation. It might require years before an opportunity would occur for Suzuki to repay him personally. In that case he may be offered an obligation of a person who already owes Suzuki a comparable obligation. This new manager, Mr. Mori, may be in a position to compensate for Mr. Kato's losses immediately, if Suzuki handles the situation skillfully. Suzuki can treat the obligation as a fungible commodity and reach into his stock and even out the rough edges produced by such complex changes.

At least some of the contingent aspect to the transaction remains, even the case of immediate repayments. If Mr. Mori's concession to Mr. Kato proves extraordinarily valuable to Kato, then all would recognize that Kato would actually owe Suzuki a compensating obligation in the future. The amount would be subject to continual recalculation as events change the values of obligations granted.

Clearly the intermediary role is crucial to development activities. Intermediaries such as Mr. Suzuki are the prime movers in bringing together diverse managers, knowledge, and resources, creating the joint understanding of the long-term profit potential, compensating for short-term losses of individual managers and units, and unifying action and purpose among those involved in the deal.

The skills and attributes necessary for an intermediary are the same skills and attributes necessary for any successful network relationship. The intermediary must earn credibility and obligation from members of his network. But he must also be able to persuade them to accept each others' obligations. He must also have the skill to choose network members who are located in functions that might be creatively and profitably combined in innovative ways. An intermediary must possess formidable communications skills. Not only must he have a range of shared understandings with each individual member of his network, he must be able to cross-fertilize those understandings and create a common shared experience and vocabulary for the group.

The intermediary must be a judge of personality, able to read signals, and also know whose signals could be read best by whom. He cannot ask two managers who are personally incompatible to work closely together. He must know who would be excited by whose ideas or experiences, and who wouldn't.

Intermediation allows a manager to become involved in far more activity than he could be if he had to negotiate everything personally. The doubling effect increases his proportional rewards. But substantial risk is present. If the deals don't work out as intended, he could find himself owing substantial obligation. The risk is particularly acute because he cannot be personally involved in everything. He has to have faith in the ability of the managers he has brought together to work things out successfully. Of course in addition to faith, if he hears of trouble developing, he can choose to intervene actively, applying then his credibility, insight, and obligation to the most difficult problems.

Successful intermediation is desirable from the point of view of both the firm and the would-be intermediary. A combination of personal incentives and corporate goals is the key factor in the ability of the emergent organization to produce a steady stream of development opportunities, overcoming the many obstacles to integrating such a highly differentiated organization.

As we noted, it is often superiors who act as intermediaries for subordinates. But this is not necessarily always the case. The seniority-based system at the sogo shosha may contain subordinates who are in fact more widely respected and known than their nominal superiors. As we noted, there is every incentive for the superior to facilitate, not obstruct, the capable subordinate in such situations.

Far more important than formal status to the success of an intermediary is the initial accumulation of a substantial stock of credibility and obligation and the creation of a network of managers who are both capable and well-placed within the firm. If development, the key activity of a sogo shosha, is to occur regularly, then there must be a mechanism for regularly creating critical masses of credibility and obligation in the hands of managers who can create and augment valuable networks.

Self-Reinforcing Dynamics: Networks, Power, and Promotion

After a few years in a sogo shosha a young manager like Mr. Tanaka comes to understand the value of network relationships with other managers of high credibility like Mr. Sato. Not only does high credibility ensure that Sato's obligations will be paid off, it indicates that Sato will be able to attract a wide group of other managers, who, like Tanaka, wish to have high-credibility network members. Thus Sato's network is likely to be extensive.

A manager with an extensive network like Sato is a highly desirable network member. He can bring enhanced opportunities to other managers. Acting as an intermediary, Sato can introduce Tanaka to new, high-credibility managers who can enter Tanaka's network. Network relationships with high-credibility managers can lead to an expansion of Tanaka's own network.

The obligation of a high-credibility manager with a large network tends to be worth more than other managers' obligations, and it also is more likely to appreciate in value over time. The larger a manager's network, the more people and resources he can mobilize by expending his obligation. This enables him to repay an obligation faster by offering the services of someone in his extensive network who owes him an obligation.

This process has a strong tendency toward self-reinforcement. As more people are attracted to the high-credibility manager, his obligation becomes worth more. This in turn attracts more people. The more people who think highly of him, the more people will know of his high credibility and will in turn become interested in establishing potential relationships with him.

The lucky manager in this position finds people bringing him information and opportunities, in the hope of establishing or using a network relationship with him. Because he sees more opportunities, he has the chance to develop the ability to distinguish between good and mediocre opportunities and people. This enables him to augment further his credibility and obligation stock by offering his valued opinions to others.

This process corresponds exactly to the growth in the abilities that is required for promotion to the higher executive class ranks. In other words, the rise in credibility and network size may well be the single most important determinant of promotability in sogo shosha management ranks, particularly for positions above section chief. Of course the speed of promotion to section chief is also determined by the perceived ability to rise further in the organization.

Recall that above the level of the section, there is no formal handling of operations. The hierarchy, in other words, exists to facilitate the integration of the work carried out by the lower-level line units, the sections. This view of course fits well with the traditional function of an authoritarian hierarchy as an integrative mechanism. However, the actual process by which the hierarchy brings about the integration of the sogo shosha contrasts strongly with the process in an authoritarian hierarchy. It is not the formal authority of a superior that enables him to coordinate the work of subordinates by fiat. Rather, his personal credibility assures them that any informal understanding about the short- and long-term division of resources generated by their efforts will be perceived as roughly equitable.

Promotion decisions for department chief and higher-level managers require the concurrence of the personnel department and perhaps some top-level corporate executives, with the final decision authority for these line promotions sometimes resting officially with the president. It was not possible to explore individual promotion decisions at the senior levels of the firms, due to the obvious sensitivity of these matters. However, it would seem inevitable that when the president or other top-level executives seek to check on the qualifications of a manager under consideration for promotion, they would have to make direct and indirect inquiries about the abilities of the manager. Members of the manager's network would be in the best position to provide the most complete evaluation, for they have worked with him. Presumably in most cases they would lend support to his promotion, for it is usually in their interest to have a network member receive promotions. In this way an extensive network made up of well-regarded individuals enhances the promotability of a manager.*

The structure of age and rank in the sogo shosha is such that there is ample time for a widespread assessment of a manager's network to be made before promotion to senior levels takes place. Approximately fifteen years is required before promotion to section chief is achieved by even the fastest rising manager. For promotion to department chief, the next full level of the hierarchy, twenty years appears to be the practical minimum. At each stage in the promotion process, there are many opportunities for a manager to demonstrate his ability to use his networks to integrate and form new businesses.

Networks are the basic resource a manager has to produce profitable business for the firm. Therefore most likely those

* The tendency of network members to lend support to one another can easily lead to the formation of competing self-conscious factions, each bitterly contesting every promotion not in its own favor. Avoiding factionalism is a constant challenge to top management.

managers with the best networks will also have the best record of business development, for without networks a manager is severely handicapped in structuring deals.

The more deals a manager is able to bring about using his network, the more committed will network members be to his promotion. The higher he is promoted, the greater value of their network tie to him. The fact that they devote more of their limited time and energies to working with him, rather than with other managers, means that they have a stake in his promotion. Thus they are likely to provide support that will filter upward and provide an indication to senior managers as to the consensus on the abilities and promotability of the particular manager in question. Thus do networks influence promotion.

Networks and Factions

There is an obvious danger that networks could be so grouped as to form rival factions made up of clusters of managers at parallel positions throughout the firm, with each faction arrayed against the other in competition for attractive deals, promotions, and other rewards. Sogo shosha managers are much aware of the dangers of factionalism and have reported in our interviews that important factions do not exist in their firms.

Factionalism is a prominent feature of many Japanese bureaucracies, so it is worthwhile to look at the reasons for the reported lack of factionalism in the sogo shosha. The fact that a firm is so widespread, and that new deals require initiative from either the buying or selling unit, encourages a greater diversity of linkages than if it were a centralized bureaucracy with all of its staff in one location. If a manager in Hiroshima needs to find a copper source in Chile, he may have no alternative than to go through the sole copper manager in Santiago, regardless of that manager's factional affiliation. If they are able to make a deal, then both managers will have a mutual benefit to share. Decentralized initiative thus creates opportunities for cross-cutting ties, which would weaken factions.

Sogo Shosha managers have an extraordinary range of contacts with many other Japanese companies. They are in a position where they can observe the debilitating nature of factional conflict. Therefore they probably have an unusual degree of awareness of the dangers of factionalism. Furthermore they understand that in their business a manager is severely handicapped if his access to some areas of the firm is curtailed. Personally, and from the standpoint of the interests of the firm as a whole, they see factions as a danger and are wary of any nascent factions.

All the sogo shosha have absorbed managers of many similar trading firms during the reconsolidation phase of the sogo shosha sector in the 1950s (see chapter 2). During this period it was essential to discourage factionalism if the firm was ever to be able to operate coherently and reap the benefits of size.

Thus the senior managers in particular are very wary of factions and experiment in transfer and promotion patterns that encourage cross-cutting ties whenever factionalism threatens to develop. Ultimately it is this strong consciousness, along with the need for decentralized initiative and the individual manager's need to have access to the greatest number of other managers, that serves to keep factionalism in check.

The most obvious divisions in the sogo shosha organization could occur in product areas that tend to have relatively self-contained rotational patterns and deal with very different environments. In a period of less than twenty years—a little more than half the career span of a manager—the textile business has gone from rich profitability to threadbare survival. The six sogo shosha firms have had to manage the gradual liquidation of their textile businesses which comprised once one of their largest product areas.

The declining fortunes of the textile sector in Japan has been due to factors largely beyond the control of any sogo shosha. Of course the firms have taken actions to protect their own involvement in the sector. The promotion of foreign investment in mills in low-wage areas is one example of this. To some extent the textile divisions have been able to adapt. Nevertheless, the importance of textiles to Japan and the sogo shosha has been declining in ways that the sogo shosha cannot change.

For the younger managers assigned to textiles, in particular, this has been a depressing prospect. They do not wish to see their future tied to a declining segment of the firm—where promotions will be particularly difficult due to a lack of openings in upper-level positions and an excess number of experienced senior managers. Thus young managers have every incentive for finding ways to link their fortunes to other product areas. For example, by active involvement in promoting synthetic fibers, a younger textile manager in the 1950s or 1960s could work with chemical and machinery units of the firm as well as clients involved in these areas. Or, by becoming involved with machinery, he could gradually expand his competence to include nontextile machinery.

The sogo shosha has no particular wish to keep a surplus of young members involved in declining sectors. Expanding sectors can always use good talent. Thus to some extent it is possible for a younger manager to maneuver his way out of a declining sector by means of his own initiative. Senior managers in the textile division might be unhappy about all of this, but they evidently were able to see that the long-range fortunes of the firm were best tied to other sectors. Issue-by-issue skirmishes most certainly must have occurred. But the industry succeeded in transferring resources out of textiles. Veterans of the textile sector can be found working in a wide variety of other positions, mainly staff positions.

Prestige among product areas is largely a matter of that area's growth record and prospects. The faster an area is growing, the more opportunities managers in that area will have to offer deals to other managers in the firm. Particularly in basic industries, such as petrochemicals and metals where the products can be used in almost any other product sector, the opportunities to offer deals to other managers have been particularly abundant.

13

Interfirm Coordination

Networks Outside the Trading Operations

Having identified work networks as a pervasive and fundamental process of management at the sogo shosha, we can expect similar patterns of interaction to be found linking the sogo shosha with other firms in its product systems. Although weaker than network ties within the trading network, these external networks can nevertheless play a significant role in the coordination of separate firms, which is among the important functions of a sogo shosha.

Integrating Subsidiaries and Affiliates

A network of subsidiaries and affiliates made up of hundreds of firms in Japan and overseas performs activities related to trade but not so closely integrated to the operations of the entire trading network as to require inclusion in the same organization. Delegating peripheral operations to different corporate entities in the form of subsidiaries and affiliates has the great advantage that it allows the core staff to be kept relatively smaller than it would be if it had to manage these other operations directly. It also keeps the core staff "purer"; it has few nontrading activities. If the core staff were expanded to manage the subsidiaries and affiliates directly, it would become significantly more difficult for individuals to have networks large enough to maintain the current level of integration.

Both formal and informal mechanisms exist for integrating the subsidiaries and affiliates. The formal mechanisms consist of three different channels for reporting information to the trading network. None of these is relied on extensively, however. Informal mechanisms sort out and unify the information being dispersed via the formal channels.

The first formal link is related to legal ownership. For subsidiaries and affiliates overseas, ownership lies in the hands of the locally incorporated trading subsidiary. Overseas affiliates send reports to one of the six regional general managers. These reports are relatively brief, on the order of shareholder reports.

The second formal link for subsidiaries, overseas and domestic, is to a staff unit at the corporate headquarters which monitors developments to bring significant matters to the attention of senior management. This staff unit typically receives operating reports twice a year and also three-year business plans. Additionally it would have the right to screen all proposed investments, product changes, and other major decisions of affiliates and subsidiaries. The type of review and approval is similar to that conducted by the staff of a highly decentralized U.S. conglomerate, which attends to only a few key financial measures. Typically, however, the headquarters staff units are too small to supervise closely the hundreds of affiliates and subsidiaries, with their tens of thousands of employees. Naturally the firms with special problems receive the lion's share of their attention.

The third, and most important formal link to the trading network, runs to the product line group most closely linked to the business area of the subsidiary or affiliate. The product groups hold the primary responsibility for the profits and losses of subsidiaries and affiliates. The product groups receive the same reports as the affiliates division but also get monthly operating reports. This gives them more immediate information on developments in the subsidiaries and affiliates.

The informal links that grow out of this third and most important formal tie with the trading network provides an even more important channel of integration and control. Core staff members from the product groups may be temporarily loaned to the subsidiaries.[1] Currently about 15 percent of the total core staff is on loan to subsidiaries and affiliates. Of course not every loanee goes from a line group to a subsidiary that the line group supervises, but this is the most common case.

A person loaned out to a subsidiary or affiliate will be able to use his personal network of contacts throughout the firm to great advantage. Contacts in the trading network may notify him of market changes, technical developments, or other information they come across, which may be useful, even vital, to the subsidiary's business. When the subsidiary needs to mobilize consensus support within the parent trading company for a major move, for instance, the personal network in the parent may again prove very useful. The personal credibility of the person loaned out, as well as debts of obligation he may hold, may be used to ensure support.

Figure 13.1 presents a schematic of the predominant relationships under this informal system. Subsidiaries and affiliates are linked to a specific product group as the group's staff members are loaned out to them. These staff members enable the subsidiaries and affiliates to make use of the well-established links that integrate the sogo shosha product organizations. Thus subsidiaries and affiliates make a kind of secondary use of integrating systems of the trading organizations.

From the point of view of the parent, particularly the line division most closely related to the subsidiary's business, the loaned-out manager serves as an excellent informal conduit of information, coordination, and control. He is likely to be quite influential in the subsidiary because of his access to the parent. He can subtly use this position to influence the strategy and operations of the subsidiary in ways favorable to the interests of line units in the parent.

Most people on loan to a subsidiary anticipate being returned to the trading network within a fairly short time. For those whose assignments to subsidiaries come late in their careers, the bulk of their careers will have been spent in the parent, and they are likely to identify more strongly with it. Thus the person loaned out usually represents the interests of the parent to the subsidiary.

The "loanee" is in an excellent position to pick up various kinds of information that may be useful to the trading network. In this way he can at least partially repay the obligations he incurs when calling on members of his network to help the subsidiary. It should be kept in mind, however, that most subsidiaries deal with relatively well-defined and fairly specific areas of business, so the opportunities for extensive collection of information important to others will be limited. Therefore most people on loan fear that they will end up with a net deficit of obligation for the period of stay in the subsidiary. They

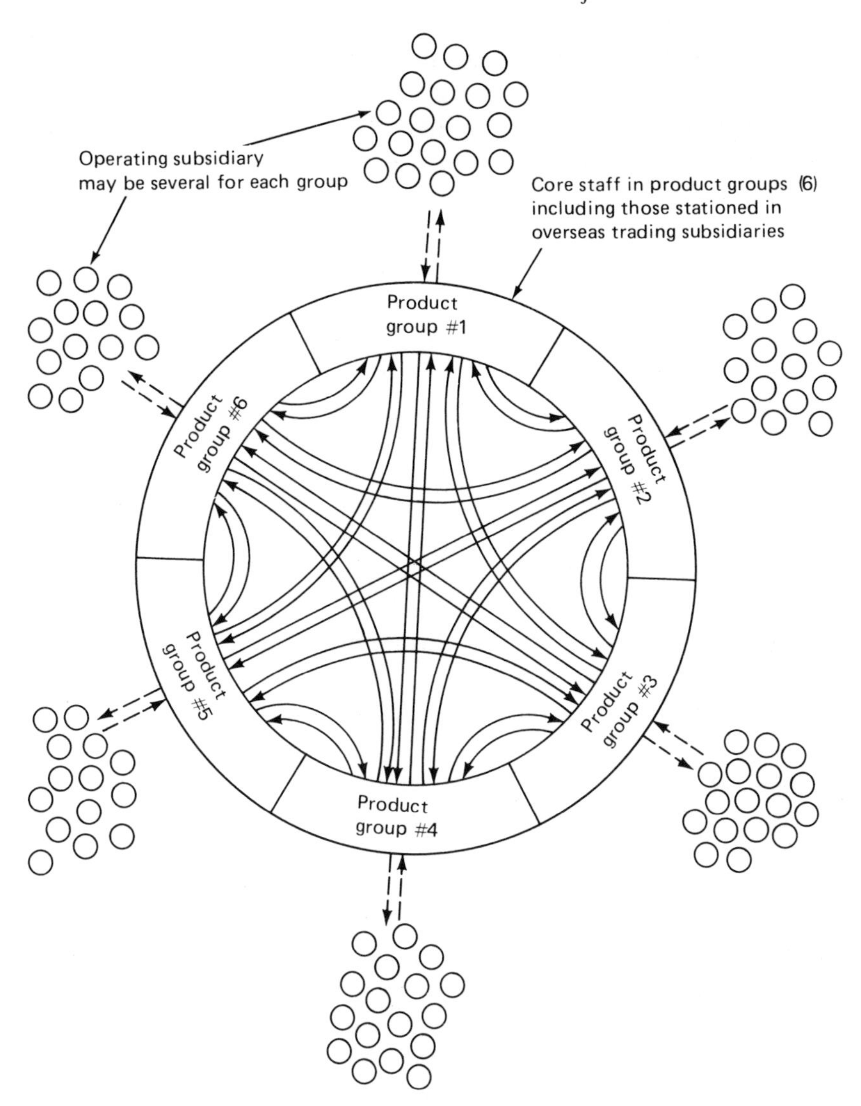

Figure 13.1
Schematic of product group, subsidiary, and affiliate patterns of coordination at a sogo shosha

simply won't be able to pass along information and influence equal to that which they receive. This may be an important underlying reason for the policy of limiting most stays in subsidiaries to a period of about three years.

In addition to these other functions the network of subsidiaries and affiliates serves to leverage the scarce resource of core staff members. Each one can manage his own personal network within the subsidiary and serve as a link between the network and his former network in the trading system. The subsidiaries also provide a place for those core staff members whose talents would not be best used within the trading system. Since the company has an obligation to provide careers for all those it hires into the core staff, and since not even the most rigorous selection process can ensure that everyone hired will be able to meet the many demands placed on those in the parent company, the subsidiaries serve the useful function of offering a wide variety of positions that do not make all of the same demands as those placed on a line manager.

Networks Outside the Firm: Parallel Hierarchies[2]

Thus far we have seen that networks of personal contacts within the firm function as the heart of the informal managerial system. Without these networks the organization would be unable to perform many of the more sophisticated or subtle tasks of coordinating its economic strategy. In this section we will examine the informal personal networks made up of persons *outside* of the firm, which the sogo shosha's management are able to use as mechanisms of integration beyond the formal boundaries of the firm. Because of their great importance in sustaining the business of a sogo shosha, they are worthy of careful examination.

In structuring its personnel system around permanent employment, seniority, and lack of individual job slots, the sogo shosha follows the norm for Japanese administrative and managerial organizations, both private and governmental. This fact has important consequences for the nature of institutional relations between a sogo shosha and its clients. The same patterns would also apply to a sogo shosha's relations with its major lenders or relevant government bureaucracies.

The management structures of all these bureaucracies can be thought of as "parallel hierarchies." That is, people who entered each bureaucracy can be expected to have contemporaries who entered the others in the same year and who are at approximately the same levels of responsibility and discretion. These parallel seniority structures have a powerful effect on the behavior of individuals within these parallel hierarchies in forming ties with each other. Moreover, because seniority-based promotion is so common in Japan, these contemporaries can be expected to be promoted at roughly similar rates. These ties profoundly influence the nature of overall relations between a sogo shosha and client organizations.

Recall that a young core staff member in a line section will usually be assigned to delivery duties first, putting him in direct contact with members of client organizations. In large organizations invariably some of the people a young core staff member deals with in such assignments are in positions comparable to his: young elite recruits, graduates of top universities, slated to rise gradually to significant high-level responsibilities in their firms. There are many reasons why it would be mutually advantageous for these young candidates for future responsibilities in the two firms to form close and enduring ties for the duration of their respective careers.

First, the relationship between the sogo shosha and its client is a long-term one. It is therefore likely that young managers in both firms can reasonably anticipate that they will be dealing with each other on a personal basis for the rest of their careers. This profoundly influences their behavior toward each other. Both will be quite willing to make a personal investment in fostering good relations and getting to understand each other's position in their respective organizations. And given the long-term nature of the relationship, both will be anxious to avoid even the appearance of untrustworthy behavior. If they make enemies of each other, it will handicap their performance and promotability from then on.

Although the ties between these two persons might become very close, their relationship is far more a business tie than a friendship. The attraction between them is at first largely based on each other's position and future prospects, especially as indicated by educational background. In the Japanese culture personal relations with business associates are given far greater emphasis than in the United States. But this does not mean that friendships determine with whom one does business. Rather, it means that ties with business associates are carefully cultivated, and that a person's moral character is considered before entering into a deep business relationship.

One might reasonably wonder how it could be possible that two young managers could anticipate dealing with each other personally over a twenty-five-year span, if both are in large organizations that transfer personnel on a regular basis. A partial answer is that in a sogo shosha transfers usually take place *within* a single product division, in part to facilitate the formation of network ties with peers in client organizations. A young manager initially assigned to petrochemicals can expect to deal with the same petrochemical client firms for at least the first fifteen or twenty years of his career. He may be transferred overseas and lose physical proximity to his contacts in those firms, but it is more than likely that he will keep in touch via letter writing, telex, and visits when he comes back to Japan on business. He will want to maintain carefully these relationships because he know that his contacts will gradually become more important within their firms, as they, like him, develop seniority.

Of course a great deal of mutual choice goes on in the formation of outside networks, just as in the case of networks within the sogo shosha. Young managers who perceive each other as especially competent will be attracted by the fact that each will someday be in a position to perform valuable services for the other. From the perspective of the young manager in the client firm, it is quite important to have a well-placed contact within the sogo shosha. The contact can provide valuable information and insight, which could enable the young manager in the client firm to distinguish himself and thus enhance his career prospects. Similarly the sogo shosha manager who has access to information from a well-placed contact in the client also is able to improve his performance. Once these network members are selected, interactions may occur with great frequency, both on and off the job.

It is interesting to note that both the individual manager and the firm benefit from the high qualities of personal networks. The client firm is able to get preferred access to important data and services from the sogo shosha. The sogo shosha gets faster and more accurate data from the client, enhancing its competitive ability in relation to the other sogo shosha. Thus both firms are, if anything, favorable toward the formation of networks linking the members of their staffs.

Naturally not all networks are equal in their quality and effectiveness, just as not all members of an organization are equally competent. A network of less competent and less well-placed individuals in a client firm does little good for a sogo shosha. How then does a sogo shosha help to ensure that the outside networks formed by its managers will be of high quality? Of course many factors are involved in such a complex interpersonal phenomenon, but a highly significant influence lies in the system of elite universities in Japan and in the propensity of graduates of the same university to use this common attribute as the basis for personal ties.

Educational Background and Outside Networks

We have discussed the highly competitive, "meritocratic" process by which ambitious young Japanese gain admission to an elite university. The university serves as a kind of conduit to a post-graduation job with a highly prestigious firm or government agency. A sogo shosha, as one of Japan's most desirable employers, is in the fortunate position of being able to attract large numbers of elite university graduates. However, many other firms and government agencies, even some smaller ones, also draw these graduates, often putting them on a kind of seniority-driven escalator to top management positions. For companies that engage in more routine, standardized tasks of manufacturing, the relative number of elite managers required may be smaller. Such companies need not recruit all white-collar employees from elite schools, but a small number may be hired and put in positions from the start that would provide good background for eventual top-level responsibilities.

The dominance of the graduates of a few leading universities in the highest levels of the major companies in Japan is overwhelming. The preeminence of Japan's top schools is unmatched in the United States. For better or worse, a graduate of one of the leading universities who is hired by one of a sogo shosha's clients is very likely to rise further and faster than most employees, within the constraints of his firm's seniority-based promotion system. The young core staff member who is experiencing his first contacts with a particular client organization can therefore quickly get a fairly rough idea of who is likely ultimately to wield more power and influence at the client firm in later years, merely by learning who the graduates of the elite schools are. At least the kind of university one graduated from is useful as an initial screening device.

In order to be accepted as an equal by a person of this background, it is very helpful if the core staff member is also a product of an elite school. This is a kind of minimum qualification, although not a sufficient condition. If the two happened to attend the same university, they can far more readily form a lasting and valuable tie. For Japanese people a common attribute is exceedingly important in forming personal ties. It forms a permanent group context for a relationship. Graduation from the same school is just the sort of common attribute made to order for forming the kind of tiese that can be activated for a useful personal network. It is not necessary that the two people have known each other in college for them to be able to form a strong tie. The mere fact of common membership in the group of graduates is enough to spark the formation of a tie. So the elite educational origins of sogo shosha personnel greatly assist them in forming personal networks with members of client organization who are slated to rise to the most important posts in their respective parallel hierarchies. These are, of course, precisely the kinds of people who can be very helpful as part of a core staff member's outside network.

Structuring Networks

Of course the process of building outside networks goes on throughout the manager's career. The process is complicated by the fact that networks exist on a "horizontal" plane (among people of approximately equal age and status) and on a "vertical" plane (between superior and subordinate). Outside networks tend to be relatively horizontal, for there is no rivalry for promotion between status equals in different companies, whereas networks within a firm tend to be relatively vertical in nature. Thus a manager's outside network is made up primarily of people with whom he deals in client firms, who tend to be about his own age. But the members of his outside network have their own networks in their own firms, which are more vertical, composed of superiors and subordinates. Therefore a manager can gain access to vertical networks within his client companies through his ties to contemporaries, who can use their own networks on his behalf.

Much of the information a sogo shosha needs to obtain from a client cannot be regularized into a formal communications pattern. For example, if a sogo shosha serves as a marketing agent, it needs to be closely tied into client management thinking about changes in the product line, investment in new plant, changes in emphasis of product lines, and many other areas. By nature this kind of information must be obtained informally. Since the consensus style of management requires extensive consultation before decisions are taken, if a sogo shosha manager has a personal network of contacts within a client firm, network members can hear about and pass on information on impending decisions, or those just being considered. Ability to mobilize these informal channels is regarded as a legitimate and effective business practice, rather than gossip or unethical use of inside information.

Because of the long-term nature of sogo shosha-client relations, mechanisms similar to those described for internal networks operate to prevent abuses of inside information passed between client and sogo shosha. Each network member has an interest in maintaining the relationship, for it gives him an advantage in performing his own work. Furthermore both sogo shosha and client are interested in seeing their relations run smoothly: there is an enormous investment of time and energy in building numerous network connections between them at all levels of the two firms. So, a trader who abused a client confidence to produce a large short-term profit would find himself heavily censured within his own firm.

14

Challenges Facing the Sogo Shosha

The Changing Nature of the Japanese Economy

As we have seen, the sogo shosha's worldwide operations are deeply rooted in the Japanese economy. In fact the sogo shosha serves as a primary distributor, purchasing agent, and financier for a number of Japan's industries in domestic as well as international markets. The sogo shosha was ideally suited to the high-growth period of the 1950s and 1960s, during which Japan pushed hard to expand capital-intensive heavy industries. By the early 1970s these industries had begun to show signs of maturity as the domestic demand for their products became saturated. Moreover a sudden and dramatic rise in energy prices put Japan into a disadvantageous position in these industries, intensifying the need to restructure the Japanese economy away from heavy toward what MITI (Ministry of International Trade and Industry) calls knowledge-intensive industries. At the same time Japan began to encounter new competition in a number of industries, including steel and chemicals, from newly industrialized nations, particularly Korea and Brazil. This meant a substantially lower rate of growth in the export of these commodities. The slowdown of the domestic economy in the 1970s also had a severe impact on the sogo shosha[1] For one thing, the basic economics of the sogo shosha are built around a high rate of capacity utilization, including a rapid turnover of handled goods and an ever-increasing volume of products to be traded. With slow or negative growth the economic and operational leverage of the sogo shosha began working against it in these fields. Thus the developments of the 1970s have brought about a fundamental change.

Financing Product System Members

The maturation of, or even decline in, the demand in many of the basic industries in which the sogo shosha played the key role began to threaten the viability of many of the product systems. Recall that during the high-growth period, the sogo shosha sought to build product systems in a number of key industries. As we have seen, a typical product system has a large complement of small- to medium-size enterprises performing processing, fabrication, distribution, and other related activities in the respective value chain. The sogo shosha's ability to provide financing served as a key instrument of control. These small- to medium-size enterprises were the weakest link in the system. With weak financial, technological marketing, or other resources of their own, they had no choice but to turn to the sogo shosha as their sponsor.

The sugar-refining industry provides an example. By the mid-1970s it had become clear that this industry had reached maturity in Japan, and its long-term prospects were bleak. The sogo shosha had traditionally played a major role, particularly in the procurement of raw sugar overseas for Japanese sugar refineries. This function had come to represent a substantial business for the sogo shosha, which in the process had developed a network of captive refineries. Anxious to capture an ever-increasing share of the market so that it could supply a greater amount of raw sugar, each sogo shosha encouraged its affiliated firms to expand their capacity aggressively. With the industry reaching maturity, by the mid-1970s overcapacity had become chronic.

Faced with virtually no growth in the consumption of sugar in the domestic market, saddled with a substantial overcapacity in refining, and locked into long-term contracts with major suppliers of raw sugar overseas, the sogo shosha found themselves in a difficult situation. To support the weak members of the product system, the sogo shosha had to extend substantial amounts of credit to keep them from failing. Today the returns on these resources are low to negative, thus damaging to the sogo shosha's profits and financial wealth. A similar situation has occurred in a number of other industries, ranging from steel to textiles and chemicals.

The foregoing example illustrates some of the fundamental problems currently facing the sogo shosha. Its traditional strengths have been in commodity businesses which are quickly reaching maturity. Also the individual sogo shosha's desire to increase its market share, particularly through the use of financial power, has often resulted in chronic overcapacity, as rival firms match investments with one another. Moreover, as noted earlier, the industries in which the sogo shosha's financial power can be most effectively exercised are those dominated by smaller firms, but the decline in the rate of growth in the Japanese economy and the increasing maturity of these industries mean that the sogo shosha have found it necessary to continue to provide financial support, with poor prospects for a satisfactory return.

In these circumstances the sogo shosha firms now find it necessary to deploy their financial strengths not to facilitate or create business as originally intended but to keep their affiliated firms in declining industries afloat. This is a costly proposition for the sogo shosha and puts further pressure on their profitability. The sogo shosha face a serious dilemma here. Understandably they are reluctant to let the weaker members of the product system go bankrupt; they would prefer to continue to support them as long as possible in the hope that they will recover in the future.

Problems in New Ventures

Another factor that has had a serious impact on the performance of the sogo shosha is the result of ill-conceived or poorly implemented new ventures. We have described earlier the need for the sogo shosha to expand and diversify into new businesses. The record of the sogo shosha in such activities during the past decade has been mixed. One area in which they diversified actively in the early 1970s was real estate and housing.

Shortly after he took office, Prime Minister Tanaka proposed a plan to undertake a major redevelopment of Japan, and real estate appeared to offer real growth possibilities because of the great potential demand for housing. The sogo shosha rushed into the real estate business. Caught up in a boom, they moved aggressively—in many cases too aggressively, for they did not possess the necessary skills for real estate development. For a number of the sogo shosha, entry into this field represented an opportunistic and speculative, rather than a well-planned, strategic move. The fall of the Tanaka government and a decline in the economic growth rate dealt fatal blows to the industry, and most sogo shosha were left with substantial real estate holdings. At the height of the boom it was estimated that the six major sogo shosha had total real estate holdings of over ¥350 billion, or $1.4 billion, and annual interest payment alone on these holdings was estimated to be around $120 million.

The increasingly demanding business environment began to take a significant toll in the financial performance of the major sogo shosha. The aggregate sales of the nine sogo shosha between 1976 and 1979 remained flat. Their sales did pick up in 1980 and increased about 30 percent between 1980 and 1983, but profit levels remained virtually unchanged. The net profit as a percentage of total sales failed to increase significantly—a real pressure on margin in the face of intense competition. Particularly disturbing was a steady decline in profit from trading.

Impact on Organizational Demography

The developments discussed have had a rather serious impact on the internal organization and personnel system of the sogo shosha. We have noted that the sogo shosha's primary strength lies in the bundle of skills nurtured within the sogo shosha through its personnel system. During each of the high-growth years, every sogo shosha aggressively recruited a large number of new graduates. The leading five sogo shosha together hired 799 young men as management trainees in 1968, and between 1970 and 1974 the five companies took on over a thousand college graduates each year. In 1971, the peak year, the number reached 1,400.

Earlier we noted the sogo shosha's rather distinct management system. Unlike the staffs of manufacturing concerns where there are many blue-collar workers, the male employees who constitute the core staff are all exclusively college-educated managers. The sogo shosha can be characterized as one of the world's largest professional organizations, for there are few firms comparable in size to a Japanese sogo shosha with such a preponderance of professional employees. Mitsubishi and Mitsui each have more than 10,000 employees. The declining rate of economic growth is creating serious consequences for the traditional personnel practices of permanent employment and the seniority-based promotion system. The seniority reward system demands that employees be given titles commensurate with their age. During the high-growth era advancement opportunities were plentiful. As the sogo shosha expanded their existing businesses and diversified into new products and markets, new sections (*ka*) and departments were created. Branches or subsidiaries were established, both in Japan and abroad, creating even more positions. Possibilities for rapid advancement, together with opportunities to work abroad, made the sogo shosha an extremely attractive place of employment. The recent developments we have just examined have radically altered this situation. Furthermore the lure of foreign assignments is losing its once strong appeal among today's affluent youth, who enjoy many more options for international travel, both personal and professional.

Beginning in the mid-1970s, the sogo shosha reduced the number of recruits drastically. In fact there were one or two years in which some sogo shosha did not take on a single male college graduate. Such an adjustment, however drastic, nevertheless could not solve another fundamental personnel problem: that the large number of employees recruited during the high-growth era is now approaching the age level at which, under the seniority-based reward system, they must be given appropriate titles and positions. This is particularly important in Japan, since one's title or position in the company has far greater social meaning than it does in the United States.

Sogo shosha employees in general tend to be particularly aggressive, ambitious, and capable. Career advancement to them is an important source of motivation and incentive. The combination of the declining growth rate and the large number of employees within the middle-management ranks eligible for promotion means that competition for advancement is becoming intensified.

The fewer opportunities for advancement and for exciting assignments have had an impact on the morale of the existing management and have made it much more difficult to recruit bright college graduates. Certainly for college students the sogo shosha has lost some of the luster that it enjoyed in the earlier decades.

These are the challenges facing the sogo shosha in the mid-1980s. The sogo shosha is a major business institution in Japan, playing a vital role in importing essential raw materials, including iron ores, basic foods and oil, and exporting such strategic products as steel. It is hardly conceivable therefore that it will entirely lose its economic viability. Yet, for the reasons examined, the environment within which the sogo shosha must function in the 1980s is less than hospitable.

Responses: Rationalization

The sogo shosha have been highly cognizant of these new challenges, and since the mid-1970s they have taken a variety of steps. Faced with the declining growth rate and increasing pressure on profits, they took measures to rationalize their operations. These included divesting ill-conceived new ventures, withdrawing financial support from marginal suppliers, and reducing the headcount by limiting the number of new recruits and encouraging early retirement.

Another step was to restructure many losing businesses by spinning them off as independent subsidiaries. Such an action was intended to give the problem company a greater sense of accountability, thus forcing it to become more responsive to the market. As independent entities, such companies often have lower costs and overhead.

Large-Scale Investments

In addition to these defensive measures, the sogo shosha have begun to take a number of more positive steps. First, the sogo shosha have begun to stress large-scale foreign direct investment in major industries in key countries, with the intent of improving their profitability from investment. This is a departure from past strategy, in which investment was smaller in scale and viewed merely as a means to supplement trading activities. With their global networks and their excellent access to funds, the sogo shosha are in a unique position to undertake major investments to increase their leverage in the existing product system and/or to diversify their sources of earnings.

One example of this new strategy is the acquisition by Mitsui of major grain elevator facilities from Cook Industries, a large grain-trading firm in the United States.[2] As we noted in an earlier chapter, Mitsui, along with other major sogo shosha, has been active in grain trading, but until this acquisition the sogo shosha had lacked a strong base in the United States. The United States is an important source of grains, and the six leading American companies, including Cook, had controlled 90 percent of the grain export from the United States.

In this single acquisition, which cost the company around $55 million, Mitsui was able to increase its presence in the grain market substantially. Upon acquisition, Mitsui entered into a management contract with Continental Grain, which would undoubtedly serve to give Mitsui employees opportunities to learn about the management of grain elevator facilities. Since Mitsui's acquisition of grain elevators, other sogo shosha have purchased U.S. elevators.

Such large-scale investments bring with them substantial costs and risks. It has been widely reported that the financial results of these large-scale investments in grain export facilities have been low profits or even substantial losses. Over the past several years American grain exports have faced serious difficulties due to the strength of the U.S. dollar and the aggressiveness of other exporting nations. So the sogo shosha firms, as new players in the operation of domestic grain-buying facilities, have undoubtedly paid a steep price for their inexperience in such a difficult market.

Yet it is not necessarily true that the move into domestic U.S. grain elevators was a mistake. Over a longer period of time these may prove to be excellent investments, as cycles of production, currency values, and other factors change. The more important point is that the strategy of moving into large-scale investments overseas brings with it large-scale risks. The increasing "lumpiness" of the risks a sogo shosha faces—the larger scale of exposure compared to sogo shosha resources—limits some of the advantages of the portfolio effect, which the sogo shosha has enjoyed in its risk management.

New Product Development Efforts

Another new strategic thrust is in the direction of seeking new products that fit the distinctive competence of the sogo shosha. Given the changing structure of Japanese industry, such opportunities for the sogo shosha are not abundant. One of the most attractive product groups is in the area of energy, particularly crude oil. Japan's nearly total dependence on external sources for crude oil is well known. Throughout the high-growth era, the Japanese government experienced difficulties in promoting rapid growth of wholly Japanese-owned and managed oil-refining firms. They had also tried without much success to achieve dominance over the subsidiaries of the multinational oil majors.

About half of the total refining capacity in Japan is owned by subsidiaries of the international companies, which in turn supply crude oil from their own sources. The Japanese government, notably MITI, first promoted the growth of nationally owned refining firms and then the development of at least partially Japanese-owned crude oil sources. In the wake of the first oil crisis, with the weakening influence of the international majors, the sogo shosha saw new opportunities in oil trading. They have pursued this strategy in a variety of ways, most significantly in their increasingly heavy involvement in the import of crude oil for the Japanese-owned refineries.

As the oil-producing countries began to seek their own outlets for their crude oil, the sogo shosha's role took on increasing importance. In the aftermath of the second oil crisis in 1979, the international oil companies once again reduced their sales to their Japanese affiliates, particularly to wholly Japanese-owned refineries. This created an excellent opportunity for the sogo shosha to enhance their position with the Japanese oil-refining firms, which had been heavily dependent on the majors for their crude supply and which were ill-equipped to undertake their own procurement. The sogo shosha moved quickly into this vacuum, and soon they had made substantial inroads into the Japanese oil industry. The sogo shosha's growing importance in oil trading is evident from the fact that by the early 1980s the nine sogo shosha were responsible for over 50 percent of the total crude oil supplied to Japan. Particularly important is the role of Mitsubishi Shoji, which alone is responsible for about 15 percent of Japan's total crude oil import.

The sogo shosha, as an institution, is well suited to dealing in crude oil. Oil is a commodity with fluctuating prices; the customer's demand for a particular type and grade must be matched by available supply. Through its international network the sogo shosha can scan the world market, and its network also enables the sogo shosha to engage in oil trading on a global basis. In oil trading logistics also play an important role; also the size of each transaction is quite large.

Involvement with the oil industry has not been without its risks and problems, however. In particular, sogo shosha involvement in the domestic Japanese refining industry has been costly. Japanese refineries have not generally been profitable in recent years, for they face many of the problems of overcapacity, inefficient facilities, and stagnant markets which also bedevil the U.S. and European refining industries. As the Japanese industry has restructured, sogo shosha equity transactions in affiliated refineries in their bank and *zaibatsu* groups have imposed significant costs on various firms.*[3]

Third-Country Trade

Another major strategy of the sogo shosha in recent years is to emphasize third-country trade, a pattern of trade that does not involve Japan. Third-country trading is not new to the sogo shosha. Prior to World War II Mitsui was quite active in third-country trading in cotton. Also in the postwar decades the sogo shosha engaged in third-country trade from time to time. In the past, however, third-country trade was largely an outgrowth of opportunistic responses to particular market conditions. During the high-growth era the sogo shosha were heavily preoccupied with trade to and from Japan, and third-country trade was not actively sought. But with the present renewed emphasis on this type of activity, third-country trade now accounts for as much as 15 percent of the sogo shosha's total sales. With its fixed investment in a global network and broad product and market coverage, the sogo shosha can engage in third-country trade on an incremental cost basis, a powerful competitive advantage.

* Particularly interesting has been the involvement of Mitsubishi Shoji in Mitsubishi Oil. Mitsubishi Oil had been a joint venture with Getty Oil, a major U.S.-based supplier of crude oil, and various Mitsubishi companies; the arrangement dated back to 1931. However, when Getty Oil was acquired by Texaco, a major side effect occurred in Japan, where Texaco already owned a major stake in Caltex, an important rival of Mitsubishi Oil. Because Texaco was likely to sell its holdings in Mitsubishi Oil, to help pay for its acquisition of Getty, the threat existed that outside, potentially hostile or difficult owners might control 50 percent of a Mitsubishi Group company. To avoid this possibility, the Mitsubishi Group of companies jointly agreed to acquire Getty's half ownership of Mitsubishi Oil at a premium over market prices. Mitsubishi Shoji's purchase share was 20 percent, four times larger than that of any other Mitsubishi Group company. Although Mitsubishi Shoji may expect to benefit by increased dealings with Mitsubishi Oil, the transaction caused a ¥7.6 billion extraordinary charge to earnings in fiscal 1984, equal to over a third of the corporation's net profits for the year.

An increasing number of large-scale investments in raw material ventures and processing facilities abroad in which the sogo shosha has begun to take a larger share of the investment have provided both the need and the opportunities for third-country trade. Many of these investments require a certain minimum scale, which is likely to involve markets beyond Japan. The demand for products such as minerals, chemicals, grain, and pulp tends to fluctuate from time to time; this is another reason it is desirable to have access to markets beyond Japan.

As a part of its emphasis on third-country strategy, the sogo shosha has begun to seek to represent American and other foreign manufacturers. For example, recently Mitsubishi Shoji entered into a ten-year contract with Diamond Shamrock to market vinyl chloride monomer. To promote third-country trading in chemicals in Southeast Asia, Mitsubishi has built major storage facilities in Singapore. Similarly Mitsui and C. Itoh represent Union Carbide and Celanese, respectively, in markets outside of the United States (see table 14.1).

The sogo shosha can also serve as an effective marketing intermediary for newly emerging industries in developing countries. For example, Mexico has been expanding its production capacities of ethylene, and it has been equally active in building downstream operations. The sogo shosha have been energetically promoting the export of Mexico's petrochemical products to various parts of the world.

Opportunities for third-country trading are found in textile products as well. Cotton and wool have been popular items traded by the sogo shosha on a third-country basis for some time. For example, the sogo shosha purchase more than one-

Table 14.1
Third-country trade: percent of total sales of the leading sogo shosha

	1973	1979	1983	1984
Mitsubishi	6.2	6.1	8.9	11.7
Mitsui	6.3	7.9	14.8	16.0
C. Itoh	6.2	12.0	15.1	17.7
Marubeni	5.1	13.3	15.7	16.9
Sumitomo	9.9	5.2	8.2	11.5
Nissho-Iwai	10.1	9.9	22.5	21.1

third of the total wool sold in Australia, and about 40 percent of what they buy is sold by the sogo shosha to markets other than Japan. In the textile field some of the sogo shosha have been active for some time in building networks of supply sources and manufacturers to promote third-country trading. Third-country trading is also an excellent way for the sogo shosha to strengthen their ties with their clients. For example, Komatsu, a leading manufacturer of construction equipment recently exported $42 million worth of this equipment to Algeria. The terms included the payment in crude oil amounting to some 1.4 million barrels. Nichimen helped put together the deal.

The foregoing illustrates the expanding scope of third-country trade. As is evident from the examples cited, the products involved are standard commodities that are traded on an international scale. It is significant that in selected product areas, the sogo shosha is emerging as a powerful force in trading on a global basis.

Construction Projects

Another new strategic thrust of the sogo shosha has been to place increasing emphasis on selling major construction projects. These projects range from the installation of large chemical or steel plants to the construction of subway systems, airports, and waste disposal facilities. Most of these projects are concentrated in developing countries. The sogo shosha is well suited to manage large-scale consortia of enterprises. It has extensive contacts with a variety of businesses, and typically it enjoys a strong position in each business group, with excellent ties to key private as well as governmental financial institutions.

The sogo shosha can mobilize American and European suppliers by financing opportunities as well. Its extensive presence in developing countries is an all-important asset in identifying new opportunities for projects and in negotiating with potential customers, which are likely to be governmental agencies. The sogo shosha's global network can provide logistical support to the participating firms in any country once a project gets underway. It can also hold a strong bargaining position vis-à-vis the local government. Large-scale turnkey plant construction projects or infrastructure development is therefore attractive to the sogo shosha. Such projects can have the additional advantage for the sogo shosha of enhancing their presence in these countries.

Countertrade

Pushing countertrade, or barter arrangements, is another new strategy of the sogo shosha. Saddled with a perennial shortage of hard currency, a number of developing countries as well as Eastern Bloc countries often insist on counterpurchase obligations as prerequisites to their import. For example, C. Itoh, Nissho-Iwai and Nikki, a construction engineering company, sold the construction of a petroleum-refining facility in Indonesia which meant a substantial amount of export of plant equipment to Indonesia. The contract stipulated that a certain percentage of import be paid through purchase of Indonesian goods other than crude oil and natural gas. Major products offered were lumber, tuna, shrimp, and palm oil. The profitability of the project depended to a large extent on the price at which the sogo shosha could export these products from Indonesia. Indeed, its ability to take on such large-scale counterpurchase deals gives the sogo shosha a significant competitive edge.

High-Technology Products

Another major new strategy move is to enter high-technology fields. Keenly aware of the shift of the Japanese economy to high-technology industries, the sogo shosha have been seeking opportunities to expand into these fields. Entry barriers, however, are high. High-technology products, ranging from semiconductors, computers, and telecommunications to biotechnologies, require in-depth product knowledge, specialized marketing skills, and service capabilities. The sogo shosha lack these skills in most of the promising high-technology fields. One field where the sogo shosha does enjoy some expertise is biotechnology because of its long-standing involvement in grains. To date, the sogo shosha have largely concentrated on the development of new seeds. Japanese traditional seed producers are typically small and fragmented and do not possess the skills or capital to engage in the large-scale R & D efforts needed to exploit advances in biotechnology. C. Itoh, for example, recently entered into an agreement with a leading seed producer in Denmark to undertake jointly the development of new seeds. The project seeks to develop new seeds suitable for Japan, using an experimental farm in the United States. Furthermore the joint venture has plans to undertake a major project to develop seeds suitable for use in China.

Another high-technology field the sogo shosha has targeted is the computer and telecommunications sector. In this area the sogo shosha can perform a number of useful functions. One is the import of computer communications technology developed in the United States. Mistui, for example, became AT&T's agent in Japan to promote VAN, the company's network system. At the time of this writing, Mitsubishi was negotiating with IBM to play a similar role in the sale of IBM's own network, IN, in Japan. Successful marketing of communication networks requires the participation of a large number of users across a spectrum of different industries, including manufacturing, distribution, and other services. The sogo shosha, by occupying a key position in a particular group of companies, can play a strategic role in marketing a network that can link a number of major companies in the group. It also presents promising business opportunities in marketing communication networks to Japanese customers. The recent great technical advances in the field of communications can be a source of a new competitive edge by facilitating information flow and exchange. A number of the sogo shosha have invested considerable resources in the study of how state-of-the-art technology could be used to improve their global communications capability. This expanding field presents both threats and opportunities for the sogo shosha.

Some of the sogo shosha have successfully established subsidiaries specializing in marketing a limited line of electronic products. Among the most successful in this area is Kanematsu-Gosho, the eighth largest firm. The company established Kanematsu Electronics which markets office equipment throughout the world. This subsidiary has been so successful that at the time of this writing it was planning to go public soon, with substantial capital gains for the parent company.

Both the biotechnology and computer-telecommunications sectors hold great promise to emerge as central business fields for the sogo shosha in coming decades. Both sectors are fast-growing and promise to become basic industries in the future. Both are characterized by some very large producers, complemented by large numbers of medium and small companies. And in both sectors there are great opportunities to manage an international division of labor in research, production, and distribution of finished products.

But there are also obstacles that may impede the success of the sogo shosha in becoming product systems manager in these sectors. For one thing, the large Japanese producers in the computer-telecommunications sector, such as Fujitsu, Hitachi, and NEC, are already highly internationalized companies that are unaccustomed to relying on the sogo shosha for extensive services. Unlike Japanese firms in the steel, machinery, chemical, and other sectors whose development the sogo shosha had overseen, these high-technology companies do not see themselves as needing the help of a more experienced partner in order to "catch up" with their American or European peers. In fact in many fields they see themselves as leaders. The old pattern of the sogo shosha importing technologies and raw materials and exporting finished products will not work as well in the new sectors.

It may well be that the sogo shosha's role in these new sectors will involve much more important roles for non-Japanese major clients. By combining its ability to help American or European producers to market their high-technology goods and services in Japan, with its abilities to mobilize smaller Japanese firms as component suppliers and to scan lower-wage third countries as potential sources of components, the sogo shosha could possibly become major players in truly internationalized high-technology production systems of the future. It remains an open question as to whether vertically integrated high-technology firms will predominate in the industries of the future or whether there will be a major role for the sogo shosha as systems integrator.

Related to this, the sogo shosha are pursuing investment in new start-up high-technology companies in the United States. This strategy offers several advantages. One is that the sogo shosha, with their extensive contacts and presences in the United States, are in a position to identify potentially attractive opportunities. With their excellent credit ratings, they can raise funds at low cost, which in turn can be invested in new start-up companies. The sogo shosha can also market their products or ideas in Japan or to other companies. This concept is particularly appealing to major Japanese companies which are finding it increasingly difficult to acquire advanced technology from large American companies through licensing.

To strengthen their position in high-technology fields, the sogo shosha has been actively recruiting college graduates with a technical education. In recent years about 20 percent of the college graduates hired by the sogo shosha have had technical backgrounds.

Financial Services

Other major new areas are financial services. In 1984 Mitsui, Marubeni and C. Itoh announced the establishment of subsidiaries in New York and London which were to expand into the growing area of financial services. Mitsubishi followed with a major investment in 1985. The new organizations are designed to assume not only some of the traditional financing functions of the sogo shosha but to take on a number of new activities, such as fund raising in foreign markets, marketing of securities, and investment management. The new organization can be quite important in supporting third-country trade, since low-cost financing from Japan does not apply to third-country trading.

Another new area in which the sogo shosha can combine several of its distinctive competences is in leasing capital equipment, from plant machinery to commercial aircraft. For example, in 1984 Mitsubishi leased a fleet of Boeing 767s to Qantas Airlines. Insurance provides still another avenue of new business opportunities. For example, Mitsubishi recently established a casualty insurance company in Bermuda. Bermuda was selected because of the country's favorable laws governing the insurance industry. The company was designed to handle its own freight insurance and the reinsurance of casualty coverage of major projects.

Faced with rather fundamental changes in the business environment, as we have seen, the sogo shosha have embarked on a number of new policy ventures. Can they implement these measures effectively? Will they be sufficient to revitalize the sogo shosha? So far the series of new strategic thrusts has had only a limited impact on the product mix. In the mid-1980s the breakdown of the major commodities handled consisted of four traditional product categories—machinery (23.1 percent), metals (23 percent), foodstuffs (11.5 percent), and textiles (7.1

percent). These constituted the bulk of their business. Most of the machinery products consisted of those with mature technology. The fact that the sogo shosha were not successful in entering consumer electronics and automobiles a decade or two earlier is a sober reminder of the difficulties they are likely to encounter in attempting to make major inroads into high-technology fields and financial services. The effective implementation of these strategies requires major adjustment in some of the fundamental characteristics of the sogo shosha.

Organizational Adaptation

To pursue a new strategic thrust requiring major investments places a high premium on skills in evaluating business opportunities and risks. The traditional career path within the sogo shosha has not given much emphasis to the development of formal analytical skills. Line management personnel, while skilled in trading activities, are not accustomed to making rigorous business analyses. Those in corporate staff positions, in such departments as finance or planning, either lack the experience needed to make critical assessments of major new business opportunities or are not in positions of strong influence in the making of final decisions. Moreover the sogo shosha's traditional organization, with its power concentrated in the product sector, makes a critical and objective assessment of major investment opportunities difficult.

An effective pursuit of this new strategy also requires changes in internal managerial practices, particularly in the traditional method of resource allocation. In small investments in the past, the initiative came largely from the product groups, which identified an investment opportunity, structured the investment, and funded it. However, as the sogo shosha moves into large-scale investment, the continued reliance on this bottom-up approach, which had worked so well in trading and small activities, is not likely to be appropriate. The resources required for a single investment are so substantial that only selective investments can be and should be funded.

Here the sogo shosha faces a serious dilemma. The very orientation, in fact the strengths, of the sogo shosha lies in its bottom-up system, where those lowest in the organization, and therefore closest to the market, can and do generate a substantial amount of new business in the existing field. In the traditional business lines this system is effective and appropriate. However, for large projects, particularly in new fields, direction from top management is necessary. Herein lies the dilemma. The top management is excellent in mobilizing the resources and energy of the organization and provides an encouraging climate for product or commodity experts who can aggressively search for new opportunities. In the traditional sogo shosha organization the top management seldom has to shape explicitly the corporate direction. The new strategy therefore calls for a redefinition of the task of top management. Given the strengths of the sogo shosha's culture, and the fact that top management is very much a product of the system, such a redefinition will be difficult for top management to make and for those under them to accept.

Diversification into new areas such as the high-technology fields of computers and communication networks raises a fundamental question about the role of the sogo shosha in such new product systems. What does or can the sogo shosha bring to these systems? The answer is by no means clear. In high-technology fields the sogo shosha is particularly handicapped by its lack of a strong technical staff. It is true, as we have seen that, for the past decade the sogo shosha have been making considerable efforts to expand their technical staffs. Some sogo shosha have established special staff groups to deal with high-technology industries, with an eye toward building a critical mass. However, the technical staff at the sogo shosha typically is diluted by being spread over many fields. Moreover, since the sogo shosha is without R & D or manufacturing facilities of its own, the technical staff is likely to find it difficult to keep abreast of the latest developments and to continue to develop their own skills. It is virtually impossible to build a strong technical staff overnight. Technical careers at the sogo shosha can hardly be considered to represent the mainstream of an industry. All these factors make it difficult for the sogo shosha to recruit highly qualified technical personnel. All the sogo shosha can expect then, at least in the short run, is to build sufficient technical competence to evaluate technology. This can be a serious if not a fatal handicap in the long-term viability of the sogo shosha in high-technology fields. For this reason and others, it will be very difficult for the sogo shosha to play a lead role in state-of-the-art high-technology sectors.

Localization Overseas

Another major challenge facing the sogo shosha in implementing the new strategic thrust is that of building strong local management in key countries. Traditionally the sogo shosha have filled the key positions in their overseas branches and subsidiaries with members of the core staff sent from Japan. The reasons for the extensive reliance on them have been already discussed. The staffing pattern has been consistent with the sogo shosha's strategy and its organizational philosophy. On the one hand, the pursuit of the new strategic thrusts, particularly with their increased emphasis on major investments and third-country trade, will require strong local management. Overseas clients and markets must be cultivated far more aggressively than in the past, and new investment opportunities must be identified, evaluated, and negotiated. Once the acquisitions or new investments are made, they must be managed. The performance of the new business efforts and investments must be monitored and evaluated carefully.

On the other hand, effective implementation of third-country trading or countertrade demands close systemwide integration and coordination. Particularly in the early stages of the development of a new business opportunity across countries, it is likely that the relevant manager will have to invest a considerable amount of time and energy in gathering information, testing the concepts, exploring new opportunities, and assessing risks without immediate tangible benefits to his organization. To implement the project, the particular manager will often require the assistance of a number of his associates throughout the organization, who too must be willing to expend considerable effort in consummating the deal, often going beyond their already heavily taxed daily schedule. We have seen that the traditional value system of the sogo shosha does an excellent job of cultivating a set of values that encourages such behavior.

The management problem posed by the new business thrusts is a difficult one. To be able to represent major U.S. chemical companies in the export market, for example, it would be highly desirable for the sogo shosha to have on its staff an American executive with a strong background in the industry, in general, and in international trading of chemical products, in particular. But effective implementation of third-country trading or countertrade will likely require an intimate familiarity with the workings of the sogo shosha and, most important, an ability to mobilize key managers assigned to various parts of the world. Information must be gathered and evaluated from several places quickly. The chemical manager in the United States, for example, must be able to deal with his counterparts in various key markets throughout the world. Under similar conditions a Japanese manager with twenty years' experience would rely on his personal network. Chances are that the American manager, however technically competent he is, without the benefit of a long maturation within the sogo shosha, would not have a network in the Philippines, Thailand, or Brazil. On what basis would he mobilize them? How could he induce his counterparts to make the efforts required to consummate a deal?

However, for the reasons noted, it would be difficult to find or develop a full complement of the skills required for effectively pursuing the new strategies among the core personnel alone. Some of the skills are country specific. For example, it would be difficult for the members of the core staff on assignment from Japan to gain as intimate knowledge of local management and financial practices. To put it another way, whether or not the sogo shosha can achieve its strategy depends to a large degree on their ability to build and, more important, integrate strong local management teams into the entire corporate system.

The extensive use of local nationals is rather common among American multinationals. In fact many American multinationals take great pride in doing so. This practice offers several advantages, including lower cost, higher morale, local expertise, and the goodwill of the host government, just to mention a few. The sogo shosha management is well aware of these advantages. They recognize the need, but they must overcome a number of barriers. Compared with their Japanese counterparts, American multinationals enjoy several inherent advantages in this area. English is the common business language, and this is a decided advantage for recruiting and integrating capable local nationals. Moreover the American managerial system, with its strong predilection for the clear delineation of authority, for rules, standard operating procedures, and well-defined tasks, is built around explicitly defined and more universal standards.

In contrast, the sogo shosha face a more difficult environment. For one thing, they exhibit few of the characteristics that are typically associated with large American multinationals. Even more basic is the fact that the institution of the sogo shosha itself is unique to Japan, and its managerial system is deeply rooted in the basic Japanese environment. In fact the very core of the sogo shosha's operations, and a dimension of its competitive strength, lies in its effective use of informal networks that rely on shared Japanese culture and the closed-end nature of the core staff employment system for their effectiveness. This is the essential reason for the extensive use of the members of the core staff throughout the system.

The effective employment of local nationals is one of the sogo shosha's highest priorities, not only because of the advantages discussed earlier but also because a number of countries are pressuring the firms to do so. In the United States, for example, it is becoming increasingly difficult for sogo shosha firms to obtain work visas for expatriate Japanese to staff the offices of their American subsidiaries. Moreover, two important discrimination cases have been filed, *Lisa Avagliano* et al. v. *Sumitomo Shoji America, Inc.*, which alleges sex discrimination, and *Michael E. Spiess* et al. v. *C. Itoh & Co. (America)*, which alleges racial discrimination against Caucasian males.[4] These cases are working their way slowly through the federal courts, with a variety of complex legal issues at stake. In other countries different types of pressures apply. For example, in several South American countries governments require that 75 percent, 80 percent, or more of the payroll go to local nationals.

However, the sogo shosha cannot immediately accommodate the large-scale integration of local nationals into their mainstream trading activities without destroying the very basis of their effectiveness. Even though the successful implementation of the new strategy depends to a large extent on their ability to recruit qualified local nationals, the companies must move more slowly than many would prefer. This poses a fundamental dilemma for the sogo shosha's management.

The sogo shosha owes much of its success to its organizational capability, its ability to create an effective, distinct subsystem within the broad context of Japanese culture, labor markets, and other factors that allows for efficient coordination and integration without inhibiting entrepreneurship. Acculturation and lifetime commitment to the subsystem is essential for membership in it. Thus sharing the basic Japanese cultural traits is a necessary, but not a sufficient, condition for membership in the core staff. Potential staff members must still be willing to go through extensive socialization into the sogo shosha subsystem.[5] It is obvious that there are very few non-Japanese who are both able and willing to do this.

Three solutions suggest themselves. The first is to search for non-Japanese nationals who can be acculturated into the existing sogo shosha system, a task that will be difficult at best. The uniqueness of Japanese culture is well recognized, and so is the difficulty of the Japanese language. The viability of this approach as an enduring solution requires that there be a pool of individuals who are motivated and interested in working in the Japanese system under virtually the same conditions as a native-born Japanese would. Perceived favoritism to non-Japanese would certainly handicap them in gaining acceptance. The requirement does not stop there. Such individuals must be professionally qualified. On the whole the Japanese personnel who work for the sogo shosha are well educated and highly disciplined; it would be reasonable to require similar qualifications in foreign nationals. The practical limitations of this solution are obvious.

The second solution is just as radical: to change the sogo shosha's managerial system from its traditionally Japanese, or highly particularistic, approach to a more universalistic or more Western approach. Once again a sudden transformation of this kind cannot be accomplished without destroying the very foundations of the sogo shosha. Such a radical transition cannot be achieved by edict.

The only feasible approach then is the gradual evolution of a hybrid that can accommodate the need for developing local management capabilities without destroying the system. Toward this end the sogo shosha are taking several steps. First, virtually all sogo shosha have intensified their search for well-educated and highly qualified local nationals. This is particularly true in the United States and Europe. Successful recruitment and development of qualified nationals is a difficult and time-consuming process, but it has begun.

Another step has been to train and develop selected members of the Japanese core staff so that they may gain understanding of the Western, particularly the American, management approach, with the goal that these men could serve as an effective bridge between their more traditional peers and the capable and experienced third-country nationals. The sogo shosha, particularly the major ones, were among the first to send their promising young managers to the United States and Europe for graduate training in business administration, and to send experienced senior managers to various university executive programs abroad. The number of employees who can attend these programs is limited, to be sure, but over time the impact of such a systematic effort can be quite significant. Through these programs the Japanese employees can obtain a different kind of international experience from that which they gain from foreign assignments. A combination of academic training abroad and international assignments can reinforce each other to broaden their perspective and training. Academic training does not automatically transform them into effective managers in the Western setting of course, but it is a way to complement their on-the-job experience.

A third step that the sogo shosha are taking is to attempt to use local nationals to staff key positions in the affiliates and subsidiaries that are not directly related to trading, which are the functions that require the closest integration and coordination with other parts of the organization. Though recognizing the difficulty of accommodating local nationals immediately into responsible positions in trading, this approach gives the sogo shosha experience in managing local nationals and gives the local nationals opportunities to gain some insight into the sogo shosha. These subsidiaries and affiliates perform well-defined activities, and because it is not necessary to integrate them closely into the world trading network, these managers do not need to have extensive networks in the core staff, nor do they have to make decisions that affect other areas of the firm.

It is quite possible that over time, particularly in large countries such as the United States, the legal and administrative structure of sogo shosha operations will be radically transformed. Instead of a single wholly owned trading subsidiary as the chief vehicle for operations, there may emerge a much more extensive network of wholly and partially owned subsidiaries and affiliates, performing more specialized tasks and staffed largely by indigenous managers.[6] Depending on the legal and tax ramifications, direct branches of the Japanese parent may be used to coordinate the interdependencies among these subsidiaries and affiliates, and between them and the sogo shosha's global network. The direct branches might be staffed largely by Japanese core staff members but may also include some non-Japanese personnel who have a career-long commitment to the sogo shosha system and who are acculturating themselves to it.

An essential point to be recognized in regard to recruiting and advancing local nationals is that it is a slow and gradual process, given the magnitude of the changes that must be made and given the fact that a sudden change is neither feasible nor practical without drastic consequences that could destroy the very foundation of the sogo shosha as it exists today. The transition must be carefully managed so as to maintain the economic viability and competitiveness of the enterprise.

Consolidation of the Sogo Shosha Sector

One point relevant to the future viability of the sogo shosha yet to be discussed concerns the structure of the industry. It is questionable whether all nine sogo shosha can survive.[7] As we noted in chapter 2, in the postwar decades the sogo shosha have gone through a series of shakeouts and consolidations. Mergers and acquisitions reduced the number to nine. Are the nine still too many? There are forces at work that suggest that further consolidation may be in the offing.

The disparity in size among the companies is quite wide. In terms of total sales in 1984, Mitsubishi is four times as large as Nichimen, the smallest of the nine. Even Nissho-Iwai, the sixth largest, is almost half the size of Mitsubishi. To put it another way, the combined sales of the bottom four companies is about the same as that of each of the top two, Mitsubishi and Mitsui, respectively. Mitsubishi and Mitsui account for more than one-third of the total sales and employees of all the sogo shosha and 40 percent of the total assets. In contrast, the sales per employee of Nichimen is about half that of Sumitomo, the third largest.

In stable businesses such as steel it would be virtually impossible for any sogo shosha to expand its market share of the business. In new fields such as energy, in which the leaders have already established a stake, smaller companies face substantial entry barriers. Availability of capital alone presents a formidable problem! Still, two of the smaller sogo shosha, Kanematsu and Tomen, derive nearly a quarter of their total sales from textiles and related products. These comparisons are very sobering.

Can Japan continue to support the nine sogo shosha? Or, can the smaller sogo shosha, particularly the three at the bottom, survive? Recall the fundamental characteristics of the business, namely the importance of the economies of scale and the difficulty of product differentiation. Smaller firms will have to find their special niches. It would be all but impossible for them to compete head-on with Mitsubishi and Mitsui. The management of the smaller sogo shosha argue that because of their size they have traditionally had to be aggressive in looking for new business opportunities, since they could not depend on stable long-term relationships with major customers to the extent that their larger competitors did. They believe that flexibility and strong entrepreneurship will serve them well in the future. There is some fragmentary evidence that this argument is valid in some cases, but is it universally applicable?

Restructuring, in the form of mergers, will be a real possibility. Indeed, the recent history of the sogo shosha is a history of consolidation and mergers. Past experience suggests, however, that such consolidations are not likely to go smoothly. They usually take the form of one company in drastic straits being absorbed by another. Historically there have been few consolidations that were planned and managed so as to gain strategic advantages through combination. If the past pattern continues, the coming decades will be likely to present serious challenges for the smaller sogo shosha. Of course, even those that survive the probable shakeouts will have to undergo transformation in a number of areas.

It would be a mistake at this point in history to write an obituary for the institution of the sogo shosha. The sogo shosha has successfully transformed itself before in the face of challenges. The key question is: Will the sogo shosha be able to adapt again? The multitude and the magnitude of the changes facing the sogo shosha are formidable. Not only must the sogo shosha continue to find new ideas, products, business lines, markets, and clients to keep itself alive, the sogo shosha now faces a different kind of challenge. It must internationalize its business strategies and its basic organizational approach. No longer can it be a Japan-centered bridge of information, money, ideas, physical goods, and entrepreneurship. The success of the transformations already underway will depend on the sogo shosha having room for more non-Japanese businesses, people, ideas, and clients, as well as for new types of Japanese.

The top management of sogo shosha firms has relatively few powerful tools with which to undertake the transformation already underway. There are many "givens" of the status quo that will take a long time to change, especially those changes related to basic organizational issues. Maintaining the viability of the old-style sogo shosha business while experimenting with ways of identifying and building the new sogo shosha will be a demanding task. There is no guarantee of survival for any firm, or even for the sector as a whole.

Methodological Note

We have been conducting research on the sogo shosha for over a decade. Each of us has previously written and published on the subject. Yoshino (1968) looked at the sogo shosha in the context of business groupings, Yoshino (1971) treated the role of sogo shosha in Japanese domestic distribution systems, and Yoshino (1976) examined the role of sogo shosha in Japan's foreign direct investment. In 1976 Yoshino invited Lifson to join him in an internal consulting and research project in a sogo shosha firm, and this led to a subsequent collaboration in a joint research project conducted under the auspices of the Fairbank Center for East Asian Research at Harvard. Lifson's doctoral dissertation (1978) was produced during this latter project. Since that time, individually and jointly, we have pursued the topic through several research projects. Throughout the long process the primary mode of investigation has been in-depth interviewing, usually in the Japanese language, of sogo shosha personnel. Almost three hundred such interviews, most of them between one and two hours, provided the core of the data used in this study.

We have conducted concerted interviews at two of the six largest sogo shosha. The first of these began as a consulting project, producing an internal study. Of necessity, both the identity of the firm and the specifics of the data in that report must remain proprietary to the firm that sponsored the study, But our insights, hypotheses, and questions could not be expunged or ignored, even had we desired to do so.

The second project was conducted by Lifson at Mitsubishi Corporation. Some of the results of that study were published as a case series by Harvard Business School, Lifson (1981a and 1981b). Since these data are now public, it has been possible to cite published portions in this work. In both firms we spoke to a broad range of people at all levels in the hierarchy, encompassing a wide variation of products, staff functions, and perspectives on the sogo shosha. Sogo shosha personnel were formally interviewed in Tokyo and Osaka, Japan, Tapei, Taiwan, Hong Kong, New York, Los Angeles, San Francisco, and Atlanta. In addition, due to the extensive travels of sogo shosha personnel, we have been able to speak with others stationed in every continent save Antarctica (where there are no sogo shosha outposts, yet).

In both firms we had access to documents about organizational and management issues (though not individuals' personnel files). In both firms we enjoyed access to and the support of top management. Without such cooperation, this study would have been impossible.

But there were limits to our research efforts in these firms. We were interested in understanding patterns of business and organizational life, but we did not pursue the specifics of ongoing business deals (unless volunteered by an interviewee as an example). The distinction was vitally important. A sogo shosha is of necessity a closed organization. Its members handle business data of great value to outsiders. The acquisition of these data is one of their principal activities. For outside researchers to poke after the specifics of confidential business transactions and plans can readily strike a sensitive nerve. We avoided this as much as possible, often declaring ourselves explicitly uninterested in the details of current plans and transactions. Confidentiality of sensitive information was promised by the researchers. Only data sanitized of any possible sensitive identification with an individual or with a firm would be used.

The establishment of a basic trust, that the interviewer would not use information in any way that would harm the subject, was essential in obtaining real views on a variety of strategic, operational, and organizational issues. In most of the interviews there was an agreement not to quote the subject directly without written permission.

The basic interviewing technique was clinical probing of aspects of the firms' strategy, operations, and organization. As patterns and hypotheses emerged, the interviews grew more structured. Our interviewing was supplemented with interviews conducted by Professor Hiroyuki Itami of Hitotsubashi University and Professor Haruo Takagi of Keio University Graduate School of Business Administration. In their interviews a structure of topics and patterns to pursue was outlined, but no formal questionnaire or protocol was followed. We reviewed and discussed these interviews with Itami and Takagi and benefited from their insights, hypotheses, and analyses, but the organization and writing of the material was our doing. Throughout the project we have together enjoyed frequent discussion, comparison and evaluation of data and concepts, jointly grappling with the complexities and subtleties of our subject. The division of labor in writing was as follows: Yoshino produced drafts of chapters 2 and 14, and portions of 3 and 4, and Lifson produced drafts of the remaining material. Each then read and suggested revisions of the other's chapters.

We made extensive use of corporate documents in the course of research. These included organizational charts, manuals, directories, personnel planning documents, internal company publications, and a variety of orders, memoranda, charts, graphs, and files.

There have been many less formal contacts with members of sogo shosha organizations. Both of us have had members of sogo shosha firms as students in MBA and executive programs at Harvard Business School and various corporate management development courses. In many cases these longer-term relationships have proved especially valuable, providing insight into the nature of the reality of the sogo shosha. In addition we have maintained social contacts of various sorts in which it has been possible to glean various data, each fact becoming another small piece to fit into an enormous puzzle. We have had chances to discuss and compare our tentative findings with the views and insights of members of all six firms.

Extensive use has been made of published materials. Research in the academic and business literature preceded the initial interviewing and has been continuing throughout the project. Works in the fields of economics, sociology, anthropology, political science, psychology, history, business policy, marketing, organizational behavior, and control have been drawn on extensively. In addition to books in the United States, Japan, Germany, and Italy, we have reviewed a variety of economic and trade journals for large and small pieces of information on the sogo shosha and their activities.

Many people outside of the sogo shosha have been interviewed, formally and informally, on their views and experiences. These include large and small clients in the United States and Japan, bankers, government officials, members of U.S., European, and Asian trading firms, and other business managers.

Our choice of methodological approach reflects our belief that the sogo shosha required an interdisciplinary, multidimensional approach. It is a complex institutional phenomenon that must be understood in the context of many factors. Our central concern was to discover the hows and whys of the sogo shosha. Why does an organization like this exist? How does it manage itself? How does such an organization make money? What must it do well? How do things currently operate? How is people's work organized? But we also wished to relate these institutional questions to broader issues of the economy, society, politics, and organization. Establishing lines of inquiry across the variety of people we interviewed and the range of literature and issues we reviewed required flexibility in approach.

There are many lines of potentially valuable research on the sogo shosha we did not pursue. Any study, even one of this length, requires that priorities be set and choices made. The sogo shosha is a multifaceted institution, affecting large numbers of people, and the questions that remain unanswered are very important.

We trust that the community of sogo shosha researchers will grow steadily from its current small base. There will be much room for more refined and focused inquiries and we hope that our analysis will prove useful to those who follow.

Bibliographic Notes

Chapter 1

1. The quotation at the top of the page is from Lifson (1981a).

2. The data on the largest non-U.S. firms comes from *Forbes* magazine (July 2, 1984, p. 134).

3. The estimate of 10 percent of U.S. exports comes from Wiegner (1983). Our estimate of sogo shosha share of world trade is derived from *International Financial Statistics* (1984).

4. The sogo shosha as organizer of trade is featured in Kikuri (1973). Other general overviews of the sogo shosha as an institution can be found in Tsurumi (1980), Young (1979), Yoshihara (1984), Yoshino (1973), and Oki (1978).

5. On the Export Trading Company Act see Tsurumi (1982). On Sears World Trade and its problems, see Dizard (1984). On the copying of sogo shosha, see Sarathy (1983).

Chapter 2

1. For two contrasting views of Japan's modernization process, see Reischauer (1965) and Norman (1940).

2. Wallerstein (1974) asserts that modernity or modernization consists of the growing interrelatedness of formerly isolated actors all over the world. This framework highlights the importance of linkages, specifically for the institutions that establish and maintain global systems; Yamamura (1976) and Yoshihara (1984) provide good historical accounts of the origins and development of the early sogo shosha. Yoshino (1968) covers the development of the managerial system in Japan. Roberts (1973) traces the development of the Mitsui family businesses from the seventeenth century onward.

3. Wray (1984) traces the development of Mitsubishi, with a focus on the sogo shosha's shipping line operations of the *zaibatsu.*

4. On the development of Suzuki, see Nakane (1970).

5. For information on the development of second tier companies, see Sakudo (1973) and Miyamoto, Togai, and Mishima (1976).

6. Nakagawa (1966) deserves much credit for developing a comparative framework for understanding the sogo shosha's role in the industrialization of Japan.

7. Trade figures are from Oki (1978).

8. Economic data are from Japan, Office of Prime Minister (1966 and 1972).

9. Economic data are from Japan, Department of Finance (1935) and Japan, Ministry of International Trade and Industry (1974).

10. See Japan Fair Trade Commission (1974) for a critical look at sogo shosha holdings in other firms.

11. Hadley (1970) examines the breakup and reemergence of *zaibatsu* groups. Other treatments of the postwar business structure and system can be found in Yoshino (1963), and Caves and Uekusa (1976).

Chapter 3

1. On the systems perspective, see Katz and Kahn (1966).

2. For the product systems of sogo shosha, see Lifson (1978, 1981c). For examples of sogo shosha participation in many different industries, see Uchida (1982).

3. On the analysis of the merits and demerits of markets and hierarchies, see Williamson (1977) and Ouchi (1980). Roehl (1981) provides a valuable consideration of transactions cost literature as related to the sogo shosha.

4. For information on Nippon Steel and the Japanese steel industry, see Nikko Research Center (1982).

5. On sogo shosha survival strategies, see Tsurumi (1980).

6. On sogo shosha financing, see Sasago (1979).

Chapter 4

1. On oligopoly, see Stinger (1964).

2. The service life cycle concept (Lifson 1978) owes much to the theory of the product life cycle. See Vernon (1966), Levitt (1965), Cox (1967), Wells (1972), and Wasson (1974). On the chicken business in Japan, see Tsurumi (1977) and Marubeni (1977).

3. On the Isuzu-GM-C. Itoh deal, see Mainichi Shimbunsha (1973). On Mitsui-Iran, see Caldwell (1981).

4. For sogo shosha involvement in grains, see Toyo Keizai (1981) and Eaton (1983). On the Mitsugoro agricultural development project in Indonesia, see Rix (1978) and Tsurumi (1977).

Chapter 5

1. Some theorists, such as Galbraith (1972), see information processing as a central determinant of organization.

2. This use of structure is somewhat broader than how the term is usually employed. For example, Kotter, Schlesinger, and Sathe (1979) limit structure to the following: job definitions, subunit definitions, hierarchy, rules, plans, committees, and task forces. They would separately categorize measurement systems and reward systems, for example.

3. Homans' use of the terms "required system" and "emergent system," which he applies to small groups, bear some resemblance to the present comparison (Homans, 1950). But he distinguishes between the "external" system and the "internal" system, which also captures some of the difference between formal and emergent. Dalton (1959) proposes the term "unofficial" organization which corresponds to our use of "emergent." Whatever the terminology employed, it is clear that we are not the first to recognize that this dimension of organization can be extremely significant.

4. Meyer (1968) outlines two similar polar options: control by people and control by rules.

5. On the "classical model," see Perrow (1972).

6. On professions and professionals, see Parsons (1958).

7. On organization and culture, see Evan (1975), Hofstede (1978), and Roberts (1970). On comparative studies, see Waldo (1969).

8. The 164 definitions are from Kroeber and Kluckhohn (1952), and Taylor (1924). On holistic perspectives, see Perrow (1972) and Selznick (1957).

9. Crozier (1964, p. 8) is the source of the quotation.

10. Parsons (1968, p. 437) is the source of "shared basis of normative order."

11. The role of culture in legal proceedings is succinctly explained in Kawashima (1963). On traditional dispute resolution and culture, see Sansom (1962) and Haring (1963).

12. Group control of individual behavior was strongest in the family, as noted in Watanabe (1963). On contracts, see Van Zandt (1976) and Lodge (1975).

13. Kawashima (1963, pp. 50–57), from which the quotation is drawn.

14. On the Japanese language, see Kunihiro (1973, 1976) and Peng (1975).

15. For further discussion of the relationship of language to society in Japan, see Nakamura (1960) and Doi (1966).

16. On leadership and managerial style, see Rohlen (1974).

17. On the hiring of recent graduates, see Cole (1971).

Chapter 6

1. On matrix organizations, see Davis and Lawrence (1977), Goggin (1975), and Ames (1972). Tsurumi (1976, pp. 148–150) provides an example of matrix balance in the Mitsui Company.

2. On subsidiaries and affiliates, see Lifson (1981a).

Chapter 7

1. The quotation is from Lifson (1981a).

2. Ibid.

3. Ibid.

4. See Learned, Christensen, Andrews, and Guth (1962).

5. On the theory and practice of capital budgeting, see Hunt, Williams, and Donaldson (1971).

Chapter 8

1. On recruitment, see Rohlen (1974) and Lifson (1981a).

2. On entrance rituals, see Rohlen (1974).

3. The quotation is from Lifson (1981a).

Chapter 9

1. On foreign postings, see Lifson (1976 and 1981b).

2. On overseas localization issues, see Lifson (1981b).

3. The work of Vladimir Pucik (1981) on career patterns in Japanese companies, including sogo shosha, was very helpful in analyzing sogo shosha careers.

Chapter 10

1. The quotation is from Rohlen (1974). On the section as a work unit, see also Rohlen (1976).

2. On vertical ties, see Nakane (1970).

3. On *amae*, see Doi (1966).

4. On learning by experience, see Tanaka (1981).

5. On the functionalities of loose coupling, see Glassman (1973).

6. Dalton (1959).

Chapter 11

1. On the "small world method" of tracing networks, see Schotland (1976). On the development of the network perspective, see Lincoln and Miller (1979) and Tichy, Tushman, and Fombrun (1979). The typology of sociometric and ethnographic is from Lincoln and Miller (1979). On networks, see also Mitchell (1978).

2. For examples of the sociometric approach, see Cartwright (1959), Blau (1962), and Rice and Mitchell (1973).

3. For examples of the ethnographic approach, see Barnes (1954, 1968), Kapfere (1969), and Boissevain and Mitchell (1973).

4. E. P. Hollander's (1958) concept of "idiosyncracy credit" is related to the concept of obligation as it is used here.

5. On commitment, see Becker (1960).

6. On the process of working out standards in an interpersonal work relationship of importance, see Gabarro (1979).

7. Benedict (1946) centers much of her explanation of Japanese culture on concepts of obligation.

8. The definition of *on* is from Lebra (1969). Also see Doi (1966, 1973). Atsumi (1979) explores the rituals of obligatory socializing. The sense of obligation and its developments into reciprocal commitment is well illustrated in Befu (1968). The analysis of "strategy signals" in face-to-face interaction

in Duncan, Brunner, and Fiske (1979) is useful in conceptualizing the nature of the interpersonal obligation assessment process.

9. The conceptualization of commitment comes from Schelling (1960).

10. The study on capital budgeting is that of Bower (1970).

Chapter 12

1. The utility of a large network is discussed in Granovetter (1973).

2. On "linking pin," see Likert (1961). On vertical relationships, see Nakane (1970).

Chapter 13

1. Clark's (1979) discussion on loaning out employees to subsidiaries in a medium-size industrial firm is instructive.

2. The term parallel hierarchies was first brought to our attention by Professor Harrison White. For its application to the sogo shosha and to other situations in Japan, see Lifson (1978, 1984).

Chapter 14

1. Following the 1973 oil crisis, criticism of the sogo shosha was severe, see Umezu (1975). When sogo shosha sales growth began to slow down after 1978, dire predictions began appearing; see Hiraiwa (1978). By 1982 it was obvious that some sort of transformation was necessary for sogo shosha survival. The *Nihon Keizai Shimbun* (a national business daily) published an outspoken article on the "season of winter" of the sogo shosha Nikkei business (1983). The term has come into wide use. See also Tsurumi (1980) and Abegglen and Stalk (1983).

2. On the Mitsui grain elevators, see *Japan Economic Journal* (May 12, 1981) and *New York Times* (September 6, 1982) as well as MacKnight (1983) on the Japanese role in the U.S. grain business.

3. On the Getty Oil Deal, see *Japan Economic Journal* (August 14, 1984).

4. On the case *Lisa M. Avagliano* et al. v. *Sumitomo Shoji America, Inc.* 102 S.Ct 2374 (1982), see 102 *Supreme Court Reporter*, pp. 2374–2382, for latest decision as of this writing. Also on this case, see Lewin (1982). On the case *Michael E. Spiess, Jack Hardy, and Benjamin F. Rountree* v. *C. Itoh & Company (America)* 643 F 2d 353 (1981), see 643 *Federal Reporter*, 2d. Series, pp. 353–372, for latest decision as of this writing. See also the discussion of the *Spiess* et al. v. *C. Itoh* in Sethi, Namiki, and Swanson (1984).

5. See Tsurumi's (1980) discussion of hiring non-Japanese nationals.

6. See Misato (1984) on the spin-off of subsidiaries.

7. See Umezu (1982) on mergers among the sogo shosha. See also Tsurumi's (1980) discussion of consolidation and Arita (1982).

References Cited

Abegglen, James, and George Stalk. "Japanese Trading Companies: A Dying Industry?" *Wall Street Journal*, July 18, 1983.

Ames, Charles. "The Dilemma of Product/Market Management." *Harvard Business Review* 49, 1974.

Arita Kyosuke. *Sogo Shosha: Mirai no Kozo* [Sogo Shosha: The Future Composition]. Tokyo: Nihon Keizai Shimbunsha, 1982.

Atsumi, Reiko. "Tsukiai: Obligatory Personal Relations of Japanese White Collar Company Employees." *Human Relations* 38, No. 1, 1979.

Barnes, John A. "Class and Committees in a Norwegian Island Parish." *Human Relations* 7, No. 1, 1954.

Barnes, John A. "Networks and Political Process." In Marc Swartz, ed., *Local Level Politics*. Chicago: Aldine, 1968.

Becker, Howard S. "Notes on the Concept of Commitment." *American Journal of Sociology* LXVI, No. 1, 1960.

Befu, Harumi. "Gift-Giving in Modernizing Japan." *Monumenta Nipponica*, 23, 1968.

Benedict, Ruth. *The Chrysanthemum and the Sword*. Boston: Houghton Mifflin, 1946.

Blau, Peter. "Patterns of Choice in Interpersonal Relations." *American Sociological Review* 27, 1962.

Boissevain, J., and J. C. Mitchell, eds. *Network Analysis: Studies in Human Interaction*. The Hague: Mouton, 1973.

Caldwell, Martha Ann. "The Dilema of Japan's Oil Dependency." In R. A. Morse, ed., *The Politics of Japan's Energy Strategy* Berkeley: University of California Press, 1981.

Cartwright, D. "The Potential Contribution of Graph Theory to Organization Theory." In Masso Hare, ed., *Modern Organizational Theory*. New York: Wiley, 1959.

Caves, Richard, and Masu Uekusa. *Industrial Organization in Japan*. Washington: The Brookings Institution, 1976.

Clark, Rodney. *The Japanese Company*. New Haven: Yale, 1979.

Cole, Robert. *Japanese Blue Collar*. Berkeley: University of California, 1971.

Cox, William E., Jr. "Product Life Cycles as Marketing Models." *Journal of Business* 40, 1967, pp. 375–384.

Crozier, Michel. *The Bureaucratic Phenomenon.* Chicago: University of Chicago, 1964.

Dalton, Melville. *Men Who Manage.* New York: Wiley, 1959.

Davis, Stanley, and Paul Lawrence. *Matrix.* Reading, Mass.: Addison-Wesley, 1977.

Dizard, John W. "Sears' Humbled Trading Empire." *Fortune,* June 25, 1984.

Doi, Takeo. "*Amae:* A Key Concept for Understanding Japanese Personality." In Robert Smith and Robert Beardley, eds., *Japanese Culture.* Chicago: Aldine, 1962.

Doi, Takeo. "Giri-Ninjo: An Interpretation." *Psychologia* 9, 1966.

Doi, Takeo. *The Anatomy of Dependence.* Tokyo: Kodansha, 1973.

Duncan, Stanley, Lawrence Brunner, and Donald Fiske. "Strategy Signals in Face-to-Face Interaction." *Journal of Personality and Social Psychology* 37, No. 2, 1979.

Eaton, Linda. "The Sogo Shosha: Japanese Traders to the World." In *Food Systems Update.* Washington, D.C.: Food Systems Associates, February 1983.

Evan, William. "Culture and Organizational Systems." *Organization and Administrative Sciences* 5, 1975.

Gabarro, John. "Socialization at the Top: How CEO's and Subordinates Evolve Interpersonal Contracts." *Organizational Dynamics* Winter, 1979.

Galbraith, Jay. "Organizational Design: An Information Processing View." In Jay Lorsch and Paul Lawrence, eds., *Organizational Planning: Concepts and Cases.* Homewood, Ill.: Irwin, 1972.

Glassman, Robert. "Persistence and Loose Coupling in Living Systems." *Behavioral Science* 18, 1973, pp. 83–98.

Goggin, William. "How the Multidimensional Matrix Works at Dow-Corning." *Harvard Business Review* 52, 1975.

Granovetter, Mark. "The Strength of Weak Ties." *American Journal of Sociology* 78, No. 6, 1973, pp. 1360–1380.

Hadley, Eleanor. *Antitrust in Japan.* Princeton: Princeton University, 1970.

Haring, D. "Japanese National Character: Cultural Anthropology, Psychoanalysis, and History." *The Yale Review* 42, 1963.

Hiraiwa, Takeo. *Sogo Shosha no Hateshinai Kuro* [The Boundless Distress of the Sogo Shosha]. Tokyo: Aki Shobo, 1978.

Hofstede, G. "Culture and Organization: A Literature Review Survey." *Enterprise Management* 1, 1978.

Hollander, E. P. "Conformity, Status, and Idiosyncracy Credit." *Psychological Review* 65, No. 2, 1958.

Homans, George. *The Human Group.* New York: Harcourt, Brace, 1950.

Hunt, Pearson, Charles Williams, and Gordon Donaldson. *Basic Business Finance.* Homewood, Ill.: Irwin, 1971.

Japan, Bureau of Statistics. *Kihon Tokei Nenkan* [Japan Statistical Yearbook]. Tokyo: Office of the Prime Minister, 1966.

Japan, Bureau of Statistics. *Kihon Tokei Nenkan* [Japan Statistical Yearbook]. Tokyo: Office of the Prime Minister, 1972.

Japan, Department of Finance. *Gaikoku Boeki Geppo* [Monthly Report of Japan's Foreign Trade], January, 1935.

Japan, Fair Trade Commission. *Sogo Shosha ni Kansuru Dai Ni Kai Chosa Hokoku* [A Report on the Sogo Shosha: Volume Two]. Tokyo: Japan Fair Trade Commission, 1975.

Japan, Ministry of International Trade and Industry. *Tsu Sho Hakusho* [White Paper on International Trade], 1974.

Japan, Office of the Prime Minister. *Kokumin Seikatsu ni Kansuru Seron Chosa 43 Nen* [A Public Opinion Survey on National Life]. Tokyo: Office of the Prime Minister, 1968.

Japan Economic Journal "Big Japanese Traders Pin Hope on Grain Dealings, but 'Watch Out.'" May 12, 1981, p. 14.

Japan Economic Journal. "Mitsubishi Group Shows its Characteristic Solidarity." August 14, 1984, p. 8.

Katsura, Y. "Sangyo Kigyo no Ikasei to Shosa" [Development of Industrial Firms and the Shosha], 1971.

Katz, Daniel, and Robert Kahn. *The Social Psychology of Organizations.* New York: Wiley, 1966.

Kawashima, T. "Dispute Resolution in Japan." In A. von Mehren, ed., *Law in Japan.* Cambridge: Harvard University, 1963.

Kikuri, Ryusuke. "Shosha: Organizers of the World Economy." *Japan Interpreter* 8, No. 3, 1973, pp. 353–373.

Kapferer, B. "Norms and the Manipulation of Relationships in a Work Context." In J. Clyde Mitchell, ed., *Social Networks in Urban Situations.* Manchester, U.K.: Manchester University Press, 1969.

Kroeber, A. L., and C. Kluckhohn. *Culture: A Critical Review of Definitions.* Cambridge: Peabody Museum of Harvard University, 1952.

Kunihiro, Masao. "Indigenous Barriers to Communication." *The Japan Interpreter* 8, 1973.

Kunihiro, Masao. "The Japanese Language and Intercultural Communication." *The Japan Interpreter* 10, 1976.

Learned, E., C. Christensen, K. Andrews, and W. Guth. *Business Policy: Text and Cases.* Homewood, Ill.: Irwin, 1965.

Lebra, Takie. "Reciprocity and the Asymmetric Principle: An Analytical Analysis of the Japanese Concept of *On.*" *Psychologia* 12, 1969.

Lebra, Takie. *Japanese Patterns of Behavior.* Honolulu: East-West Center, 1976.

Levitt, Theodore. "Exploit the Product Life Cycle." *Harvard Business Review* November–December 1965, pp. 81–94.

Lewin, Tamar, "A Complex Sex Bias Case." *New York Times,* April 8, 1982, p. D1.

Lifson, Thomas. *The Sogo Shosha: Strategy, Structure, and Culture.* Unpublished Ph.D. dissertation, Harvard University, 1978.

Lifson, Thomas. "An Emergent Administrative System: Interpersonal Networks in a Japanese General Trading Firm." Harvard Business School Working Paper #79-55, 1979.

Lifson, Thomas, *Mitsubishi Corporation (A)* Boston: HBS Case Services #9-482-050, 1981a.

Lifson, Thomas. *Mitsubishi Corporation (B)* Boston: HBS Case Srvices #9-482-051, 1981b.

Lifson, Thomas, "A Theoretical Model of Japan's Sogo Shosha (General Trading Firms)." *Proceedings of the Academy of Management,* 1981.

Lifson, Thomas, "What Do Japanese Corporate Customers Want?" In *U.S.-Japan Relations: A New Era.* Cambridge: Harvard University Program on U.S.—Japan Relations, 1984.

Likert, Rensis. *New Patterns of Management.* New York: McGraw-Hill, 1961.

Lincoln, James R., and Jon Miller. "Work and Friendship Ties in Organizations: A Comparative Analysis of Relational Networks." *Administrative Sciences Quarterly* 24, June 1979.

Lodge, George. *The New American Ideology.* New York: Alfred A. Knopf, 1975.

MacKnight, Susan. "The Growing Internationalization of the U.S. Grain Trade." Japan Economic Institute Report No. 34A, September 9, 1983.

Mainichi Shimbunsha. "Nippon no Shosha: Itoh Chu Shoji" [Trading Companies of Japan: C. Itoh], 1973.

Marubeni Corporation. *Marubeni Business Bulletin* 53, November 1977.

Misato, Y. *Sogo Shosha no Hokai* [The Sogo Shosha in Decline]. Tokyo: Bancho Shobo, 1984.

Mitchell, J. Clyde. "Networks, Norms, and Institutions." In J. Boissevain and J. C. Mitchell, eds., *Network Analysis and Human Interaction.* The Hague: Mouton, 1973.

Miyamoto, Mataji, Yoshio Togai, and Yasuo Mishima, eds. *Sogo Shosha no Keieishi* [The Managerial History of the Sogo Shosha]. Tokyo: Toyo Keizai Publishing Co., 1976.

Meyer, Marshall. "Two Authority Structure of Bureaucratic Organization." *Administrative Sciences Quarterly* 13, 1968.

Nakamura, H. *The Ways of Thinking of Eastern Peoples.* Tokyo: Japan National Commission of UNESCO, 1960.

Nakane, Chie. *Japanese Society.* Berkeley: University of California, 1970.

New York Times. "Japanese Gaining in U.S. Grain Trade," September 6, 1982, pp. 33, 36.

Nikkei Business. *Shosha: Fuyu no Jidai* [The Age of Winter of the Sogo Shosha]. Tokyo: Nihon Keizai Shimbunsha, 1983.

Nikko Research Center. "Nippon Seitetsu no Kenkyu" [Research on Nippon Steel]. Tokyo: Nikko Research Center, 1982.

Norman, E. H. *Japan's Emergence as a Modern State.* New York: Institute of Pacific Relations, 1940.

Oki, Yasu. *Sogo Shosha to Sekai Keizai* [Sogo Shosha and the World Economy]. Tokyo: Tokyo University, 1975.

Oki, Yasu. "Inside View of the Sogo Shosha." *Japan Quarterly* XXV, No. 2 (April–June), pp. 161–168, 1978.

Ouchi, William. "A Framework for Understanding Organizational Failure." In John R. Kimberly and Robert Miles, eds., *Organizational Life Cycle.* San Francisco: Jossey-Bass, 1980.

Parsons, Talcott. "The Professions and Social Structure." In T. Parsons, ed., *Essays in Sociological Theory: Pure and Applied.* Glencoe, Ill.: The Free Press, 1958.

Parsons, Talcott. "Social Integration." *International Encyclopedia of the Social Sciences,* Vol. 7. New York: Macmillan, 1968.

Peng, F. *Language in Japanese Society.* Tokyo: Tokyo University, 1975.

Perrow, Charles. *Complex Organizations.* Glenview, Ill.: Scott-Foresman, 1972.

Pucik, Vladimir. "Promotions and Intraorganizational Status Differentiations among Japanese Managers." *Proceedings of the Academy of Management,* 1981.

Reischauer, E. O. *The United States and Japan.* Cambridge: Harvard University, 1965.

Rice, Linda E., and Terrence R. Mitchell. "Structural Determinants of Individual Behavior in Civilization." *Administrative Sciences Quarterly* 18, 1973.

Rix, Alan. "The Mitsugoro Project: Japanese Aid Policy and Indonesia." *Pacific Affairs* 52, 1979.

Roberts, Kathleen. "On Looking for an Elephant: An Evaluation of Cross-Cultural Research Related to Organizations." *Psychological Bulletin* 74, 1970.

Roberts, John. *Mitsui: Three Centuries of Japanese Business.* New York: Weatherhill, 1973.

Roehl, Thomas. "The General Trading Companies: a Transactions Cost Analysis of Their Function in the Japanese Economy." Paper presented, at the Academy of International Business, Montreal, October 16, 1981.

Rohlen, Thomas. *For Harmony and Strength.* Berkeley: University of California, 1974.

Rohlen, Thomas. "The Work Group in Japanese Organization." In E. Vogel, ed., *Modern Japanese Organization and Decision-Making.* Berkeley: University of California, 1976.

Sakudo, Y. "Senmon Shosha Kara Sogo Shosha eno Michi" [Transformation from Specialized Trader to General Trading Company], 1973.

Sansom, George. *Japan: A Short Cultural History.* New York: Appleton-Century-Crofts, 1962.

Sarathy, Ravi. "Japanese Trading Companies: Can They Be Copied?" Northeastern University College of Business Administration Working Paper 83–25, 1983.

Sasago, Katsuya. *Shosha Kinyu* [Trading Company Finance]. Tokyo: Kyoikusha, 1979.

Schelling, Thomas. *The Strategy of Conflict.* Cambridge: Harvard University, 1960.

Selznick, Phillip. *Leadership in Administration.* Evanston, Ill.: Row-Peterson, 1957.

Sethi, S. Prakash, Nobuaki Namiki, and Carl Swanson. *The False Promise of the Japanese Miracle.* Marshfield, Mass.: Pitman, 1984.

Stinger, G. J. "A Theory of Oligopoly." *Journal of Political Economy* 72, February 1964, pp. 44–61.

Tanaka, Hiroshi. "New Employee Education in Japan." *Personnel Journal,* January 1981.

Toyo Keizai. "Ote Shosha no Kokusai Kokumotsu Senryaku" [Major Trading Companies' International Grain Strategies]. *Toyo Keizai,* March 14, 1981.

Tsurumi, Yoshi. *Multinational Management: Business Strategy and Government Policy.* Cambridge, Mass.: Ballinger, 1977.

Tsurumi, Yoshi. *Sogoshosha: Engines of Export-Based Growth.* Montreal: Institute for Research on Public Policy, 1980.

Tsurumi, Yoshi. "Export Trading Company Act of the U.S.: The Beginning of a New Industrial Policy." *Pacific Basin Quarterly* 8, Fall 1982.

Uchida, Yoshihide. *Sangyokai Shiriizu: Shosha* [Series on Industry: Trading Companies]. Tokyo: Kyoikusha Shinsho, 1982.

Umezu, Kazuro, *Shosha.* Tokyo: Kyoikusha, 1975.

Umezu, Kazuro. *Shosha: Saihen no Jidai* [The Restructuring of the Shosha]. Tokyo: Diamondo-sha, 1982.

Van Zandt, Howard. "How to Negotiate in Japan." *Harvard Business Review* 48, 1976.

Vernon, Raymond. "International Investment and International Trade in the Product Life Cycle." *Quarterly Journal of Economics* LXXX, May 1966, pp. 190–207.

Waldo, Dwight. "Theory of Organization: Status and Problems." In A. Etziono, ed., *Readings on Modern Organizations.* Englewood Cliffs, N.J.: Prentice-Hall, 1969.

Wallerstein, Immanuel. *The Modern World System.* New York: Academic Press, 1974.

Wasson, Chester R. *Dyynamic Competitive Strategy and Product Life Cycles.* St. Charles, Ill.: Challenge Books, 1974.

Watanabe, Y. "The Family and the Law: The Individualistic Premise and Modern Japanese Family Law." In A. von Mehren, ed., *Law in Japan.* Cambridge: Harvard University, 1963.

Wiegner, Kathleen. "Outward Bound." *Forbes,* July 4, 1983, pp. 96–99.

Williamson, Oliver. *Markets and Hierarchies.* New York: The Free Press, 1977.

Wray, William. *Mitsubishi and the NYK: Business Strategy in the Japanese Shipping Industry.* Cambridge: Harvard University Press, 1984.

Yamamura, Kozo. "General Trading Companies in Japan: Their Origins and Growth." In Hugh Patrick, ed., *Japanese Industrialization and its Social Consequences.* Berkeley: University of California, 1976.

Yoshihara, Kunio. *Sogo Shosha: The Vanguard of the Japanese Economy.* Oxford, U.K.: Oxford University Press, 1981.

Yoshino, Michael Y. *Japan's Managerial System: Tradition and Innovation.* Cambridge: The MIT Press, 1968.

Yoshino, Michael Y. "Note on the Japanese Trading Company." HBS Case Services #9-374-136, 1973.

Yoshino, Michael Y. *The Japanese Marketing System: Adaptations and Innovations.* Cambridge: The MIT Press, 1971.

Yoshino, Michael Y. *Japan's Multinational Firms.* Cambridge: Harvard University, 1976.

Young, Alexander. *The Sogo Shosha: Japan's Multinational Trading Companies.* Boulder, Colo.: Westview, 1978.

Wells, Louis T., Jr. "International Trade: The Product Life Cycle Approach." In L. Wells, ed., *The Product Life Cycle in International Trade.* Boston: Division of Research, Harvard Business School, 1972.

Index